Recovering Their Stories

Recovering Their Stories

US CATHOLIC WOMEN IN THE TWENTIETH CENTURY

Sandra Yocum and Nicholas K. Rademacher, Editors

FORDHAM UNIVERSITY PRESS
New York 2024

Fordham University Press has no responsibility for the persistence or accuracy of URLs for external or third-party Internet websites referred to in this publication and does not guarantee that any content on such websites is, or will remain, accurate or appropriate.

Fordham University Press also publishes its books in a variety of electronic formats. Some content that appears in print may not be available in electronic books.

Visit us online at www.fordhampress.com.

Library of Congress Cataloging-in-Publication Data available online at https://catalog.loc.gov.

Printed in the United States of America

26 25 24   5 4 3 2 1

First edition

Contents

Recovering Their Stories

Introduction

NICHOLAS K. RADEMACHER AND SANDRA YOCUM

Catholic laywomen have made important, significant, and lasting contributions to the Catholic Church and US society and culture, and, yet, these contributions have been largely overlooked. Over three decades ago, Christopher Kauffman made a similar observation. In his preface to *American Catholic Women: A Historical Exploration* (1989), Kauffman explained that he had decided to dedicate one volume to Catholic women in his bicentennial series on the history of the Catholic Church in America "[b]ecause there are so few secondary works on Catholic women." Unlike other volumes in the series with single authors, as Kauffman explained further, this one had an editor, Karen Kennelly, "because one author could not do justice to a general history of Catholic women." Indeed, Kauffman understated the challenge that remains.[1] The commendable work of more recent scholars has brought to light the diversity of women's contributions to Catholic life in the United States and highlights how much remains to be explored, especially about Catholic laywomen.[2] Even while scholarship on women in religion and Catholic women religious, more specifically, has flourished recently, few secondary sources are dedicated to the contributions of American Catholic laywomen. Like Karen Kennelly's edited volume, this collection of essays brings together scholars dedicated to making their modest contribution to doing justice to the history of Catholic women in the US.

While we have sought to provide an inclusive perspective on Catholic laywomen in the twentieth century, including women from diverse racial, ethnic, geographic, and socioeconomic backgrounds, we recognize that there is much more work to be done. We anticipate that this volume will encourage additional explorations into the lives and contributions to church and society of Catholic laywomen representative of the diverse voices and perspectives of the Catholic Church in the US.

The contributors to this volume illustrate the interdisciplinary demands of this kind of scholarship. They are scholars who work in distinct but related disciplines, including African American studies, Catholic studies, historical and liturgical theology, and religious studies, among other fields. Taken together, their work provides an opportunity for readers to look for patterns, areas of convergence, and areas of divergence across the depth and breadth of American Catholic laywomen's experience and contributions to church, culture, and society in the US. For example, the authors included in this volume look closely at various sources that reveal the rich and diverse dimensions of Catholic laywomen's lives; the authors' studies of these sources bring to light different themes that emerged in these women's personal and public lives; and they invite readers into the public and private spaces where the lives and ministries of Catholic laywomen unfolded.

We have detected a number of thematic convergences in these essays. No doubt there are more. All these women claim the imaginative force of the Catholic tradition in devotional and sacramental life in dialogue with intellectual currents of their day. They were leaders, each in her own way. They were evangelists for the Catholic faith that enlivened their lives, and they were theologians, even though very few claimed that title. Some cultivated Christocentric Marian devotion along with rich expressions of their membership in the Mystical Body of Christ. Others authorized jazz Masses, crafted and curated Catholic literary magazines, promoted and created contemporary religious artwork, and facilitated innovative church architectural design. Still others sponsored state legislation for workers' rights, supported women's health, fostered the international women's movement, and worked tirelessly for interracial justice. Their relationships with clergy varied by context. In some situations, they clashed with them, and in others, they negotiated with and even collaborated with clergy. In summary, each of these women featured in this volume sought to create a distinct, alternative culture imbued with a lively Catholic faith and thereby influence the broader culture through the arts, through scholarship, through social justice initiatives, both interpersonal and structural. They sought to create a new order.

One of the fascinating aspects of bringing these women together in a single volume is how much they diverge in the particular ways they received and creatively adapted the tradition and then handed it on to their peers and the rising generation. Contemporary scholars now receive their legacy and communicate it to a contemporary audience. Yet, telling the stories of Catholic laywomen is challenging.

Scholarship on the history of Catholic laywomen remains difficult in large part because primary sources can be difficult to locate, if they have been preserved at all. Still, one of the scholarly pleasures of doing this kind of research is discovering and engaging the varied sources which these women produced and promoted. The authors have located a wide variety of sources, from private to public material, that appear in the chapters of this volume: diaries, devotional objects, marginalia, doodles in notebooks or on scraps of paper, correspondence, memoirs, cookbooks, monthly columns in popular Catholic periodicals, Catholic high school textbooks, dissertations, scholarly articles, handcrafted liturgical art, architectural plans and the buildings that resulted, NFP manuals, websites, documentaries, and, in several cases, memories captured in oral histories.

These sources reveal women who are "spiritual seekers," both before and during their participation in the Catholic tradition, through their music and correspondence, their teaching, scholarship, and writing for a general public, critical engagement in feminist movements, their work promoting racial and worker justice, contributions to the liturgical movement and liturgical arts, or their participation and leadership in natural family planning and reproductive justice concerns. All of these women emerge as leaders who serve with authority in sacred and public spaces. The sources also reveal different expressions of their deep love and conflict in their engagement with the Catholic tradition, as they creatively struggled with the limitations imposed on them as laywomen in the church.

These essays, arranged alphabetically by author's name, introduce us to these laywomen as they enact their Catholic commitments in a surprising variety of spaces and places. Here we have Mary Lou Williams in front of a piano in her Manhattan apartment composing letters. In "'Pray for Good Sounds': Black Catholic Practice, Friendship, and Irreverence in the Intimate Correspondence of Mary Lou Williams," Vaughn Booker examines thirty-two letters to and from Mary Lou Williams, jazz artist and Catholic convert, and her circle of Black and religious friends. The letters disclose "intimate, confessional conversations" about lives shaped by spiritual struggles, Catholic ritual practice, the love for and art of jazz, concerns for Black freedom social struggles and so much more, communicated with a mixture of seriousness, humor, and a touch of irreverence.

St. Benet's Book Store is the site for Brian Clites's essay, "Nina Polcyn: Living Art and Laywomen's Leadership at St. Benet's Bookstore." Polcyn, who took over Chicago's St. Benet's Book Store from another laywoman, Sarah O'Neill, created "a third space" in which she, in the company of other laywomen, exercised leadership in mid-twentieth century national movements of Catholic Action and liturgical renewal, including introducing Catholics to handcrafted rather than mass-produced liturgical and devotional art.

The sacred home of the Lakota, amidst the vast expanse of prairies punctuated with striated masses of rock formations, provides the place for Lucy Looks Twice to remember her father's spiritual legacy. In his essay, "Lucy Looks Twice: The Agency of Lay Lakota Catholic Women, and the Legacy of Nicholas Black Elk," Damian Costello examines the influence of Lucy Looks Twice in bringing to light the deep Catholic faith of her father, Black Elk, Lakota holy man and Catholic catechist. Costello describes the space created for laywomen's agency in spiritual matters in the early Lakota Catholicism that shaped Looks Twice's own faith, which she had received from her father.

Dolores Huerta enacts her life-long quest for justice through escalating actions: lighting candles in cathedral chapels, organizing workers in the field, engaging in public protests, and shepherding legislation through the statehouse. As beautifully expressed in the chapter title, "Dolores Huerta Haciendo Más Caras: Navigating a Catholic World Not Scripted for Her," Neomi De Anda creatively employs Gloria Anzaldúa's *haciendo caras* (making faces/making soul) to explore the life of Dolores Huerta as a Catholic woman leader. De Anda brings to light how Huerta's lifetime of activism promoting social justice and systemic change remains rooted in her Catholic faith, even as she publicly challenges specific church teachings.

On playgrounds and at reproductive health conferences, successive generations of Catholic women explore natural family planning (NFP). In her essay, "Catholic Laywomen's Natural Family Planning across Three Generations," Katherine Dugan's essay presents a brief, but dense, history of a network through three generations of laywomen's engagement with NFP. Taken together, their lives illustrate the creative ways in which laywomen navigate both cultural and Catholic commitments to family planning in light of *Humanae Vitae*.

In art studios and the open cookbooks in Catholic women's kitchens, Katharine Harmon focuses on the role of laywomen who emulated Mary as Christ-bearer. In her essay, "Our Lady of the Liturgical Movement? Rejecting and Reclaiming Marian Devotion by American Catholic Laywomen," Harmon explores how laywomen facilitated social transformation and unity in the church as scholars, artists, activists, and homemakers. They labored in a number of different contexts to challenge and reintegrate traditional Marian devotion. They "preferred a more broadly social understanding of Mary, rather than an individualized relationship." Indeed, they understood Mary as a "universal mother with no bounds of ethnicity, place, or race" who had an essential role in salvation history.

At her typewriter composing her popular columns and fictional biographies, Katherine Burton sought to communicate the transformative power of the Catholic faith that she had experienced, convinced that it was "for and, therefore, should be about everyone." In her essay, "The Catholic Novel: Book Reviews in Katherine Burton's 'Woman to Woman' Columns, 1933–1942," Annie Huey explores Burton's contribution to the Catholic literary revival through her book reviews as featured in her column, "Woman to Woman." Burton commended to her readers those novels, whether written by Catholics or not, that she believed could anchor readers otherwise adrift in the modern world.

Maureen O'Connell takes readers to the streets of Philadelphia at midcentury, around the parish Church of the Gesu and the halls of city government. In her essay, "'We Are Not Here to Convict but to Convince': A Catholic Laywoman's Witness to Anti-Racism in Twentieth-Century Philadelphia," O'Connell reveals the otherwise overlooked life and legacy of Anna McGarry, a woman who, in all of her "ordinariness," worked for racial justice and equity in the City of Brotherly Love and Sisterly Affection. McGarry broke with the conspicuous silence of her lay Catholic female counterparts. As O'Connell maintains, given McGarry's ordinariness, "she might be exactly the heroine white Catholic women need right now."

Wealthy and influential Catholic women spearheaded the building of distinctive, modern liturgical spaces in the Arizona desert, the Bay Area, and a Houston college campus. In her essay, "Laywomen as Church Patrons: Clare Boothe Luce, Marguerite Brunswig Staude, and Dominique de Menil," Catherine Osborne turns our attention to the work of three wealthy laywomen who funded and, in turn, controlled the aesthetic decisions of church design, closely working with the artists, architects, and builders. Once the buildings were complete, however, the clergy's sense of ownership over these liturgical spaces ended the women's influence in respecting the integrity of the original designs. Osborne points to the broader implications of this power dynamic with respect to the circumscribed influence of all laywomen in the church to which they have given so generously.

Ellen Tarry and Ann Harrigan discerned a commitment to extend the initiatives of the Catholic interracial movement by co-founding Friendship House in Chicago in 1940. In "The Road to Friendship House: Ellen Tarry and Ann Harrigan Discern an Interracial Vocation in the US Catholic Landscape," Nicholas K. Rademacher chronicles the prayerful reflection that led Tarry, a journalist and author living amidst the Harlem Renaissance, and Harrigan, a teacher in the New York public school system, to sacrifice for a time their vibrant lives in New York City to undertake the arduous work of founding an interracial center in the Midwest.

The American branch of the Grail Movement, planted in the fertile soil of southwest Ohio in the 1940s, came to exert global influence across Europe, Africa, and Oceania. In her essay, "From Grailville to the Universe: How the Grail Movement Widened the Possibilities for American Catholic Laywomen," Marian Ronan traces the history of the Grail movement across the globe and across time, from the early decades of the twentieth century to the contemporary period. She also highlights the ambiguities of the movement, as a group of Catholic laywomen who make promises but not vows of chastity, poverty, and obedience; as a group that was once exclusively Catholic and is now ecumenical in its membership; and as a movement that has both a rural and an urban presence. In tracing this history and noting these ambiguities, Ronan points to the ways in which Grailville might inspire similarly creative endeavors among laywomen today.

The Mystical Body proves to be a capacious place in Sandra Yocum's essay, "Laywomen Enacting the Mystical Body." She employs Michel de Certeau's imaginative depiction of "place" and "space" to consider how a wide variety of laywomen transformed their place in the Mystical Body of Christ into a space of agency and faith-in-action. Yocum then traces how some laywomen found the space of the Mystical Body of Christ too constraining for their newfound agency. Many of the women featured in the previous essays serve as additional exemplars of women who transformed their place in the Mystical Body into a space of agency in faith.

Taken together, the women in this volume comprise only a small sample of the laywomen whose contributions to Catholic life and thought in the US need to be discovered and documented. Even this small sample highlights the importance of recovering women's stories in order to expand our understanding of their influence in the church both locally and across the globe. We are grateful to the scholars who through patience and perseverance contributed to this project. The project, envisioned just prior to the pandemic, came to fruition through virtual conferences and ongoing mutual support of each other's projects through electronic media. In spite of the hardships, these scholars have contributed important articles. We look forward to further collaboration among the scholars included in this volume and others working in this area.

The image on the cover of this volume, "Tower of Women," was created by Sr. Helen David Brancato, IHM, in 2019. Sr. Helen is an artist, educator, and activist who has invested a lifetime exploring themes of justice and peace. She "genuinely sees people in their lived reality and has the ability to capture these moments through the medium of art." In her work as a painter, printmaker and illustrator, she emphasizes "mercy and compassion as central to approaching the human condition" and she challenges those who view her art "to ponder and reflect on the holiness that surrounds us."[3] Of "Tower of Women," Sr. Helen explained, the "woman carries in her all of the other women who have gone before her and, as she moves resolutely into the unknown, she weaves together and leaves as a legacy their stories."[4] In a similar manner, we hope that this volume contributes to the diverse and ever-expanding tapestry of the legacy of Catholic laywomen—in their lived reality—in the US and around the world.

Notes

1. Karen Kennelly, ed. *American Catholic Women: A Historical Exploration* (New York: Macmillan, 1989).

2. Mary Henold's *The Laywoman Project: Remaking Catholic Womanhood in the Vatican II Era* (Chapel Hill: University of North Carolina Press, 2020) is one such notable exception. Henold studies the influence of "everyday Catholic

laywomen" after the Second Vatican Council. Other works, like Kathy Sprows Cummings' *New Women of the Old Faith: Gender and Catholicism in the Progressive Era* (Chapel Hill: University of North Carolina Press, 2009), provide sustained exploration of the important contributions of laywomen alongside women religious or other figures in the church.

3. See Barbara O'Neill, IHM, "Blessed are They Who Show Mercy: Mercy Shall be Theirs," *Impact: Sisters, Servants of the Immaculate Heart of Mary* (Fall 2020): 4.

4. Sr. Helen David Brancato, conversation with Nicholas K. Rademacher and Michelle Sherman, 2019. "Tower of Women" is in the private collection of Nicholas K. Rademacher and Michelle Sherman.

"Pray for good sounds"

Black Catholic Practice, Friendship, and Irreverence in the Intimate Correspondence of Mary Lou Williams

VAUGHN A. BOOKER

. . . You see, my sister, not only do I pray (you got me *praying* again)—pretty sneaky broad, you are—ask me to pray for you!! How could I refuse??? Prayer is a funny thing. It sneaks up on you. I cannot say that I stopped *believing*—no! The truth is that I didn't *feel* right praying. Of course, since the break-up of my marriage [with Ezio Bedin] (although we are very good friends) and the human mistakes of a couple of priests, I became bitter and refused to have anything further to do with the Church. Not with God, mind you, but the Church!

. . . Since I have begun prayer again, I have more hope. People are full of fine words—but man alone can do nothing! I read "Anima Christi" and it sure sounds as if it were written with *me* in mind![1]

This excerpt comes from a letter that jazz and classical pianist Hazel Scott (1920–1981) wrote to fellow jazz pianist, arranger, and composer Mary Lou Williams (1910–1981) on September 5, 1965. Written correspondence between the two Black women pianists was critical to their friendship. As biographer Karen Chilton notes, "Hazel vented her frustration over her failed second marriage and other matters of personal importance in letters to her friend Mary Lou Williams. . . . Confiding the most intimate details of her life, Hazel sought Williams's listening ear and spiritual counsel. The letters became a form of prayer and confession."[2] Scott's correspondence followed the release of *Black Christ of the Andes*, Williams's landmark album of sacred jazz that Scott had praised in a previous letter. Scott was on a religious journey that eventually led to her embrace of the Bahá'í faith. But as she journeyed, she corresponded and prayed alongside fellow Black Catholics—her "dear sister" Mary Lou Williams and dancer Lorraine "Lo" Gillespie (1920–2004), who was married to, and manager for, jazz trumpeter and eventual Bahá'í member John Birks "Dizzy" Gillespie (1917–1993). An excerpt from an earlier letter that Scott sent to Williams on November 19, 1963, reflects the two spiritual

Black women confiding in each other while navigating a religious institution in which white men were the authorities:

Hi Mary,

Pray for me dear. Because of two priests—who after all are only men and can make mistakes like all of us—I have not gone to confession or even to mass in one year! *I cannot be a hypocrite.* God knows, I need *help.* And I pray on my knees at home. He hears me and knows that at least I am not a liar and a hypocrite, even if I am a sinner.

One priest betrayed the secret of the confessional and another lied to me in front of a witness who knew better. I don't want to go into any details except that if more priests were like Father Woods there would be a lot more good Catholics!

You are a blessed person. Blessed and pure in heart. God help me to carry on, day in, day out, and to have the strength to believe that He will not let me down.[3]

Mary Lou Williams, ten years older than Hazel Scott, was many things to her—she was a consistent financial supporter in times of few professional performing opportunities,[4] a fellow spiritual journeyer exploring Roman Catholicism, and a lighthearted Black sister who understood her frustrations with being a Black woman in the jazz industry and a Black neophyte in the Catholic Church. In her profession, Williams was respected as a boogie-woogie virtuoso as well as a pioneer and mentor in bebop music and sacred jazz. Many other musicians, family members, and friends only experienced the stern and serious side of Williams the Catholic, and because they viewed her as a religious fanatic who informally proselytized around Harlem, they often avoided conversing with her. Friends and Catholic clergy even associated her diligent labor to establish the Bel Canto Foundation to support struggling jazz musicians with the perception of her fanaticism.[5] However, certain close Black Catholic friends felt Williams's embrace of the sacred alongside her sustained enjoyment of the profane and irreverent in person, on the telephone, and through mail correspondence. This close circle included Scott, Lorraine Gillespie, jazz bassist Eustis Guillemet (1934–2021), and the Black Franciscan friar, Brother Mario Hancock (1937–2005).[6]

This essay highlights Mary Lou Williams's correspondence with two Black spiritual companions, Hazel Scott and Mario Hancock, while she stayed in Copenhagen, in Pittsburgh, and in her Hamilton Terrace apartment home in New York City between 1963 and 1970.[7] Beyond communicating with ordained white Catholics and women religious, Williams's letters also demonstrate her work to construct and maintain intimate and confessional conversations with other Black women, and with Black men religious, as they navigated spiritual life in a white religious hierarchy. Secondarily, as this set of Black folks collaboratively developed their relationships with God, saints, departed priests, and each other, their letters also reveal that irreverent humor, amid religious and spiritual cultivation, was important to their friendships.

At times, Williams and her friends wrote weekly letters. Other times, they sent back-to-back letters each day. The letters often combined with in-person and telephone conversations, as many of Williams's references indicate that the letter's content continued a previous conversation. Of this set of intimate conversation partners, it is likely that Mario Hancock knew that Williams was preserving the correspondence she received from others. Although all the available letters now sit in Williams's archival collection at Rutgers University's Institute of Jazz Studies, Hancock initially gave his letters from Williams to musicologist Tammy Kernodle, who worked to restore as many as possible at Miami University. As Kernodle writes, "I learned so much about Williams's humor, passion for life, and her personal struggles from those letters and the time I spent with Brother Mario."[8]

Centering Williams's written correspondence spotlights the cultivation of religious sensibilities that occur through friendship as a category of social relationship and affective orientation, as historian of Catholicism and theorist of religion Brenna Moore has advocated for the study of religion. An "intermediary realm between the individual and society" that relies on "training in the arts of relationships" and is also entangled with the dynamics of race, gender, and class, intimate friendship produces an "affective intensity," in Moore's analysis, which is impactful for "generating religious experience, deepening or losing faith, and converting or returning to the religion of [people's] childhoods." This essay on Mary Lou Williams's correspondence demonstrates that letters between religious and spiritual compatriots can highlight the interpersonal, discursive ways that "religion is felt, apprehended, even contested bodily, and it is also rendered real *between* bodies, among family and friends in contexts of intimacy." For this study of Williams's intimate religious circle of friends, Moore offers a capacious conception of intimate friendship as it relates to religion, one that goes beyond "just face-to-face *amis*" to represent the experiences that constitute religious and spiritual relations to human and nonhuman beings (including Catholic saints like Martin de Porres and the foreboding spirits that Williams embraced Catholic ritual to ward off), across states of consciousness, and with various modes of recall: "dreams of friends, memories of them, and imagined conversations, often provoking feelings for one another so intense that it was almost as good as (and sometimes even better) than the real thing."[9]

Centering this written correspondence also illuminates letter writing as a medium for "confessional intimacy"—what sociocultural anthropologist of religion Todne Thomas defines as "reflexive interactions among spiritual kin" in white-dominated religions "that allow them to navigate the racial and moral demands" of their white lay counterparts and ordained authorities.[10] Arising from her ethnography of African American and Afro-Caribbean evangelicals in Atlanta, Thomas details the "spaces where church members could air different emotions, reflections, and criticisms" of evangelical family norms.[11] Thomas's study of Black evangelical counter-narratives and counter-practices relates to the epistolary communications of Williams and her friends, because the confessional intimacy of both evangelical and Catholic Black communities across time and space "emerges in the conversational realm of spiritual or extra-institutional spaces of lived religious experience between close kin, whether familial or spiritual."[12] Moreover, Williams's correspondence created epistolary "spaces for revelation, nonjudgmental support, and contexts for a subjective and intersubjective coherence" between Black Catholic seekers and believers outside the surveillance of institutional spaces and channels, which evinces "the power of the spiritual to govern modes of sociality that are not always beholden to institutional ideologies."[13]

This essay focuses on the religious content of Williams's correspondence with Scott and Hancock to highlight one internationally prominent Black Catholic woman's navigation of spiritual and material battles, along with her deployment of spiritual resources and regular communication with Black friends allied in (or adjacent to) the faith, within a global Christian Church with a clear gender hierarchy and an implicit racial hierarchy that faced the prospect of desegregation in the US. Before discussing this Black Catholic correspondence, alongside the religious experiences and practices it illuminates, it is important to account for the Afro-Peruvian Catholic saint who compelled many African-descended peoples in the twentieth century to embrace the religion.

Saintly Correspondence—Martín de Porres

Some of us are for suffering—This keeps us close to God—

I use to get angry & disgusted to see you slaving for "Whitie" but St. Martin came to my mind. To perform miracles he must have caught hell & this was during slavery. I get a pitiful feeling when I think of him—yet a strong one when I think of God & how he performs miracles & what's involved.

[. . .]

All my life, my suffering was great—starvation, slapped, beaten, lied upon, was called crazy for loving in the 30s especially those who mistreated me—was always getting hung up with bad people—trying to change them to good—but since I became Catholic (they *really* know the liturgy) A sound came that they are helped when dying—You dig— no matter how much you pray for someone bad, they are more successful and never change, but our prayers help them to at least make purgatory.

I have been with some fantastically wild souls since coming to Copenhagen. . . . Both have died, but God took mercy on them and gave them peace—& spoiled me with a $5,000.00 grant (inspiration to continue my suffering for souls).

—Letter from Mary Lou Williams to Mario Hancock, July or September [month unknown] 4, 1970, pp. 1–2.

For many Catholics of African descent, their religious communities included not only earthly sister- and brotherhoods but also spiritual ones. More than the muse for her 1962 hymn *Black Christ (Hymn in Honor of St. Martín de Porres)* and 1964 album *Black Christ of the Andes*, with a first track that celebrated his tale (lyrics composed by Williams's beloved Jesuit friend, Father Anthony S. Woods), for Williams, the Afro-Peruvian Dominican St. Martín de Porres (1579–1639) was a hallowed Catholic compatriot. Musicologist Gayle Murchison writes that de Porres functioned in history "as an especially important symbol and inspiration for African American acolytes, novitiates, and priests to encourage them in their commitment to the Church. In adopting Martín as her patron saint, Williams was following a well-established tradition."[14] As Moore writes, the cult of de Porres "was emerging in the 1930s among antiracist and Black Catholics in different pockets of the United States. . . . Martín de Porres was an important member of the 'spiritual family' gathered at the Harlem Friendship House in the early 1940s when [Claude] McKay came."[15] Spencer Williams (1893–1969), the African American producer, director, and star of several independent Black-audience religious films, created *Brother Martin, Servant of Jesus* (1942), his first explicitly Roman Catholic film. Historian of African American religions Judith Weisenfeld wrote that Williams's "interest in the cross, the crossroads, and the intercessory activities of divine and demonic beings" is present in *Brother Martin*'s story of Uncle Jed, a Black Catholic played by Williams, telling his niece that de Porres saved his life because he "did something for Blessed Martin." Although there are no known extant copies of *Brother Martin*, Weisenfeld notes that the film's advertising trailer promises to reveal to the viewer "the mysteries of Brother Martin's holy religion" while also showcasing Black and white Catholic devotion, including soldiers seeking his guidance and protection by carrying medals and relics during World War II.[16]

Writing for the *Negro Digest*'s Black readership in 1948, Thelma Pearson described de Porres as "the precursor of social service and one of the greatest symbols of interracial brotherhood." For an African American audience, Pearson extended the saintly narratives of benevolence and spiritual foresight that de Porres's life had acquired: "Contrary to the practice of the day, Martin attended all the sick whether they could pay or not. He worked unbelievably long hours—giving most of his earnings to care for those less fortunate than himself." Pearson added, "The poor and the rich knew his psychic ability that gave him the power to read their thoughts, to describe actions he had not observed but that had happened. . . . Always he tried to be most inconspicuous, saying: 'I could do nothing without Christ!'"[17] Both the claim of a person of African descent's spirit of service and his spiritual gift of extrasensory perception resonated with Williams's beliefs about her own calling and spiritual gifts as she sought to define her Catholic identity. With an optimistic tone about the anti-racist potential of de Porres's canonization, based upon the claim that white men praying to de Porres "drops away old prejudices," Pearson concluded her article: "When Martin de Porres receives this singular religious honor, he will be the first Negro from the New World to be raised to sainthood. He will take his place beside St. Benedict the Moor; St. Moses, the Ethiopian Hermit; the twenty-two Blessed Martyrs of Uganda; St. Augustine, the great Doctor of the Church and St. Monica his saintly mother . . . in these too coursed the blood of Africa."[18] A moral exemplar whom Pope John XXIII canonized in 1962, de Porres's life modeled what Williams and other Black Catholics who sought to draw closer to God must expect to endure from the world and the Church, as both operated under structures of white supremacy.

Historian of religion Erin Kathleen Rowe offers insight into the construction of de Porres's hagiography that reveals its enduring appeal to Catholics like Williams. Although not an enslaved subject, the "deep color prejudice" and verbal abuse de Porres received from Creole Spanish Catholics served to affirm the psychological hardships Williams had experienced and relayed in her letters.[19] Additionally, Rowe identifies the trope of "subversive humility" in de Porres's purported statements: "While he preferred to heal the poor, he was often called to minister to the mighty. . . . . Subversive humility occurred sporadically in the vidas of saints, who frequently professed obedience while ignoring earthly authority in favor of the divine."[20] For Williams, who viewed jazz music as a divine, healing gift, de Porres's reputation for healing abilities amid a contested relationship with Creole Spanish Catholic authorities would certainly resonate with her advocacy of jazz music's healing, therapeutic potential. Her Bel Canto Foundation effort to realize this potential required, then, the white Catholic Church hierarchy's vigorous financial and liturgical support.

As his spiritual compatriot, Williams found parallels with de Porres in her struggles and her gifts. According to Rowe, "Martin's hagiographer describes his extreme penitential practices in graphic language that explicitly compares his bodily suffering to that of the martyrs."[21] Williams practiced frequent daily Mass attendance and extensive periods of praying and fasting that her friends and priestly authorities considered extreme. Without flagellation or bloodshed, she put her own body through extreme rituals to demonstrate her pure devotion to God. Martin's spiritual practices occurred primarily within domestic (kitchen labor) and care (hospital labor) arenas, menial work that fed into the trope of "heroic humility".[22] For years, Williams opened up her Hamilton Terrace apartment in her labor to house, feed, and provide what would later bear the name music therapy to unemployed jazz musicians and jazz musicians struggling with substance abuse. Lastly, as Williams told an oral history interviewer in June 1973, "I have been a very psychic person. I was born a psychic person."[23] Consequently, it is also likely that de Porres's purported ability to "slip out of [his] body and travel freely, a gift that correlated with Central African beliefs," confirmed for Williams her belief that she possessed extrasensory spiritual gifts, as discussed later in this essay.[24]

Murchison notes that "[s]ince the middle of the nineteenth century, Dominicans and Josephites . . . had offered Martin to African American Catholics in the United States as a symbol of comfort and consolation for the oppressed and downtrodden."[25] It is also important to acknowledge the historical dynamics of racial hierarchy as they factor into the dissemination of an exemplary Catholic suffering servant of African descent for the purpose of African American proselytization. Scholar Chris Garces offers a critical portrait of the Spanish Catholic structure that afforded de Porres brotherhood status by situating it contextually in early-seventeenth-century Lima, Peru. Garces observes an "interspecies racism" in this context: people of African descent, not considered species equals to Creole Spanish subjects, "reperform[ed] their colonized status as beasts of burden or as subjects normally unworthy of civil recognition."[26] The hagiographic narrative of de Porres's life represents him as emblematic of African-descended people who "carried out the city's most tedious chores and managed the city's beasts of burden, serving as mediating agents between those who gave orders and those who acted upon them."[27] To accept Catholic fellowship under these racialized circumstances meant becoming a religious brother or sister "on the exclusive condition that all accept a God-given role as inferior subjects who should grow accustomed to a life of unrelenting toil."[28] Consequently, Catholics like Williams, who gravitate toward de Porres's hagiography as exemplary, become subject to a racial logic that relegates them to a status as "burdened" Catholics; their labor never elevates their status in the eyes of Church hierarchy. In her letters, Williams's expressed private frustrations often reflected both her inability to transcend this oppressive structure, try as she did, and the appealing power of the de Porres narrative of a life of service as such a burdened, Black Catholic.

As Farrah Jasmine Griffin notes in her study of Black women artists in the World War II era, Williams's "sense of spirituality, deeply informed by a kind of organic mysticism, called her to act in the world to alleviate human suffering. . . . [M]ost often she was engaged in individual, one-on-one efforts to free people of debt, addiction, violence, and homelessness."[29] Williams adored and related to de Porres, and her life and letters reflect how she found herself in this inferior position often as she sought visibility for her perceived calling to create a charitable foundation (to no avail) and recognition for her work to pioneer sacred jazz (which came belatedly, and contrasted the popular success of her contemporary, Duke Ellington, and his Sacred Concerts).[30]

Seeking Correspondences—Letters from Hazel Scott

In addition to Williams's professional ambition as a jazz artist who conveyed spiritual feelings and ideas through her compositions, improvisations, and song lyrics, her experience as an adolescent in Afro-Protestant religious life, followed by an adulthood as a theistic, spiritual person, shaped her approach to institutional religious authority before embracing Roman Catholicism. Williams was born in Atlanta with a veil/caul, and as religion scholar Yvonne Chireau notes, southern African Americans interpreted such births "as evidence that one was gifted with enhanced insight into the invisible realm."[31] As I have written previously, Williams "claimed that she had religious visions as a child. She likely had religious family members who encouraged the notion that she wielded spiritual gifts."[32] In adulthood, as Griffin writes, "Williams had a long-standing interest in the zodiac. At this stage in her life she hungered for spiritual meaning and guidance, but she did not have a sense of religiosity. For her, music was a spiritual medium, a conduit to something outside of herself as well as a vehicle for expressing a sense of the spiritual, if not the divine." This spiritual orientation entailed significant community building among jazz musicians and concern for others' suffering, precedents for her Bel Canto Foundation work in later decades. Griffin continues, "Williams found community in the context of New York nightlife, a world in which sex, drugs, and money were in great supply. But the scene also provided fellowship, warmth, love, and transcendence."[33]

She shared this orientation not only with her closest friends in the jazz arena, Dizzy Gillespie, Lorraine Gillespie, and Hazel Scott, who were also religious and spiritual seekers, but also with Eustis Guillemet, a young

FIGURE 1: Mary Lou Williams holding a score of her sacred jazz composition "Lamb of God" in front of St. Patrick's Cathedral, New York, NY, 1975. "Mary Lou Williams Jazz Mass," Jack Mitchell/Archive Photos via Getty Images.

bassist she encountered through her Bel Canto Foundation effort to support struggling jazz artists. In addition to Guillemet's embrace of Catholicism, Lorraine remained a Catholic alongside Williams, while Hazel transitioned from Catholicism to the Bahá'í faith and Dizzy embraced the Bahá'í faith without ever considering becoming Catholic. For the 1970 album *Portrait of Jenny*, Dizzy composed "Olinga" about Enoch Olinga (1926–1979), the Bahá'í religious leader from Uganda who was appointed as the youngest Hand of the Cause, the highest appointed position in the religion. Williams the Catholic covered her beloved Bahá'í friend's religious composition for her 1974 album, *Zoning*.

The virtuoso pianist Hazel Scott was Williams's close friend in the music profession, who worked to cultivate a prayerful correspondence with Williams as both famous Black women navigated personal and professional tribulation, albeit with irreverent sensibilities at times. In their correspondence between 1963 and 1969, Scott often lamented her failed pursuits of romance. In late 1963, she was in the midst of an unhappy marriage to the Italian-Swiss comedian Ezio Bedin, whom she labeled a coddled "family baby." "Maybe one day he'll grow up," Scott wrote. "Meanwhile I'm stuck with a Catholic marriage, to an infant!! / In any case, it keeps me from making any more idiotic mistakes. As long as I'm married I can't *get* married, that's for sure—no matter how often I *think* I'm in love!!!" With Williams, Scott directed her irreverent humor toward herself, the concept of true love and romance, and one of the seven Catholic sacraments. She cautioned Williams, "Love is for the birds Mary Lou. Only God's love counts. The rest is horse manure. You can quote me. Call Lo [Lorraine] and give her my love."[34] Interestingly, Scott credited Father Woods and an unnamed white priest for counseling her against marrying Bedin—as Scott reported, the second priest even remarked, "it would have been better for us to live together and not get married[.] Mary, he was not so shocking at all!! He *was* only being practical *although he was a priest.* Very rare! He saw we were crazy in love but it was not enough love of the spirit in our love to keep us safe."[35] A priest who counseled Scott and Bedin against entering holy matrimony, while encouraging a living arrangement that presumably entailed their active sex life, struck her as one of the few, practical, and reliable Church authorities she respected. Williams carried this same self-deprecating sensibility into her letters with Mario Hancock, demonstrating the intertwining of these Black women's irreverent humor, critical dispositions toward religious authority, and prayer practices.

By 1965, Scott was proclaiming her certainty that Catholic life did not suit her, albeit troubled by what it might mean to drift from Williams in this regard. Nevertheless, she conveyed her faith that God still guided and resided with her: "Mary, I'm frightened. I don't go to church. How can I? Are you sure you remember me? I go all the way. Big letters of truth are written on me for God to see so why should I try to parade as something I'm not? I can't fool God so why try to fool anybody else? You see God is in me as well."[36] Williams's non-Catholic friend believed in the power of her prayers and continued to request them when facing interpersonal battles. Financially strapped in June 1965, Scott wrote to Williams about an incident where she argued with another woman who owed her $4.00. The drummer Arthur Taylor (1929–1995) was present for this argument. When Taylor asked Scott, "What are *you* doing *NEEDING* two mille?" he elicited a significant response from her: "Needless to say since I am unfortunately not a practicing Catholic at the moment (I'm not a hypocrite, Mary), I *read* him forever and a day! He gets pretty nasty with people anyway. It was necessary for me to tell him that when I ask *him* for 'bread' then and only then he can consider himself free to cast reflexions and look at me with scorn!"[37] In her biography of Scott, Chilton describes this confrontation as Scott "cuss[ing] him out".[38] However, Chilton's account omits both the fact that Scott declared her non-Catholic identity and that she used the Black discourse of critically "reading" a well-known compatriot ("I *read* him forever and a day!"), which is a confrontational form of signification that is thoroughly evident in Black (religious *and* humor) culture.[39] In any case, in the wake of their diverging religious paths, Scott and Williams shared similar professional and interpersonal battles as famous Black musicians, a sense of humor about confronting people who questioned them, and a resort to being spiritual women committed to prayer in spite of it all.

In an August 1965 letter, Scott interpreted her life in light of the Parable of the Rich Fool (Luke 12:13–21). She assured Williams, who always requested prayers and testified to their power, that she would try to practice the Catholic ritual for her: "If you think you need prayer, and we all do, then darling, as difficult as a rosary a day may be—a selfish horrible thing to say—I should at least make the attempt! Especially since it ain't for me! *Really!*" Scott asked Williams if her ears were burning, because she had told Nina Simone and her husband Andrew Stroud "[a]bout you saying your rosary instead of cussin' out the musicians"—advice she offered to Scott in heated moments. If Scott would not commit to becoming a Catholic, or to regular Catholic rituals (like the rosary) beyond prayer, her letters to Williams reveal that she would certainly choose to repeatedly lift her Catholic sister's spirits, ask for any and all details about the sacred songwriting processes for *Black Christ of the Andes*, request that she send records of specific songs (sometimes multiple times, due to parcel theft), and encourage her to continue producing sacred jazz:

> "A Fungus Amungus—WOW!" "Dirge Blues" breaks my heart. Please, send me the Prayer for the Holy Spirit. Isn't that, the start of "Praise the Lord"? Write and tell me, 'cause it sure is a gas! What is the next? 150th Psalm? I want you to tell me *about* it! The feeling is so great. You start with "Come Holy Spirit." Well I *know*!
>
> In any case, my sister, you are about a beautiful human being![40]

The two Black women's written exchanges also involved relaying spiritual and medical recommendations for the other to practice for their well-being, and to ease their unsettled spirits in moments of acute stress: for Williams to treat foot fungus, Scott recommended foot baths, a chiropodist, and "*POTASSIUM PERMANGANATE*"; for liver issues, eating oranges; for heart troubles, relaxation, and seeing a doctor "when you get hold of some money. . . . There is no crime involved in taking care of your health." Overall, Scott instructed her dear sister that these symptoms sounded "like a general warning from your nervous system to cool your<u>self</u>. And try relaxing more."[41]

Sometime before officially embracing the Bahá'í faith, Scott also received from Williams a card with Father Woods's image following his death. In 1966, Scott wrote about its affective spiritual presence in her residence, animated by the action of her maid:

> . . . Something strange happened to me. You know the little prayer mourning card with Father Woods' picture? *Well* when you sent it, *I saw only* the *back* with his name on it and the date. Possibly—as a matter of fact, *surely* I was too weak spiritually to face the fact even though I could advise *you*! Only a couple of weeks ago I was walking through the apartment and saw the picture lying on a table and my heart jumped!

I picked it up with the *weirdest feeling* you can *imagine!* It was [as] if he heard me praying and crying and I saw his face.

Mary—it scared me to death! You see until I turned the card over and saw the *back* I had *no idea* <u>where</u> it had come from. The German girl who was cleaning here had straightened out some papers and *she* kept the picture face *up!!*

Do you realize how many times I held that card and <u>never</u> turned it over?

Requesting that Williams "Tell this to Lorraine <u>please</u>" because it was "spooky," Scott provides an emphasis on the centrality of communication (namely, of relaying profound spiritual experiences via letter, telephone, and in-person conversation) among spiritual friends, whether they bear the categories of lay, neophyte, or seeker. In reflecting on the comfort she received from her friend, Mabel Howard, when her mother died, Scott reminded Williams of the religious experience the three women shared, which also brought to mind the fainting of her son, Adam Clayton Powell III (nicknamed Skipper):

> Remember when you came to the hotel in 1954 and we had the mass for my mother and "Skipper" fainted just as the priest committed her soul? Remember the ray of light that you saw come through the high stained glass window that you noticed and Mabel and I saw it at the same time? She has reminded me of a lot of things. I had forgotten about "Skipper" passing out cold. He is weird. Father Woods used to tell me to leave Skip alone! He kept telling me that and I didn't understand. I wanted Skip to come into the Church. Father Woods told me not to *bother* him. He liked him. As a matter of fact, they liked each other.[42]

Throughout their correspondence, in which spirit, humor, lament, venting, advice, and prayer requests were always present, Scott wrote of her ambition to produce an autobiography that she wanted to live beyond a book, as a play, movie, and television series. "You know what?" Scott queried Williams. "If it is a good, funny and highly moral play, [it is] because I am a highly moral woman (you see why I'm confused??? Don't *laugh*, Mary, it's my soul). I'm attempting to joke about [it] because I am selfish enough to ask you to pray for me."[43] As Scott reckoned with her history of marriages that did not end up as she hoped, and her ongoing ambitions as a Black entertainer determined that her story had value and professional longevity, she weaved together self-deprecating humor intended to generate Williams's laughter, an admission of spiritual uncertainty, and certainty about the effectiveness of Williams's prayers in this request for her dear sister's continued spiritual support. With an intimate, confessional friendship that entailed reading and replying to each other's letters, Williams the Catholic and Scott the seeker engaged in shared commitments, consternation, charity, and comedy with each other. In working together to cultivate spiritual and religious selves, Williams and Scott anticipated that their correspondence would range a gamut of affects.

Comedic Catholic Correspondence—Letters to Brother Mario Hancock

Whether it was during her stay at the St. Lioba Kloster in Copenhagen or at her Hamilton Terrace apartment, Williams's letters to Bro. Mario Hancock are especially revealing. Bro. Mario, born Grady Hancock and a Franciscan Friar of the Atonement in Graymoor, New York, received Williams's letters while he served in administrative services in the Convent of Saint Onofrio / Onuphrius al Gianicolo in Rome, and upon his return to Newark (Hancock later served in various parish and chaplaincy roles upon moving to Washington, D.C., which included the Newman Center at the historically Black Howard University).[44] They detail her celebrations of faith, updates on struggles, requests to spiritually assist others, and notes that both Black Catholic friends had prayed for each other. In the margin of one letter, for instance, Williams indicated that the check she included was for Hancock to obtain a Papal Blessing for Louis Armstrong and Lillian Hardin Armstrong in advance of Louis's sixty-eighth birthday.[45] Many of her letters reveal that she viewed Hancock as her spiritual compatriot, rather than as an ordained superior—Williams regularly used profanities, which she occasionally censored, in her correspondence with Hancock. As she related to the Black Catholic monk with irreverent fondness, she enjoyed recounting humorously the dramas she experienced as a determined jazz musician who sought recognition from her Church, her profession, and society. For instance, after asking Hancock to contact several parish priests to invite her to perform her Mass, she shifted gears abruptly between discussing sacred matters, generous friendships, and a recent physical altercation: "I got into a fight & lost my watch. 'Lo' called tonite & said 'Dizzy' had bought me a watch—wow!! I'm too embarrass[ed] to go & get it. Wait'll I see you. You'll double up in laughter when I portray the fight. Did I send you the Entrance song I wrote for the Peace Mass?"[46]

Her September 11, 1967 letter to Hancock celebrated the Catholic conversion of one of her uncles, which she relayed took "less than 2 months" and came with his request that she take him to religious classes for neophytes.[47] She signified the irony of going on a twelve-hour fast over two days to lose weight and ending up gaining four pounds instead.[48] When seeking Hancock's blessed advice, Williams requested that he provide "spiritual sounds" in his replies: "Please give me spiritual sounds—Is it God's will that I play dated music?"[49] As I have written elsewhere, Williams articulated a concept of good spiritual sounds with multiple meanings, which resonate in this exchange as "the religious messages she received in her life during prayer or in conversation with others, and the religious truths she sought to convey to others."[50] This letter shows that she regarded Hancock's words, both spoken and written, with the potential to resonate with divine plans for her life.

Williams's letter on September 28, 1967, detailed various woes—composing songs for Duke Ellington without the expected compensation from him; kidney and bladder ailments; and the recent theft of her apartment's television, new typewriter, and luggage. She was hosting a young jazz musician in her apartment to help with composing, but she felt that his Black Power consciousness meant "the spirits around him 'ain't so hot'!" This perceived spiritual presence meant that Williams expressed that she was "out of sauce when he's around," an indication that his sociopolitical stance and expression blocked her spiritual inspiration for producing music. "It's utterly impossible to get thru, in America," lamented Williams, adding "everybody is kooked, me too." As her depressing circumstances and stresses mounted, Williams confessed to Hancock, likely with considerable dark humor, "Almost prayed to leave here—but would like to do a few more things for God. Am [tempted] to ask Him to take my sister [Grace Mickles] to heaven—feel like I'd be shunning my cares—this one is very, very heavy. It's just the right one for sweet Jesus."[51] Mickles, Williams's sister who battled alcoholism and relied on the musician for financial support, became so great a burden that she nearly induced Williams's petition for eternal freedom from these earthly woes.

Williams was confident that she had the gift of extrasensory perception. She wrote to Hancock, "I think that my mind is blocking me, now—Grace tried to commit suicide the day before I was supposed to leave—So you see." This statement suggests that Williams believed her spirit would have detected any ill vibes related to her sister's precarious mental health, had her mind not clouded her receptivity. In response to this worry, Williams fasted for twelve hours, which gave her "quite a peace."[52] Later, she informed Hancock that her beloved nephew Robbie had had a bicycle accident that resulted in "a spot on the back of his head"—and she claimed that she "saw this [life-threatening incident] while in Copenhagen."[53] When Hancock returned to the US and began looking after Robbie, a worried Williams sensed something was awry and demanded "the truth" from Hancock about Robbie—had he been disobedient or sassy (possibly smoking), and did he produce feelings of sickness in Hancock, who she claimed never became "sick, if not worried or agitated"?[54] Her correspondence with him reiterated her belief that the "bad vibrations" of an individual had the power to produce physical illness in others.

At the start of 1970, Williams updated Hancock that she "Went to confession—was getting too many things, including deaths[,] woe! Really bad—don't need it, ha! I think many of us can foresee but have to be careful."[55] During her period of religious instruction, Williams had dreams in which she encountered dead friends and relatives in her home, such as an aunt who came in chains to tell her that she had been chained down in her own house. Such dreams led her to feel "so polluted with friends or things dying or getting killed that I began to go to church and get those brown candles for the dead. I became frightened here in the house, you know, and I'd get brown candles and burn them for the dead in the house." And although she tells her interviewer in 1973 that she ceased lighting brown candles for the dead when she formally became Catholic in 1957, her conversations with Hancock on her confession reveal that such dreams and visions persisted into the early 1970s.[56]

Lastly, Williams relayed one ESP incident in her 1973 oral history interview. She dreamed that Dizzy and Lorraine discussed asking her for an expensive pocketbook that they knew Scott gifted to her for her Bel Canto fundraising. When Williams was awake, Lorraine did call her to turn down the pocketbook—unprompted by Williams. Williams returned it to Scott and viewed it as further confirmation of her spiritual abilities.[57]

On one of her writing tablets, which contained prayer lists, essays, and book notes, Williams made a note to purchase the 1919 book *Essays in Occultism, Spiritism, and Demonology* by Dean W. R. Harris. Some of Williams's notes reflected her study of Harris's *Essays*. Additionally, she expressed a belief in the spirits of the dead, angels, evil spirits, and Satan ("the man"), as well as humanity's ability to communicate with/ward them off. These beings had the ability to influence, aide, or impede humanity in the quest to realize the will of God. Williams wrote, "He who accepts inspiration of prayers (strengthen soul against attacks, etc. and to ward off temptation) and Bible rids himself of blindfold[s] and ear-pluggers to see and hear [the] existence of malign influence on human beings of the man and his rebel spirits." Although spirits and their influences were real, she also stated that "there is no such thing as good or bad luck, black magic, etc. . . . ." To ward off "bad sounds" from unwanted spiritual presences, musicians in particular must pray for good sounds. "The air around us can be musical or the whisperings of evil spirits. It's a dangerous mistake to think evil spirits do not exist. There are a great many of them to attack us. *Another reason one has to forgive friends and others*—we are control[led] either by good or bad. Prayers, charity, no sins, etc., keep good angels with us."[58] In these private writings, Williams reveals the way her religious study not only paralleled the lived and popular religious experiences of other Catholics but also paralleled discourses of "spiritual warfare" in charismatic and Holiness-Pentecostal Christianity.

Williams's perceptions were not always foreboding, however. She had visions and empathic experiences that she relayed to Hancock: "I saw success for you in music—by the way [I] also saw you very close to a dark kid & being successful but take it easy. I know you must want to see him in school right away but God has a place for him. I feel your suffering but offer it up for me (music) & your family."[59] Some of her visions and dreams received interpretations that involved her ongoing sacred jazz endeavors, an investment in spreading joy and facilitating personal healing through the gift of music. In this instance, Williams relayed to Hancock that he needed to rely on God more and tax himself less to ensure that the "dark kid" would become enrolled in school soon and that Hancock would find professional success.

Several letters to Hancock detail the messy institutional politics and economics of producing, performing, and generating income from sacred jazz within the Catholic Church. Often, Williams asked Hancock for his assistance in getting her concerts or Mass performances. Irreverence, candor, and a general air of humor mark these letters, a sign that she felt familiar enough with the Black Catholic monk to relate to him in a different manner than with white priests and nuns. Assessing the enterprising nature of religious authorities, Williams admitted, "You know, Mario I pray often for nuns & priests. They are in the commercial business and it's a mess, ha!"[60] Her May 7, 1968 letter indicated her woes engaging with clerical authorities, including the conflicted benefactor relationships she and Lorraine had with younger white male priests:

. . . Then too, in as much as I'd like to do a concert—will have to get paid—Mario you're very kind to me but other priests have used me & others to no end and they don't have to pay bills to live—Please don't get me wrong 'cause I want to help people but the USA is really rotten. The same kinda rotten tactics exist with the priests & nuns that the commercial [music] field offers over here and it's the worst, please believe me. I'll just have to make a living. Have to talk with Lorraine madly to keep her with the church. She & Dizzy send priests to school etc. She had a couple bad experiences—and believe it or not, some of the Catholic schools are closing. What do they do with all the money?[61]

"Priests are strange when they leave the priesthood," Williams told Hancock. "They usually come to me. Fr. Ledogan and Fr. Salmon are out also—But the last two are something else."[62] Williams often confided that American priests—with Father Woods having been one of the few exceptions—were not well suited to be her religious authorities, and Hancock was not the only one to receive her assessments of these white clerics. Eustis Guillemet wrote, "Hearing about these priest[s] sure is disheartening but as you say, keep on praying. Everybody is going his or her way."[63] When advising Hancock on how to retain his spiritual fortitude, one spiritually enervating hazard she assessed was priests' carefree willingness to reside in the homes of anyone without knowing their spiritual practices or fortitude: "Mario[,] through experience & observing priests—I think the worst thing that could ever happen is to be allowed to stay in people's houses—this weakens one. The spirits are asleep during the day in the corners." Reading scripture and ritual cleansing must be fortifying spiritual practices, Williams cautioned Hancock, so that he would not succumb to potentially hostile or negative spiritual influences: "One has to read the Psalms—use holy water etc. to get rid of them, because all people are not charitable. One has to get into the folds of God in a big way to sustain being with God, forever, through all this muck & mud."[64]

As she pondered in her 1973 interview, "You know what actually happened with me, I prayed so hard for priests and later on a lot of them came up with me. I don't know why I was praying so hard for them but most of my prayers—and I used to light candles for them in the church, you know."[65] Save her charitable relationship with several jazz-friendly priests, what informed Williams's negative impression of priests was her experience with their unwanted sexual advances and expressed interest in marriage, possibly to marry her. She wrote to Hancock from Pittsburgh on May 7, 1969 during a visit for her birthday: "Guess what? A friend priest from Bishop Wright's diocese asked me out to dinner tonite and he had another friend priest with him & both were begging me to talk to Bishop Wright about priests getting married. They must be 'kooked' (crazy). They said Wright loved me & would listen to me—What they meant is he'd listen to another Negro." Williams referred to Pittsburgh Bishop John J. Wright, who she considered to be "for the black man all the way" who also supported her jazz Mass. Williams described the unwanted behavior of one of the two white priests at the dinner: "One of the priests tonite had on a big, big diamond ring—B—sh—ting [Bullshitting] me that he'd like to get an act with me—kissing me in the mouth, even when I turned my head. . . . Really sickening."[66] Here, Williams discloses the converse of spiritual and religious friendships that strengthen one's commitment to a religious community. Williams identified white priest "friends" who expected that their friendship with her would result in her work to persuade Catholic bishops to allow them to act on their desires for marriage partners, in one instance, or in her sexual availability to them, despite her physical movements to protest the unwanted kissing of a white priest aggressor. In another letter to Hancock March 4, 1970, William laments:

> . . . Often I become disgusted & upset—and sick but have to carry on—
> everybody is nuts! and believe or not whenever a priest comes out of
> the Church he lands in my house. One came last nite—He was so

nervous. I couldn't sleep after he left wow! They all seem to go nuts—have to see a psycho—wow. Fr. Ledogar is out also.

I'm beginning to think most are in dire sin—They can't rest or think—who knows—I really shouldn't have said that because they are pitiful—[67]

A portrait of a sinful white Catholic clergy emerges with Williams's correspondence. Assessing her encounters with them, "problem priests" were nerve-racked, prone to arranging meetings with laity in order to make unwanted sexual advances, desperately seeking official sanctions to end priests' vows of celibacy through the use of token Black liaisons, susceptible to adversarial spiritual influences, and ultimately unsuited for their calling. These interactions justified her irreverent orientation toward their institutional religious authority.

On November 24, 1968, Williams wrote to Hancock while performing in Copenhagen:

> . . . A customer who calls himself young Hemingway came to the club every nite (drunk with a beard) called me & said, Mary I can't stay in the room when you're not playing. Seems that your music is coming from God & your heart.
>
> I laughed to myself—When I played I'd pray—'Jesus Mary Joseph help! Our Father, Hail Mary, Jesus give me patience!' The works—prayed so hard one nite my crucifix rosary 'Lo' gave me—came up out of my bra—Inez pointed at it & told me to straighten it—I looked at her & said: That's my knife! She jumped as if to say: I knew she wasn't nothing [smiley face with lips]—But she stayed her distance, ha! I feel sorry for her . . . I was a nervous wreck while there but the minute I touched the piano nobody existed but above, I think, or I went somewhere, ha! [. . .][68]

While friends like Scott may have regarded Williams as their elder spiritual sister whose sacred music reflected her deep spiritual cultivation, Hancock also received her humorous self-disclosures that revealed her playful uncertainty about her gifts and calling.

During her stay at St. Lioba Kloster in Denmark, Williams seriously contemplated a cloistered life as her next calling. Williams regarded the teachings of Trappist monk Thomas Merton (1915–1968) as spiritually formative. Merton's teachings in *The Sign of Jonas* (1953), which concerned one's ability to control desire in order to acquire knowledge and improve one's being, inspired Williams to take seriously that the Copen-hagen cloister was a space where she could feel God bringing her closer: ". . . I felt that God was saying, Be cool, see I'm doing everything to bring you closer to me." Remarking on her spiritual senses, Williams testified to Hancock, "I can see many things since I came here."[69] "[T]o tell you the truth," wrote Williams, "I am always in the habit of telling God to show me myself, often, and show me him too! This time I asked to be shown myself (Merton and Dom Columba Marmion had gotten to me, ha). This particular time I must have been sincere—bang! Ha! And guess what? I have been so full of joy and God's love at times I could kiss a mule." Williams drew a surprised facial expression on this letter, con-veying her shock at the kindness the cloister nuns showed her and how it worked to foster the joy and love that flowed from divine and self-awareness.[70] And even though Williams decided against becoming a nun, she maintained that her spiritual work in seclusion was responsible for the revived popularity that jazz musicians experienced in the late 1960s and into the 1970s. "It's something how when God does hide one, things begin moving. They [other jazz musicians] all think they started this—and once again I guess I'll have to be hidden for it to continue."[71] Her diligent prayer life, out of the spotlight, was part of God's plan and aided the flourishing of other jazz artists, she surmised.

Hancock's letters to Williams were not present in her archive at Rut-gers University during my period of study. Nevertheless, the constant correspondence reliably indicates a relationship between the two Catho-lics that reflected her other exchanges, in that they covered matters mundane, musical, institutional, political, familial, somber, spiritual, and humorous. At times, she was comfortable enough with Hancock to relay her experiences with attempted sexual assaulters beyond the priests who made advances.[72] It is very reasonable that her additional conversations with Lorraine and Scott, beyond this collection of letters, constituted a circle of Black women aware of the behaviors of certain religious authorities and varyingly irreverent toward them as a conse-quence. Observing and/or experiencing ostensibly celibate priests in their most "carnal" moments of desire would aid any disenchantment about their priestly calling. For Hancock's part, his record of responses, and the sacred or profane nature of his discourse with her, does not re-side within the archives.

Conclusion: Intimate Friendships, Irreverent Spirituality, and Religious Authority

If people consider a religious institution incapable of accommodating the *entirety* of their religious and spiritual experiences, they may regard its leadership with less totalizing authority. If the institution cannot accommodate their gender, race, or professional history—or adhere to professed standards of celibacy when interacting with laity—these barriers may add to an irreverent embrace and appraisal of the religious institution. Williams was a Black jazz professional who expressed confidence in the extrasensory spiritual gifts with which she was born. She was going to do as much (praying, fasting, candle-lighting) as she wanted, for as long as she wanted, and often against the counsel of a Catholic clergy she confidently assessed to have many morally wayward priests. While not always humorously irreverent, her practices of worship, ritual, devotion, and prayer (especially the humor and sincerity of her prayer life with others) were a mark of her irreverent religious orientation.[73] Her handwritten, in-person, and over-the-telephone correspondence with her friends Hazel Scott and Mario Hancock also constituted intimate means of binding oneself to sacred and social others—some of the work of being religious. Her intimate and confessional practices with friends were alternative and supplemental avenues to religious life beyond Mass attendance, ritual observance, and priestly consultation—the spaces of white religious authority, instruction, surveillance, and even clandestine sexual advances.

For Williams and her friends to carry intimate, confessional conversations between media (telephone and letter) and across time (writing in response to an over-the-phone or in-person conversation that just ended, or weekly / monthly / unscheduled written correspondence) is also to carry along their expressed recognition that they were Black Americans, Catholic ritual practitioners, Catholics under a white male hierarchy, jazz professionals and afficionados, transnational Black Catholics, and commentators on Black freedom social struggles. As active cultivation of selves, intimate friendships illuminate the complex intersubjectivity of religious identity and practice. Additionally, there was plenty of humor in this correspondence. Williams's letters, as well as Scott's letters to her, signified on her body, mind, soul/spirit, experiences, ritual work, jazz work, and her ordained/lay/non-Catholic interlocutors. Written laughter, hyperbole, reading (a form of signifying), profanity, self-deprecation, recounting dramatic altercations/confrontations, dark humor, playful religious doubt, and comical self-illustrations by pen constitute the presence of humor in this correspondence that also reveals the importance of an irreverent orientation toward complex religious intersubjectivity. In twentieth-century African American religious history and beyond, I have found that such irreverent communications represent "a posture of religious thought and belonging[,] between reverence and non-religiosity" that has allowed practitioners to express and sustain their theological commitments while avoiding, opposing, or subverting the norms of reverential religious behavior—especially deference to religious authority.[74] An irreverent lay Black Catholic jazz professional, Mary Lou Williams built religious community and sustained spiritual life around, beyond, and by transcending white male Catholic religious authority with her communicative friendships.

Notes

I am grateful to the Black Religious Studies Working Group for helpful feedback on this chapter.

Letter sender/recipient names are abbreviated as follows: EG = Eustis Guillemet, HS = Hazel Scott, MLW = Mary Lou Williams, MH = Mario Hancock.

1. Letter from HS to MLW, Sunday, September 5, 1965, 2–3, 7.

2. Karen Chilton, *Hazel Scott: The Pioneering Journey of a Jazz Pianist from Café Society to Hollywood to HUAC* (Ann Arbor: The University of Michigan Press, 2008), 193.

3. Letter from HS to MLW, November 19, 1963, 1–2.

4. Chilton, *Hazel Scott*, 195.

5. For a detailed discussion of Mary Lou Williams's Bel Canto Foundation effort, see Ch. 7, "Jazz Communion," and Ch. 8, "Accounting for the Vulnerable," in Vaughn A. Booker, *Lift Every Voice and Swing: Black Musicians and Religious Culture in the Jazz Century* (New York: New York University Press, 2020).

6. For more biographical information on Mary Lou Williams, Mario Hancock, and Eustis Guillemet, see Linda Dahl, *Morning Glory: A Biography of Mary Lou Williams* (New York: Pantheon, 1999); Tammy Kernodle, *Soul on Soul: The Life and Music of Mary Lou Williams* (Boston: Northeastern University Press, 2004); and Vaughn A. Booker, *Lift Every Voice and Swing: Black Musicians and Religious Culture in the Jazz Century* (New York: New York University Press, 2020). For more biographical information on Hazel Scott, see Chilton, *Hazel*

Scott. For more on Loraine and Dizzy Gillespie, see Dizzy Gillespie's autobiography co-written with Wilmot Alfred Fraser, *To Be . . . or Not . . . to Bop* (Minneapolis: University of Minnesota Press, 2009).

7. There are forty-three letters to or from Mary Lou Williams and her Black religious and spiritual friends that are available in the Mary Lou Williams Collection, Institute of Jazz Studies, Rutgers University: three from Lorraine Gillespie, six from Eustis Guillemet, twenty from Hazel Scott, and fourteen from Mary Lou Williams.

8. Tammy L. Kernodle, "Preface to the New Edition," *Soul on Soul: The Life and Music of Mary Lou Williams* (Urbana: University of Illinois Press, 2004 [2020]), xxi.

9. Brenna Moore, "Friendship and the Cultivation of Religious Sensibilities," *Journal of the American Academy of Religion* 83, no. 2 (June 2015), 439–441, 452.

10. Todne Thomas, *Kincraft: The Making of Black Evangelical Solidarity* (Durham: Duke University Press, 2021), 171.

11. Thomas, *Kincraft*, 182.

12. Thomas, *Kincraft*, 195.

13. Thomas, *Kincraft*, 197–198.

14. Gayle Murchison, "Mary Lou Williams's Hymn *Black Christ of the Andes (St. Martin de Porres)*: Vatican II, Civil Rights, and Jazz as Sacred Music," *The Musical Quarterly* 86, no. 4 (Winter 2002): 603.

15. Brenna Moore, *Kindred Spirits: Friendship and Resistance at the Edges of Modern Catholicism* (Chicago: The University of Chicago Press, 2021), 213.

16. Judith Weisenfeld, *Hollywood Be Thy Name: African American Religion in American Film, 1929–1949* (Berkeley and Los Angeles: University of California Press, 2007), 124–126.

17. Thelma Pearson, "The Negro Whom South Americans Worship," *Negro Digest* 6, no. 4 (February 1948): 89–91.

18. Pearson, "The Negro Whom South Americans Worship," 92.

19. Erin Kathleen Rowe, *Black Saints in Early Modern Global Catholicism* (New York: Cambridge University Press, 2019), 185–186.

20. Rowe, *Black Saints*, 188.

21. Rowe, *Black Saints*, 190.

22. Rowe, *Black Saints*, 210–211.

23. Williams continued, ". . . I could, if I was playing with any musician on earth—it could be Charlie Parker—I could almost hear, could hear most of the time, the next note they're going to make. All this was in my music to help me musically, because I've done some fantastic things, you know, and not studied as much as other musicians in the music field. So I think that what happened to me after I stopped playing[,] then my vision and everything went on the outside of music and I began to hear what was going to happen musically while

I was praying. Like I saw Charlie Parker's death. I felt that a strange foreign sound would enter into the strains of jazz and would destroy the heritage, would destroy jazz completely. . . . I could see all this happening while I was in Paris. It kind of frightened me. It seemed like my feelings was altogether out on the street, or what was happening in the world. I was able to make several predictions maybe 20 years ahead." Jazz Oral History Project, 142–143.

24. Rowe, *Black Saints*, 92–93.

25. Murchison, "Mary Lou Williams's Hymn *Black Christ of the Andes (St. Martin de Porres)*," 603.

26. Chris Garces, Ch. 4, "The Interspecies Logic of Race in Colonial Peru: San Martín de Porres's Animal Brotherhood," in *Sainthood and Race: Marked Flesh, Holy Flesh*, ed. Molly H. Bassett and Vincent W. Lloyd (New York: Routledge, 2015), 84.

27. Garces, "The Interspecies Logic of Race in Colonial Peru," 91.

28. Garces, "The Interspecies Logic of Race in Colonial Peru," 94–95.

29. Farrah Jasmine Griffin, *Harlem Nocturne: Women Artists and Progressive Politics during World War II* (New York: Basic Civitas Books, 2013), 140.

30. In the pursuit of prominent "celebrity converts" in the 1950s and 1960s, Duke Ellington was much more of a prized convert for various Christian denominations, including the Episcopal Church and the Roman Catholic church, than Mary Lou Williams.

31. Yvonne P. Chireau, *Black Magic: Religion and the African American Conjuring Tradition* (Berkeley: University of California Press, 2003), 23.

32. Booker, *Lift Every Voice and Swing*, 18–19.

33. Griffin, *Harlem Nocturne*, 164.

34. Letter from HS to MLW, November 19, 1963, 4.

35. Letter from HS to MLW, April 23, 1965, 7–8.

36. Letter from HS to MLW, April 23, 1965, 3–4.

37. Letter from HS to MLW, June 26, 1965, 4–5.

38. Chilton, *Hazel Scott*, 196.

39. One contemporary irony is that Scott followed this statement in her letter with a one line sentence—"*DRAG!*"—most likely in concert with her other uses of the common lament, "What a drag!" but resembling the discourse of "dragging," an intense act of Black signifying that accompanies reading.

40. Letter from HS to MLW, August 18, 1965, 3–5.

41. Letter from HS to MLW, Monday 1966, 2–3.

42. Letter from HS to MLW, Monday 1966, 1–4.

43. Letter from HS to MLW, April 23, 1965, 6.

44. "Mario Hancock Obituary," *The Star Ledger*, October 26, 2005, accessed January 26, 2023, https://obits.nj.com/us/obituaries/starledger/name/mario-hancock-obituary?id=14538317.

45. Letter from MLW to MH, June 29, 1969, 1.

46. Letter from MLW to MH, June 28, 1969, 2.

47. Letter from MLW to MH, September 11, 1967, 2–3.

48. Letter from MLW to MH, April 3, 1968, 1.

49. Letter from MLW to MH, May 23, 1968, 2.

50. Booker, *Lift Every Voice and Swing*, 94.

51. Letter from MLW to MH, September 28, 1967, 2–3, 6.

52. Letter from MLW to MH, May 7, 1968, 3.

53. Letter from MLW to MH, May 7, 1969, 7–8.

54. Letter from MLW to MH, February 16, 1970, 1–2.

55. Letter from MLW to MH, January 30, 1970, 4.

56. Williams spoke at length, "I used to pray so hard for the souls and if anybody [was dying] till when anyone died, they actually came to the house. I had an aunt that died and she was in chains. I spoke to her and asked her and she came back to me in a dream and said to me that they chained her down like that in a house. Well, they did. People took her house from her and just had her in a bed and she wasn't being fed and a lot of things. . . ." Jazz Oral History Project, 172–173.

57. Jazz Oral History Project, 174–175.

58. "Notebook—Essays on Notables," front cover.

59. Letter from MLW to MH, February 17, 1970, 4.

60. Letter from MLW to MH, January 28 or 29, 1968, 2.

61. Letter from MLW to MH, May 7, 1968, 2–3.

62. Letter from MLW to MH, May 2, 1970, 4.

63. Letter from EG to MLW, undated ca. 1966, 2–3.

64. Letter from MLW to MH, April 28, 1969, 1–2.

65. Jazz Oral History Project, 172.

66. Letter from MLW to MH, May 7, 1969, 1, 7.

67. Letter from MLW to MH, March 4, 1970, 1–2.

68. Letter from MLW to MH, November 24, 1968, 5–6.

69. Letter from MLW to MH, November 26, 1968, 1–2. Williams also remarked, "Since reading Thomas Merton—am pretty cool—back on God's time, you see at least I'm trying. The greatest blessing for my soul was to move here with the NUNS—One cannot come into HIS folds, stay outside with the world & pray, helping poor souls—someone, somewhere will try to get ya!" Letter from MLW to MH, December 13, 1968, 1.

70. Letter from MLW to MH, January 5, 1969, 1.

71. Letter from MLW to MH, April 24, 1969, 1.

72. Before her departure from Copenhagen to the U. S., Williams wrote, "Everybody is smilin'—and don't ask one of these skunks where anything is, they'll try to pull you in a hole and rape you. One said (and an old man, too!),

'You finally came to me.' I said, 'You better take your—hands off me before—in the a—By now they think I'm from Lenox Ave." Letter from MLW to MH, April 12, 1969, 2.

73. I am grateful to Chanhee Heo for helping me to articulate this point.

74. Vaughn A. Booker, "'Pulpit and Pew': African American Humor on Irreverent Religious Participation in John H. Johnson's *Negro Digest*, 1943–1950," *Journal of Africana Religions* 8, no. 1 (2020): 28.

Nina Polcyn

Living Art and Women's Leadership at St. Benet's Bookstore

BRIAN J. CLITES

St. Benet's Bookstore operated from 1924 to 1973.[1] It was a central site for the liturgical movement, women in the Catholic Worker, and many of Chicago's Catholic Action groups. The shop was much more than just a space for reading and commerce. As St. Benet's patron Adolph Schalk declared, the store's literary selections were vast, but "What ELSE St. Benet's is and does is hard to put into a brief article."[2] In short, St. Benet's was *the* place for progressive Chicago laywomen to meet one another, a "third space" that created and facilitated robust spiritual, intellectual, commercial, and artistic exchanges. The store also attracted prominent male intellectuals, including Jerome Kerwin, Andrew Greeley, Paul Tillich, Dom Mauro Inguanez, Jacques Maritain, and Martin Marty. Schalk likened it to "clearinghouse for visiting abbots, priests, authors, and converts, most of whom were indebted to [its staff] for inspiring them to see their faith through different eyes."[3]

In its early years, the bookstore hosted meetings for the Calvert Club, the Council of Catholic Women, the Sheil School of Social Studies, the Catholic Youth Organization, the Young Christian Workers, the Young Christian Students, the Catholic Labor Alliance, the League of the Divine Office, and the Vernacular Society. It was also a vital hub for the Catholic Worker movement, a meeting spot for members of Friendship House, and second only to St. John's Abbey as a center for the liturgical arts. In the 1940s, St. Benet's continued to host Chicago's growing roster of Catholic Action groups, including Cana Conference, the Christian Family Movement, and the Catholic Interracial Council. Less frequently, the bookstore hosted meetings of Benedictine oblates, women in the Grail, and the Catholic Women's Union.

For socialites, the bookstore was also a place to see and be seen. Mayor Daley routinely stopped by the store to shake hands, and even from its earliest days, St. Benet's was a popular place to find dates. "Couples use the spot as a meeting place . . . while marriages are said to be made in heaven, not a few have been known to get their start at St. Benet's."[4] Mentions of banquets and art shows hosted at St. Benet's appeared frequently in the student newspapers at Loyola, Mundelein, and DePaul. The bookstore birthed intellectual debates, liturgical experimentation, artistic creativity, and political activism.

Historians have mostly overlooked St. Benet's, as well as hundreds of less famous Catholic bookstores in the twentieth-century US. There are several exceptions, most notably Keith Peckler's *The Unread Vision* and Katharine Harmon's *There Were Also Many Women There*, each of which identifies St. Benet's and the women who ran it as crucial members of the liturgical movement.[5] In her essays on Ade Bethune, Harmon also points towards the emancipatory potential of uplifting and analyzing the handmade artwork that Catholic women produced during this period.[6] When we follow Harmon in focusing on liturgical artwork and prayers, the two features that set St. Benet's apart from other prominent Catholic bookstores, we can better understand the creative ways that laywomen collaborated with one another to carve out leadership opportunities in the decades prior to Vatican II.

Crucially, St. Benet's was a space where gender functioned differently. The women who ran the bookstore had more latitude and more liberty than most laywomen and sisters had in other Catholic spaces where women played an outsized role (e.g., parishes, schools, universities, convents). In recognition of its creative potential for Catholic women, this essay analyzes St. Benet's as a "third space," a term which emphasizes its cultural location as a site where women could cultivate religious structures and subjectivities that were differently gendered. "Third" is not a physical count of these other Catholic institutional structures. Rather, it is used here in line with Homi Bhabha's classic formulation of the term as a marker of liminal contexts where hybrid subjectivities can flourish.[7]

While nuns were running schools and hospitals, and Catholic wives were participating in Cana and the Christian Family Movement, some unwed laywomen carved out new roles in bookstores and literary magazines. Although progressive discourse at St. Benet's was sometimes controversial, the fact that it was a bookstore, and not a parish or a school or a university, gave the female staff added cover. When asked about their freedom to innovate, O'Neill's successor replied, "Bishop Sheil just felt whatever we did was wonderful . . . And I think we all had friends enough in the chancery."[8] With Sheil and Msgr. Hillenbrand's tacit approval, O'Neill made St. Benet's into a space in which women set the liturgical agenda. This dynamic of lay-women's leadership reinforces prior research identifying the arts as a frontier for lay innovation. The midcentury boom in American book culture, as Una Cadegan has observed, required "the collaboration and interdependence of hierarchy and laity."[9] Similarly, as Catherine Osborne has theorized, Catholic "hierarchy monitored aesthetic conversations less closely than the output of theologians, creating a professional and intellectual space where forbidden ideas about change, growth could reemerge earlier and with greater freedom."[10] At Catholic bookstores—nearly all of which were managed by laywomen—this artistic independence collided with emerging horizons for women's leadership.[11].

The all-female staff at St. Benet's were able to experiment with entrepreneurial roles distinctive from those available to them in other institutionally Catholic spaces. Unlike parishes, where priests mediated access to the sacred, the women of St. Benet's led their own devotional prayers and Saturday-night liturgies. Unlike Catholic homes, where the sacrality of womanhood was circumscribed within expectations of marriage and motherhood, female power at the bookstore was reconfigured around artistic and intellectual acumen. Unlike parochial schools, there were no "mothers," "sisters," or priests on staff, and the focus was on educating midlife adults. Unlike Catholic universities, the women of St. Benet's had ample leeway to diverge socially and intellectually from their male peers. And unlike cloistered convents, the spiritual labor was outward-facing and self-directed. As one guest characterized it in 1946, St. Benet's was "a place not shackled by the strict definitions of a library or a church."[12]

Sarah O'Neill: Bringing European Monasticism into the American City

Sarah Benedicta O'Neill (1869–1954) was a pioneer in the Catholic library movement.[13] A bright student, O'Neill attended Northwestern University, then taught history and languages in the Chicago public school system. In the 1890s, she enrolled in a University of Chicago course and became fascinated with lore "about how the Benedictines had saved western culture by preserving Christian and pagan learning in the Middle Ages."[14]

O'Neill made five trips to European monasteries over the coming decade, and in 1902 she was received as a Benedictine Oblate in the same subterranean chapel in which Ellen Gates Starr had consecrated herself to the rule of St. Benedict. Starr and O'Neill were foremothers of the American liturgical movement, beginning a long line of friends who joined the third order, including Maisie Ward, Ade Bethune, Dorothy Day, Nina Polcyn, Mary Perkins, John Ryan, and Pat and Patty Crowley.[15]

After returning from Italy, O'Neill became a fixture at the Chicago Calvert Club. A group of lay intellectuals associated with *Commonweal* magazine, Calvert Club members believed that Catholic literature could change American society.[16] O'Neil persuaded her Calvert friends to support her vision for opening a Catholic bookstore. In 1924, O'Neill placed a homemade sign for "O'Neill's Calvert Bookstore" in the window of her sister's house, announcing that she would be selling Catholic books and serving tea.[17] The venture was a money pit, so O'Neill's friends on the Council of Catholic Women offered to incorporate her vision into their new headquarters, which shared space with Bishop Sheil's Catholic Youth Organization (CYO) in the McCormick Building downtown. On October 31, 1931, O'Neill led five other women in consecrating the space; they knelt, recited the *Angelus,* and opened for business.[18] The store became popular, and in 1937 O'Neill formally incorporated her enterprise as "St. Benet's Library and Bookshop." After the move into the McCormick, sales increased steadily. As a measure of this newfound success, O'Neill proudly stocked bottles of the aperitif *Benedictine* behind the counter, which she would offer to distinguished guests.[19] Although O'Neill credited St. Benedict for the store's prosperity, its rise coincided with a national surge of interest in Catholic intellectual life.

American Catholic print culture exploded during the first half of the twentieth century. It not only grew in terms of the numbers of books sold but also in the proliferation of new Catholic magazines, journals, and newspapers.[20] Catholic print culture was oriented largely toward living out one's Catholicity in the secular world. This commitment was especially pronounced in the secular city, as exemplified by the Catholic Worker movement, where reading, writing, and publishing grounded founders Dorothy Day and Peter Maurin, as well as many of their friends. *The Catholic Worker* newspaper also understood print culture as a method for spreading the Works of Mercy, which exemplified solidarity with the poor.

At the time, St. Benet's was the only Midwestern store carrying *The Catholic Worker* and *Commonweal*.

Across the country, there was an urgent desire "to elevate the taste" of Catholic readers.[21] Even devotional rituals were reworked alongside this new literary participation. Prayers that were once efficacious regardless of class were now subject to the authority of more educated laypersons. As Robert Orsi has theorized, "the new words belonged to a highly educated, professionalized class of specialists in church life—teachers, liturgists, educators, administrators—whose emergence at this time reflected the confident entry of American Catholics into the middle class."[22] In producing and devouring so much print, Catholics joined Protestants in consuming the dream that reading could help them to transcend social and economic barriers.[23]

The literary boom was particularly exciting for educated Catholic laywomen. Long excluded from theological circles, including leadership positions at Catholic universities, laywomen played a number of vital roles in this new middle-class literary culture. As Jeffery Burns has observed, journalism was "perhaps the greatest outlet for Catholic laywomen" during the 1950s.[24] Although only a few Catholic women were then widely recognized as authors, many more were involved in the writing, editing, and sale of Catholic periodicals. During the late 1930s, St. Benet's achieved enough fame for O'Neill to hire a full staff to run the store during her frequent trips to European monasteries. O'Neil forged lasting friendships with the Abbot of Bruges, and Frank Sheed and Maisie Ward, the proprietors of one of the world's first lay Catholic publishing houses. When Sheed and Ward opened their New York branch in 1937, it was with O'Neill's guidance, and they repaid her tenfold by promoting St. Benet's as the national center for a new kind of Catholic "voice."[25]

The "voice" O'Neill injected into American Catholic life was decidedly gendered. Here was a woman who had, at age 55, in her sister's parlor, founded what soon became one of the most famous Catholic bookstores in the world. By 1939, St. Benet's employed more than a dozen full-time female librarians and managed a collection that exceeded the shelving space. The bookshop offered some six thousand volumes in theology, as well as forty Catholic periodicals. It carried multiple copies of Ward's 22-volume English translation of the *Summa Theologica*, rivaling the depth of even Chicago's finest university bookstores.[26]

These statistics speak to the new location's increased success, but they do not explain its sacred allure. Although St. Benet's had a world-renowned selection of books, it actually carried fewer monographs than its nearby neighbor, the Thomas More Association, which claimed to be the largest Catholic bookstore in the world.[27] To understand the phenomenon that was St. Benet's, we need to look at the ways the bookstore was transformed by O'Neill's successor, Nina Polcyn.

Nina Polcyn: "Merchant Priestess and Trafficker in Crucifixes"

Nina Polcyn (pronounced Nine-ah Pole-tsin) was born on August 21, 1914, into a poor, struggling household in the Polish district of Milwaukee.[28] Her father was a railway switchman and registered Socialist. Her parents were devoted to the Corporal Works of Mercy, "feeding the poor who came to our door."[29] Even when the Great Depression left her father unemployed, Polcyn recalled, her parents fed and housed homeless immigrants.[30] By taking on additional jobs, Polcyn paid for her tuition at Marquette University, and in 1935 she persuaded the School of Journalism to invite Dorothy Day to campus.[31]

When Day came to Marquette in 1935, she stayed with Polcyn's family. Over the week, the two women began an inimitable friendship that lasted until Dorothy's death in 1980.[32] Journalists who later wrote about Day's first visit to Polcyn characterized it as the moment when she became "a disciple of Dorothy Day;"[33] or, as another article described the visit, as a divine intervention from which "young Nina never recovered."[34] Such statements, however, overlook the influences that Polcyn had on Day; the fact that Polcyn was only gradually, over the next six years, won over by the vision of the Catholic Worker; and the extent to which Polcyn became an international force in her own right. In fact, Dorothy spent most of that first encounter speaking not to Nina but to her parents "about the work my father did as a railroad switchman."[35]

After graduating from Marquette, Polcyn convinced her parents to allow her to move to New York City to volunteer at Day's Catholic Worker house in the Bowery. The experience challenged Polcyn who, in spite of her modest upbringing, was unprepared for the grit and poverty she witnessed. Unnerved by the experience, Nina moved back to Milwaukee to write copy for Gimbel's Department Store and, finding that intellectually wanting, later accepted an appointment as a substitute high school teacher, which paid $5 a day.[36] Polcyn's trajectory after college suggests that she was torn, from the start, between Day's model of poverty and the lure of a middle-class lifestyle.[37]

In Milwaukee, Polcyn continued to gather with a group of fellow journalists in the basement of the Marquette library, including David Host, Harry Schwartz, Leonard Doyle, Larry Heaney, and Florence Weinfurter. In October 1937, they founded Holy Family House, the first Milwaukee Catholic Worker house of hospitality for the destitute.[38] Although she was very devoted to the house, Polcyn worked simultaneously as a high school teacher, from which she earned $265 per month.[39] Meanwhile, the Milwaukee house struggled constantly to maintain its finances, closing sporadically for short periods between 1937 and 1942. With the exception of those occasional closures, the house fed approximately two hundred men each day, fifty of whom were also given clothing and shelter.[40] Margaret Blaser and Joseph Petit soon joined Polcyn and her co-founders as core staff at Holy Family.[41]

Polcyn frequently left the house to accompany Day to events. Nina attended several of Father John Hugo's eight-day retreats in Oakmont, Pennsylvania, where he directed Day's inner circle in meditation on their divine mission as pacifists.[42] These early collaborations facilitated Polcyn's immersion into personalist theology and ritual. Nina was also Day's lieutenant in 1937, orchestrating local protests against Adolf Hitler and picketing the German Consulate.

In 1942, Polcyn decided to shutter the Milwaukee Catholic Worker house.[43] Day strongly objected to Polcyn's closing the house after just five years, but their friendship endured. Even as her own career in the liturgical movement blossomed over the following decade, Polcyn made frequent trips to visit Dorothy in New York, often selling the *Catholic Worker* newspaper along New York's Irish Waterfront.[44] In 1955, when Day was arrested along with twenty-nine other pacifists for the first Civil Defense protest, Polcyn disregarded Bayard Rustin's instructions to leave Dorothy in jail for a few days, instead paying her bail immediately.[45] The following year, Polcyn went even further: she sat next to Day, arms joined, at the infamous 1956 Civil Defense action in Washington Square Park (the protest that later signaled the pinnacle of Day's public career). It was one of many times when Polcyn and Day were jailed together after peace protests.

Likewise, Day was known for always staying with Polcyn during her frequent trips to the Windy City, and the two frequently travelled with one another to other cities.[46] Among numerous other journeys, Polcyn was Dorothy's personal companion for Day's well-publicized 1971 peace delegation to the Soviet Union. According to Polcyn, "We'd talked of going [to Russia] together for years, so when she got a scholarship, Dorothy called me up and asked if I could go. We had a delightful three weeks."[47] Their itinerary included meetings with politicians and activists in Moscow, Leningrad, Warsaw, Hungary, Romania, and Czechoslovakia. In Polcyn's obituary in the *National Catholic Reporter*, Robert McClory claimed that Dorothy had considered Nina her "oldest and dearest friend."[48]

After the Milwaukee house had closed, Polcyn moved to Chicago with her longtime roommate, Margaret Blaiser. Upon hearing of their arrival, Catherine de Hueck, founder of the Friendship House movement and friend of Chicago's Bishop Sheil, promised Polcyn that Sheil would pay her a handsome wage. According to a *Sun-Times* profile of Polcyn, written years later, Polcyn and Blaiser "stood in Bishop Sheil's office, flinching with pleasure as the prelate, loudly thumbing his desk with his episcopal ring, informed her in no uncertain terms that God had work for them to do in Chicago."[49] After Sheil interviewed them, "the Baroness [de Hueck] took the two women to their room in the Morrison Hotel . . . went to the window, stretched out her hands in a prophetic gesture, and proclaimed in her deep-throated Russian voice, "I give you the city of Chicago."[50]

On January 1, 1943, Polcyn was hired to manage the Sheil School of Social Studies, which endeavored to demonstrate to Chicago's working-class poor the dramatic connections between history and faith.[51] Impressed by her professional and managerial skills, Sheil soon invited Polcyn to take over St. Benet's daily operations for O'Neill, whose declining health necessitated that she scale back the store's hours.

From the moment that she assumed control of the bookstore, in 1947, to its eventual closing in 1973, Polcyn transformed St. Benet's into a vibrant center for theology, arts, and intellectual life. Above all, she imagined the bookstore as a space where the city's working- and middle-class Catholics could engage in real theological work. She later explained this mission as the manifestation of broader lay currents, describing St. Benet's as "the germ of an idea that could blossom out into a cultural oasis, something that could vivify what was happening in the Church."[52]

Gradually, Polcyn modernized not just the operation, but also its collections and aesthetics. She and Blaser now co-hosted the bookstore's weekly *Compline*. When Polcyn began foregrounding liturgical goods, O'Neill warned, "There'll be too much kitsch, and you'll burn in hell with Benzinger."[53] So Polcyn moved slowly, first hanging modern paintings on the store's walls and then gradually acquiring more artwork to sell. These changes accelerated after O'Neill's death in 1954. Later that year, Sheil left the bookstore as well, under pressure following his outspoken criticism of Senator Joseph McCarthy. Msgr. Daniel Cantwell was given control of the rest of Sheil's operations, but Msgr. Jack Egan convinced Cardinal Stritch to transfer ownership of St. Benet's entirely to Polcyn, free of charge. Polcyn became sole proprietor overnight. She relocated the store to 300 S. Wabash, at the corner intersecting Jackson, where it would remain for the next twenty-two years.

Polcyn quickly increased St. Benet's revenue tenfold. Although she was unabashedly proud of St. Benet's success, Polcyn also seemed somewhat embarrassed by her entrepreneurial instincts. Later, she self-deprecatingly referred to her role as "a merchant priestess and trafficker in crucifixes"— a phrase which reflected, I think, her perpetual unease about the relationship between faith and wealth.[54] For Polcyn, St. Benet's commodification of Catholicism was an imperfect means of supporting grassroots liturgical artists and expressing her solidarity with the poor.

"Living Art": A Personalist Response to Mass Production

Under Polcyn's ownership, the store quickly became known as much for its artwork as for its books. Original paintings and sculptures from Europe bolstered St. Benet's operating revenue, but the majority of the artwork at the store was actually produced by American painters, silversmiths, and craftswomen. Polcyn's commitment to small-scale artisans represented a subculture within the liturgical arts. Polcyn was adamant that the most sacred art was "living art," her term for handcrafted, affordable pieces that were imbued with local culture and true to the spirit of the gospels. During the 1957 Liturgy and Art workshop at St. John's Abbey, Polcyn co-founded the Living Art Group. She called for Catholics to turn their attention away from museums and toward "living art for the average layman."[55] Like Maurice Lavanoux, she saw "a hidden reservoir" of talented

American artists who were anxiously waiting for parishes to commission their work.[56]

The living art sold at St. Benet's included a wide variety of handcrafted sacred goods, including chalices, crucifixes, rings, and tabletop sculptures. Many of these were hammered from silver and adorned with glazes or semi-precious gems. Polcyn lamented that such highly-skilled Catholic artisans were rarely featured in national galleries and museums. Many of the chalices sold at St. Benet's came from the workshops of Isle von Drage and Renard Koehnemann.[57] In a conversation with Koehnemann, Polcyn stressed that they shared the philosophy "that each piece must be handmade; the designer must also be a craftsman; and each piece must be an original design."[58] Polcyn featured Koehnemann's silver chalices at St. Benet's because she appreciated their depth. "An oversize cup," Polcyn explained, "helps convey the fact that the Mass is for and by the people and not just a private devotion for the priest."[59] Polcyn's convictions squared well with the writings of Jacques Maritain, who was one of St. Benet's most famous customers, particularly Maritain's notion of the "creative intuition."[60]

St. Benet's was distinctive because Polcyn refused to carry the mass-produced devotional objects which typically generated the bulk of revenue at other Catholic bookstores. St. Benet's did not carry reproductions of old masters or factory prints of modern art, because Polcyn felt they lacked the creative integrity which made art sacred. For Polcyn, the process of *making* was itself a form of prayer.[61] St. Benet's was one of the first American galleries to sell prints by Eric Gill, who declared, "You cannot have things made by machines and pretend that they are made by human beings."[62] Although Polcyn's viewpoint resonated within the liturgical movement, her refusal to sell mass-produced objects was also a stinging rebuke of St. Benet's competitors. Most parishes purchased their chalices, crucifixes, vestments, and furnishings from the catalogues of a small but ubiquitous set of mass retailers. By insisting on carrying mostly handmade items from smaller artisans, Polcyn positioned St. Benet's as a vendor for works that she believed were more authentically sacred.

St. Benet's was also unlike most Catholic art galleries, which typically focused on "high" art. Although Polcyn sold some fine art prints, most of St. Benet's inventory was produced locally by female artists. St. Benet's offered these handmade prints in the price range of $30–$50.[63] Because she wanted the art to be used devotionally, not collected, Polcyn insisted that most of her inventory be affordable. Robert Rambusch described Polcyn's approach as "a ministry to the middle class."[64] By contrast, Rambusch wrote, other prominent Catholic art stores dealt almost exclusively in "fine works that sold in line with art gallery prices."[65] Instead of luxury and exclusivity, the artistic values preached at St. Benet's were craftsmanship, friendship, spiritual union, and community worship. This philosophy reflected Polcyn's lifelong ties to the Catholic Worker, particularly the personalist vision through which she and other Catholic Workers imagined living art as an expression of solidarity.

Seeing Christ in the Everyday Suffering of Chicago's Poor

During the 1950s, Polcyn continued to stock St. Benet's with relatively-affordable modern art. The new pieces that Polcyn selected occasionally upset customers, not merely because of their unfamiliar modernist forms, but also because she deliberately selected works that challenged Chicago's affluent Catholics to face the reality that many of the city's residents were starving and suffering.

Even objects as commonplace as a wall-hung cross could, Polcyn believed, evoke new reflections on Christ's place in the secular city. In an interview, Polcyn discussed the power of Jean Lambert-Rucki's crucifixes and Passion sculptures. The key quality of Lambert-Rucki's work, Polcyn felt, was its capacity to uplift the "truth" and "honesty" of sacrifice:

> Have you seen it before? Is it the same old thing? Does it represent a formalized, traditional figure from a conventional mold that has been used thousands and thousands of times before? If it is, chances are that it will leave you unmoved, like watching an old TV movie for the third time . . . "It's not realistic," people instinctively say. "Christ's face on the cross didn't look like *that*." Perhaps not. But the elongation of the face, the distortion, if you will, of the features by the artist, is done to convey the kind of feeling that Christ must have suffered. Like the sudden waking from a nightmare, perspectives are distorted, angles and lines are confused . . . The crucifixion, the physical suffering of it, was worse than a bad dream, and the artist tries to make us, in some small measure, understand that fact. "Pretty?" No, not exactly. But the crucifixion wasn't pretty. If the artist has helped make you in some small way come to a deeper understanding of that truth, he has succeeded,

and you will look upon the world with slightly different eyes. It's like getting a new pair of glasses . . . and we at St. Benet's try to find you exactly the right pair.[66]

Polcyn's emphasis on "truth" is an example of the broader twentieth-century trend wherein Catholic's moral aesthetics came to privilege integrity and justice over physical splendor in evaluations of beauty and goodness.[67] This tension between the comfort of the familiar and the disquieting of the unique pervaded much of the artwork that Polcyn hand-selected to sell and display at St. Benet's.

In 1962, Polcyn commissioned a new tile mosaic for the store's entryway. The modern mosaic showcased the Virgin Mary, featureless and with a dark face holding an even darker Christ child. Some customers were vocal in their disapproval, with one even going so far to accuse Polcyn of being "a handmaid of the devil."[68] Polcyn wore the story like a badge of honor, reciting it to illustrate her optimism that change was on the horizon:

> Catholicism is not a religion of the past, nor should its art be. In these exciting days of the Council when the whole Church is throbbing with a new vitality . . . it is incongruous that we would continue to be satisfied with pallid reproductions of the old masters . . . weak, sterile, theologically inadequate and cheap mass-produced monstrosities. . . . [P]opular art is a pitiful attempt to make mystery real on the surface. Nothing is left to the imagination.[69]

Modern art represented the vast potential of the Church and its ability to speak to the rapid changes of the post-war era. Polcyn envisioned the arts as part of a broader moment of possibility in which the Church was poised for growth and expansion. Just as O'Neill's generation believed that the Mystical Body of Christ could help heal the wounds of modernity, so visible in American cities, Polcyn's generation hoped that a modernized church would not only remain relevant but also lead an increasingly secularized American culture.

Among the more expensive artwork featured at St. Benet's, one set of etchings stood out as Polcyn's clear favorite, the *Miserere et Guerre* (Misery and War) series by Georges Rouault, who was among the artists she discussed most frequently in her columns for *The Critic*. It is unclear if Polcyn ever met Rouault, but they shared at least two personal friends: the priest Richard Douaire and Jacques Maritain.[70] *Miserere* contained fifty-eight etchings that depicted Christ alongside homeless Parisians and war veterans, and the black-and-white etchings rely on uncommonly bold, dark lines. Rouault had initially planned several plates about the Resurrection, but he decided instead to focus on the juxtaposition of Christ's suffering alongside almost equally haunting images of Paris's poor.

With funding from Marquette University, Polcyn curated a show on the *Miserere* series, and she personally purchased ten of Rouault's sixteen portrayals of Christ's Passion, including the final plate in the series.[71] It is a ghostly, close-up portrait of Christ's dead face, covered in blood and thorns, titled, "It is through his wounds that we are healed." Polcyn's exhibition of *Miserere* provided a glimpse into both the aesthetic form and the moral lens that came to dominate St. Benet's in the following decade.

Envisioning the Works of Mercy: Postcards and Women's Worship

In terms of sales, the 1960s were St. Benet's heyday. Fueled by the excitement and sense of wonder surrounding Vatican II, the bookstore was filled with laypersons, nuns, and priests seeking the latest theology and philosophy titles from Europe. Aesthetically, however, the artwork at St. Benet's remained focused on the poor, including the store's bestselling postcards and stationery sets.

Most of the store's stationery depicted the work of just three artists: Rita Corbin, Ade Bethune, and Fritz Eichenberg. Sometimes referred to as "the holy trinity" of Catholic Worker artists, these artists produced work that was theologically similar to Rouault's, depicting Christ among the men and women standing in the breadlines, or begging alongside migrants in the streets. These prints also shared some formal elements of Rouault's corpus, particularly the striking black-and-white format and deep, bold painterly lines. Many of Corbin, Eichenberg, and Bethune's best known prints depicted the Works of Mercy, and Polcyn preserved many of these in the papers she donated to Marquette. The stationery she sold at St. Benet's reflected Polcyn's ongoing desire to cultivate a middle-class marketplace for the Catholic Worker's aesthetics of solidarity with the poor.

Through their everyday labor of reading, cleaning, and hospitality, the staff at St. Benet's shared in the aesthetics of the Catholic Worker, particularly the sense that beauty should be sought in the wisdom of great

FIGURE 2: Nina Polcyn (left), seated behind her desk while meeting with two of her longtime staff members, Patricia Stinneford and Lois Murray, at St. Benet's main storefront, located at 300 S. Wabash Street in Chicago. This image is from Dann Herr's article, "The Gentle Firebrand," published in the April 1964 issue of *U.S. Catholic*. Reprinted with permission and licensing from *U.S. Catholic* and the Claretian Missionaries Archives.

books, in the sincerity of handwrought labor, and in mundane acts of hospitality. Maureen O'Connell has theorized these distinctive components as "creative beauty," "enlarging beauty," and "dutiful beauty."[72] Bethune's work became iconic within the Catholic Worker, particularly her ubiquitous images of the Corporal Works of Mercy and of the Holy Family at work. In one of Bethune's most widely reprinted woodcuts, "Pray and Work," the Holy Family is depicted laboring together under one small roof: Joseph is sawing a board, Jesus is chiseling a drawer, and Mary is knitting. Bethune also engraved the Latin *ora et labora*, which fellow Workers would have immediately recognized as one of Maurin's favorite phrases from the Rule of St. Benedict.

Bethune wanted to create images that would not only resonate with the laboring class, but within which workers could also see and recognize their work as holy. She also insisted on printing artwork in the Catholic Worker so that Catholics who could not read could nevertheless receive the Worker's message by spending time with the bold images on its pages. As Harmon put it in her excellent analysis of Bethune's woodcuts:

> Through her depiction of the ordinary, the work of men and women, and a truly intimate vision of Christ, Bethune's work provided a powerful visual and tactile realization of the deepest desires of the mid-twentieth century liturgical movement in the United States: to promote full and active participation on the part of the people, to deepen their understanding of the centrality of their faith with regard to their everyday lives, and to connect their worship with their work in the world, allowing the liturgy to be a true font of social regeneration.[73]

As Bethune worked and reworked her illustrations, she "gradually came to the conviction that all labor had great dignity and could reflect the works of mercy—and Christ."[74] Such images were not only theological but also political, arguing for a much-needed reevaluation of the role of women within American society more broadly.[75]

Bethune's woodcuts often depicted not just workers but also the tools of each trade. In "St. Elisabeth Takes Care of the Sick," the saint is surrounded by surgical sutures, cough syrup, and a roll of bandages. In a popular woodcut of Joseph, the carpenter is on bended knee, reaching toward a set of chisels. In addition to his head, Bethune drew Joseph's *hand* surrounded by a halo, emphasizing the blessedness of the work itself. Joseph's tools, a keyhole saw, pliers, hammer, and a handscrew vise, are distinctively modern. Bethune thus painted the saints into twentieth-century workspaces, with all their grime and grit.

In addition to stationery featuring Bethune and Corbin's artwork, Polcyn carefully saved dozens of cards by the next generation of female Catholic artists, including Meinrad Craighead prints of the divine feminine and serigraphs by Sister Corita Kent.[76] Far from frivolous, the artwork included in this correspondence helped Polcyn sustain her vision for laywomen as leaders of living art, even when they could not physically gather, as they had at St. Benet's, to pray and appreciate artwork together.[77] The St. Benet's stationery in Polcyn's archives, which she continued to use for correspondence in the 1970s and beyond, also vividly illustrates Polcyn's ongoing commitment to living art, even as other Catholics shifted away from traditional bookstore wares.

Vatican II and the Shuttering of St. Benet's

After Vatican II, Polcyn shifted her attention to broader issues of social justice. Although St. Benet's was still selling artwork, customers' tastes were rapidly shifting. "The liturgical self-consciousness that sprang up in the '30s is dead," she told the *National Catholic Reporter.*

Indeed, St. Benet's experienced the full gamut of the revolutionary spirit that marked the Catholic sixties. During Vatican II, the store's sales swelled to an all-time high, both in print materials and in artwork. But after the Council, sales declined steadily. Nevertheless, Polcyn embraced many of the changes.

> There is a great emphasis on themes, especially from the Council, the whole ecumenical spirit and the question of freedom and authority. The nun is emerging, in all of this, as a person rather than as a stereotype. There is less interest in "stationery for sisters" and more in "paper for people."[78]

By the 1970s, however, the market for the store's Catholic staples had shrunk drastically, in line with other trends like declining ordinations. "It was a roller coaster. Priests and sisters were leaving in droves. Sisters who [had] spent their lunch money at St Benet's now had to buy stockings and a permanent wave . . . and nobody was going to the convents."[79] Polcyn was not alone in her assessment of this shift; just months before she shuttered St. Benet's, Maurice Lavanoux closed down *Liturgical Arts.*

After she sold St. Benet's in 1973, Polcyn married a widower, Thomas "Gene" Moore, and moved to his house in Sauk Centre, Minnesota, where two of his children were still in high school. Polcyn took his last name, officially becoming Nina Polcyn Moore. For their wedding celebration, Nina and Gene sent a catered feast to Dorothy's Catholic Worker house. For the next four decades, they remained active within the movement, giving both time and financial donations to many of the Worker's houses of hospitality. After Day's death in 1980, Polcyn also sent checks directly to Tamar, Day's daughter, to help sustain her personal finances. Although

Sauk Centre was rather rural, its proximity to St. John's Abbey also allowed Polcyn to stay in touch with the Benedictine community.

In the 1990s, Polcyn and Gene moved to Evanston, Illinois, and she became more overtly active in groups like Chicago Catholic Women (CCW) and the Women's Ordination Conference. Polcyn was also a dear friend and mentor to Barbara Blaine, whom she met while Blaine was a Catholic Worker at St. Elizabeth's on Chicago's South Side. Polcyn spiritually shepherded Blaine through personal loss. She continued to mentor the younger Catholic Worker throughout the 1990s, when Blaine founded one of the world's first communities for victims of clergy sexual abuse, the Survivor's Network for those Abused by Priests (SNAP). One of Polcyn's last wishes, in 2007, was to donate all of her remaining assets to SNAP.[80]

Recentering Catholic Bookstores as Third Spaces

The history of St. Benet's provides a case study in how Catholic laywomen shaped postwar literary sensibilities and devotional practices through bookstores and the liturgical arts. Bookstores and art galleries played an essential role in the life of the lay apostolate, particularly as "third spaces" where women could experiment, not just as artists but also as theologians and liturgical leaders. In the decades preceding Vatican II, bookstores provided a third space where laywomen enjoyed a level of autonomy not typically allowed to women in Catholic parishes, homes, and universities. O'Neill and Polcyn were just two of many Catholic women who carved out new leadership roles during these years. Jeffrey Burns has proposed the term "emerging Catholic laywoman" to describe the liminal yet dynamic aspects of these new positions.[81] These "Catholic women of the 1950s asserted a new independence and assertiveness," Burns recognizes, even as Catholic bishops and theologians, as well as the American mainline Protestants, continued to valorize marriage, child-bearing, and domestic chores as women's most essential roles.[82]

After St. Benet's closed, Catholic artists continued to remember the success of Polcyn's vision. In 1992, for example, a layperson in San Francisco wrote to liturgical designer Robert Rambusch for advice on opening a Catholic bookstore. Rambusch instructed the inquirer to contact Polcyn, and he recalled with deep fondness and passion three other stores that had specialized in "tasteful and successful Catholic religious art" during the 1950s and 1960s: Celia Hubbard's Botolph Shop in Boston, Elouise Spaeth's Guild Bookshop in New York City, and Ethel de Souza's Junipero Serra Shop in San Francisco.[83]

Provocatively, Burns has argued that the Junipero Serra Bookstore was "perhaps the single most important place in the emergence of a liberal, activist Catholicism."[84] Like St. Benet's, Junipero Serra specialized in liturgical texts and modern religious art, while also featuring lectures by leaders of the liturgical movement, Catholic Workers, and labor organizers. "The bookshop became a central gathering place for the Catholic intelligentsia" in San Francisco, Burns concludes, and it was vital in laying "the groundwork for the reception of the Council."[85] As Rebecca Berru-Davis has shown, San Francisco's Euphemia "Effie" Charlton Fortune was at the forefront of liturgical design.[86] An exemplar of what Polcyn later called "living art," Fortune had created an entire guild of local artisans, including woodworkers, blacksmiths, silversmiths, and seamstresses, to execute her vision for St. Agnes Church in Monterrey, California.

The interplay between bookstores and liturgical artwork in San Francisco suggests that Polcyn's vision at St. Benet's may have been exemplary rather than—as Chicago Catholics had imagined it—exceptional. At St. Benet's, the staff blended O'Neill's liturgical fervor with Polcyn's roots in the personalism of the Catholic Worker. She approached new customers as both a saleswoman and as a pastor. "Really, to find the right art or book for a person is very significant," Polcyn said towards the end of her life. "There's a tremendous sense of wholeness," she continued, "in helping people find things of beauty that mirror the infinite."[87] In reflecting on St. Benet's wide appeal, which spanned four decades and encapsulated Chicago's Catholic Action movement, Polcyn retained the sense of dynamism that pervaded her pre-Conciliar world:

> It was a whole sense of really *being* the Mystical Body . . . it was just so mind-boggling and so revolutionary and so—the laity! The sense that the laity is the Church, and what is that all about? And see, these people just came to St. Benet's. They had to come to some place to develop their spirits and their minds to read. They got inspired through these movements. They got a sense of "it's all got to change and now we're a part of that." They got the yeast. They knew the bread was rising, and it just couldn't be the same. . . . We were all in it. We were all inspiring each other.[88]

Modern art represented the vast potential of the Church to speak to the rapid changes of the postwar era. Polcyn envisioned the arts as part of a broader moment of possibility in which the Church was poised for growth and expansion.

Polcyn's leadership at St. Benet's provides a glimpse into the dense and rich networks of laywomen who shaped American Catholic life in the decades preceding Vatican II. Through its promotion of women's artwork, its model of women as liturgical leaders, its insistence that theology and philosophy were the domain of both men *and* women, and its modeling of women's entrepreneurship, St. Benet's helped pave the way for the next generation of Catholic feminists, including especially Chicago's Sr. Donna Quinn, Marjorie Tuite, and the CCW.[89]

Although Polcyn's vision was gendered, she imagined laywomen as working in solidarity with women religious. In a 1958 New Year's column, Polcyn praised the blessedness of nuns who staged exceptional art exhibits without significant financial support, including Sister Thomasita of Cardinal Stritch College, Sister Helena of Alverno College, Sister Corita and Sister Magdalene of Immaculate Heart College, and Sister Helene of Siena Heights College.[90] The omission of men from this list was not incidental. In another column, at the conclusion of her glowing review of a museum-quality art show that had been staged on a shoestring budget and in the basement of a local Catholic school, Polcyn characterized the exhibit as a feminist feat, boasting, "It could only have happened because two women with boldness and audacity decided to do it."[91] In case the gendered dimension of the review had been lost on certain readers, Polcyn added, "The moral of the story is Never underestimate the power of two women."[92]

To think of St. Benet's as a library, a bookstore, or even as a Catholic gallery is to miss the point. Through their liturgical and commercial innovations at the bookstore, the women of St. Benet's lived out a distinctive vision of laywomen's leadership. Drawing on the aesthetics of the Catholic Worker, Polcyn and her staff made St. Benet's a unique space for community worship, intellectual debate, craftsmanship, socialization, and spiritual union. In the third space of Catholic bookstores, women in the lay apostolate engendered an alternative vision for Catholic womanhood and curated a more inclusive space for prayerful debate. Just as O'Neill's generation believed that the Mystical Body of Christ could help heal the wounds of modernity, so visible in American cities, Polcyn's generation recognized that laywomen were an essential component of the Church's aspiration to thrive within a rapidly changing American culture.

Notes

1. Nina Polcyn's papers are archived in distinctive collections at four institutions. The largest collection, concerning her early life and relationship with the Catholic Worker, is at the Marquette University Dorothy Day-Catholic Worker Collection (hereafter abbreviated as Marquette DD-CW). Manuscripts and images pertaining to St. Benet's are archived within the University of Notre Dame Archives, Nina Polcyn Moore Manuscripts (hereafter abbreviated UNDA CPOL). One box of materials documenting Polcyn's contributions to other Chicago organizations is maintained at the Chicago History Museum (not cited within this chapter). Finally, materials concerning Polcyn's involvement in additional Catholic Action groups are housed within the Loyola University Chicago Catholic Inter-Student Catholic Action collection (hereafter abbreviated LUC CISCA).

2. Adolph Schalk, "20th Century Bookshop," *The Voice of St. Jude* (May, 1954), 1, UNDA CPOL.

3. Schalk, "20th Century Bookshop," 2.

4. Schalk, "20th Century Bookshop," 1.

5. Keith Pecklers, *The Unread Vision: The Liturgical Movement in the United States, 1926–1955* (Collegeville, MN: Liturgical Press, 1998), 200–06; Katharine Harmon, *There Were Also Many Women There: Lay Women and the Liturgical Movement in the United States, 1926–1959* (Collegeville, MN: Liturgical Press, 2013), 147–60.

6. Katharine Harmon, "Drawing the Holy in the Ordinary: Ade Bethune, the Catholic Worker, and the Liturgical Movement," *American Catholic Studies* 123, no. 1 (2012), 1–23.

7. Homi K. Bhabha, *The Location of Culture* (London: Routledge Classics, 2004 [1994]), *e.g.,* 36–39.

8. Nina Polcyn Moore, Interview by Robert Carbonneau, C.P., July 30, 1997. Transcribed by Ann Maloney, O.P. LUCCISCA, Series 6, File 15.

9. Una M. Cadegan, *All Good Books Are Catholic Books: Print Culture, Censorship, and Modernity in Twentieth-Century America* (Ithaca, NY: Cornell University Press, 2013), 10.

10. Catherine Osborne, *American Catholics and the Church of Tomorrow* (Chicago: University of Chicago Press, 2018), 2.

11. Harmon, *There Were Also Many Women There*, 161.

12. Bob Senser, "Library in the Market Place," *The Catholic Digest Catholic Digest* 11, no. 3 (January 1947), 31–33, UNDA CPOL.

13. For a fuller account of O'Neill's biography, see Brian Clites, "Breaking the Silence: The Catholic Clergy Sexual Abuse Survivor Movement in Chicago" (PhD diss., Evanston, IL: Northwestern University, 2015).

14. Schalk, "20th Century Bookshop," 2.

15. The trend of consecrating oneself to the oblature remains strong to this day within the Catholic Worker, particularly among Workers who are most committed to Day's pacifist, anti-nuclear vision, such as Brian Terrell and Betsey Keenan of Peace House in Maloy, Iowa.

16. The Chicago Calvert Club understood itself as the Midwestern equivalent of Calvert Associates, the group of Ivy-educated New Yorkers who founded *Commonweal*. Both groups were named after George Calvert, the First Lord Baltimore and founder of Maryland. Through the influence of professor Jerome Kerwin, the Calvert Club eventually moved to the University of Chicago, where it was eventually reorganized into the Calvert House, which today serves as the campus center for Catholic liturgical and intellectual life. For a fuller history of the Calvert Associates, see Robert B. Clements, "Michael Williams and the Founding of 'The Commonweal,'" *Records of the American Catholic Historical Society* 85, no. 3 (Sep. 1974), 163–73; and Rodger Van Allen, "*Commonweal* and the Catholic Intellectual Life," *U.S. Catholic Historian* 13, no. 2 (Spring 1995), 71–86.

17. Senser, "Library in the Marketplace," 31.

18. Senser. "Library in the Market Place," 33.

19. Roy Larson, "One for the Books, She Turns a Page," *Chicago Sun-Times*, Aug. 27, 1973, S6, UNDA CPOL.

20. Cadegan, *All Good Books*, 5.

21. Cadegan, *All Good Books*, 8.

22. Robert Orsi, *Thank You, St. Jude: Women's Devotion to the Patron Saint of Hopeless Causes* (New Haven: Yale University Press), 34.

23. Matthew S. Hedstrom, *The Rise of Liberal Religion: Book Culture and American Spirituality in the Twentieth Century* (New York: Oxford University Press, 2012), 21.

24. Jeffrey Burns, "Catholic Laywomen in the Culture of American Catholicism in the 1950s," *U.S. Catholic Historian* 5, no. 3–4 (1986), 391.

25. Schalk, "20th Century Bookshop," 2.

26. Senser, "Library in the Marketplace," 32.

27. Charles Harbutt, "Chicago: The country's biggest diocese fathers a new approach to contemporary problems," *Jubilee*, September 1956, 13, UNDA CPOL.

28. After marrying at age 60, Polcyn changed her name to Nina Polcyn Moore. For consistency, and because almost all of the events narrated here took place prior to that marriage, this essay refers to Polcyn solely by her maiden name.

29. Schalk, "20th Century Bookshop," 31.

30. Dan Herr, "The Gentle Firebrand," *U.S. Catholic*, April 1964, 11, POL UNDA.

31. Schalk, "20th Century Bookshop," 1.

32. Rosalie G. Riegle, "Nina Polcyn Moore, 1914–2007," *Pie and Coffee*, February 17, 2007.

33. Roy Larson, "One for the Books," S6.

34. Herr, "The Gentle Firebrand," 11.

35. Rosalie G. Riegle, *Dorothy: Portraits by Those Who Knew Her* (Maryknoll: Orbis, 2003), 137.

36. Herr, "The Gentle Firebrand," 11.

37. Schalk, "20th Century Bookshop."

38. Herr, "The Gentle Firebrand," 12.

39. Roy Larson, "One for the Books," S6.

40. Herr, "The Gentle Firebrand," 12.

41. Herr, "The Gentle Firebrand," 12.

42. James Terence Fisher, *The Catholic Counterculture in America, 1933–1962* (Chapel Hill: University of North Carolina Press, 1989), 55–56.

43. Nina Polcyn, letter to Dorothy Day, dated "Third Sunday of Lent 1942," Marquette DD-CW, Series W17,Box 2.

44. Herr, "The Gentle Firebrand," 11.

45. Riegle, *Dorothy*, 51.

46. Riegle, *Dorothy* 204.

47. Riegle, *Dorothy*, 39.

48. Robert McClory "Bookstore Owner, Dorothy Day's Friend, Dies at 92" *National Catholic Reporter* March 2007.

49. Larson, "One for the Books," S6.

50. Larson, "One for the Books," S6.

51. Herr, "The Gentle Firebrand," 12.

52. Nina Polcyn Moore, interview by Rosalie Riegle Troester, December 1986. Marquette DD-CW, Series W-9.4, Box 11, Folder 9.

53. Nina Polcyn, Interview by Keith Pecklers, *Unread Vision*, 205.

54. Larson, "One for the Books," S6.

55. Polcyn, "Art and Artists," *The Critic* 16, no. 3 (1957), 55.

56. Nina Polcyn, quoting Lavanoux, in "Art and Artists," *The Critic* 16, no. 3 (1957), 54.

57. Polcyn, "Art and Artists," *The Critic* 16, no. 3 (1957), 55; Schalk, "20th Century Bookshop," 4.

58. Nina Polcyn, "Arts and Artists," *The Critic* 16, no. 7 (1958), 51.

59. Polcyn, "Art and Artists," *The Critic* 16, no. 7 (1958), 51.

60. Jacques Maritain, *Creative Intuition in Art and Poetry* (New York: The American Library, 1953).

61. Polcyn, *"Art and Artists,"* 51–52.

62. Eric Gill, *Art* (London: The Bodley Head, 1934), 115.

63. Kenon Heise, "St. Benet's Nina Polcyn: Medals out, peace buttons in," *National Catholic Reporter* 2, no. 24 (13 April 1966), 2. When adjusted for inflation, pieces that sold for $30 to $50 in 1966 would cost approximately $250 to $400 in 2021.

64. Rambusch, letter to Nina Polcyn Moore, February 1, 1992, Marquette DD-CW, Folder 17.

65. Rambusch, letter to Polcyn.

66. Nina Polcyn, "Is Honest Art Pretty Art?," *De Paul Magazine* (Spring 1958), 14–15, DePaul University Special Collections and Archives.

67. On the relationship between goodness, truth, and beauty in Catholic evaluations of art, see Cadegan, *All Good Books*, 29, 72.

68. Herr, "The Gentle Firebrand," 10.

69. Herr, "The Gentle Firebrand," 10.

70. See Polcyn, "Art and Artists," *The Critic* 16, no. 1 (1957), 60; and Polcyn, "Art and Artists," *The Critic* 16, no. 5 (1958), 52. Douauire was a regular at both St. Benet's and the nearby Art Institute of Chicago, and he helped both institutions acquire some of Rouault's originals. Maritain was a friend of Rouault, and the artist was one of several connections the Maritains had to Leon Bloy. For more on Bloy's significance within midcentury Catholic networks, see Brenna Moore, *Sacred Dread: Raïssa Maritain, the Allure of Suffering, and the French Catholic Revival* (Notre Dame: University of Notre Dame Press, 2013).

71. Author's interview with Dr. Peter Mayock, one of Polcyn's surviving friends and a recipient of some of these Rouault prints, January 7, 2021.

72. Maureen O'Connell, "A Harsh and Dreadful Beauty: The Aesthetic Dimension of Dorothy Day's Ethics," in *She Who Imagines* (Collegeville, MN: The Liturgical Press, 2012), 113–123.

73. Harmon, "Drawing the Holy in the Ordinary: Ade Bethune, the Catholic Worker, and the Liturgical Movement," *American Catholic Studies* 123, no. 1 (2012), 4.

74. Harmon, "Drawing the Holy in the Ordinary," 13.

75. For an alternative reading of Bethune's corpus, see Colleen McDannell, who provocatively theorizes that women in the liturgical movement gained traction by reifying images that emphasized Christ's masculinity over and above Mary's submissive stature. McDannell points to woodcuts generally attributed to Bethune as primary examples of a bearded, decidedly masculine Christ standing over and above the Blessed Mother. McDannell, *Material*

Christianity: Religion and Popular Culture in America (New Haven: Yale University Press, 1998), 177–180.

76. For a compelling analysis of why more religious historians should reflect on Sr. Corita's pop art, see Tim Dulle, "Making New Wineskins: Commemorating the Life of Corita Kent," *American Catholic Studies* 129, no. 3 (2018), 109–121.

77. On postcards as a window into religious subcultures, see Ellen Smith, "Greetings from Faith: Early Twentieth-Century American Jewish New Year Postcards," *The Visual Culture of American Religions*, 229–248. On the scholarly tendency to dismiss postcards as feminine ephemera, see Leigh Schmidt, *Consumer Rites: The Buying and Selling of American Holidays* (Princeton: Princeton University Press, 1995), 307. On the importance of recentering Catholic women's artwork within the study of material culture, see McDannell, *Material Christianity*, 234–236.

78. Polcyn, quoted in Heise, "St. Benet's Nina Polcyn: Medals out; peace buttons in," *National Catholic Reporter* 2, no. 24 (April 13, 1966), 2.

79. Nina Polcyn, Interview by Carbonneau.

80. Author's interview with Peter Mayock. For more detail on Polcyn's relationship with Blaine and her support of SNAP, see Clites, "Breaking the Silence."

81. Jeffrey Burns, "Catholic Laywomen in the Culture of American Catholicism in the 1950s," *U.S. Catholic Historian* 5, no. 3–4 (Summer-Fall 1986), 385–400.

82. Burns, "Catholic Laywomen," 389.

83. Rambusch, Letter to Nina Polcyn Moore.

84. Jeffrey Burns, "Prelude to Reform: The Church in San Francisco Before the Council," *U.S. Catholic Historian*, 23, no. 4 (2005), 1–16.

85. Burns, "Prelude to Reform," 14.

86. Rebecca M. Berru-Davis, "E. Charlton Fortune: Precursor to the Renaissance of Religious Art in the San Francisco Bay Area," *U.S. Catholic Historian* 31, no. 2 (2013), 95–118.

87. Polcyn, Interview by Carbonneau.

88. Polcyn, Interview by Carbonneau.

89. For more on the history of Chicago Catholic Women, as well as Tuite and Quinn's roles in other groups, see Mary J. Henold, *Catholic and Feminist* (Chapel Hill, NC: University of North Carolina Press, 2008).

90. Nina Polcyn, "Art and Artists," *The Critic* 16, no. 5 (1958), 52.

91. Polcyn, "Art and Artists," *The Critic* 16, no. 1 (1957), 60.

92. Polcyn, "Art and Artists," *The Critic* 16, no. 1 (1957), 60.

Lucy Looks Twice

The Agency of Lay Lakota Catholic Women, and the Legacy of Nicholas Black Elk

DAMIAN COSTELLO

We always imagine people like Lucy Looks Twice (1908–1978), an Oglala Lakota woman from Pine Ridge, to be acted on by the Church. In Looks Twice's story, we see how laywomen act on the Church, often in unexpected ways. As the main source on the Catholic life of her father Nicholas Black Elk (c.1867–1950), a prominent Lakota spiritual leader and candidate for sainthood in the Catholic Church, Looks Twice helped change the public image of her father and laid the groundwork for his cause for canonization.

At first glance, Looks Twice seems an unlikely agent of change. She lived on the outskirts of a tiny town on a remote reservation on the Northern Plains. Even if you have been to Pine Ridge Indian Reservation, you probably have not been to Manderson, the small village of about 600 located nine miles northwest of Wounded Knee.

In many ways, Looks Twice's deep faith in the face of tragedy is representative of the first generation of Lakota Catholic women born on the reservation. She was born in 1907, one of six children and the only daughter of Black Elk. Her name seems to have been related to her father's vision problems, as St. Lucy is the patron saint of those who suffer with afflictions of the eyes.[1] Three of her siblings and stepsiblings died as children. Though Looks Twice attended Holy Rosary Mission boarding school, she was a Lakota-first speaker and does not seem to have reported being negatively affected by her education experience. Leo Looks Twice, who became her husband, was Episcopalian, and her father blessed their marriage, only requiring that Leo become Catholic.[2] The couple were distantly related and Looks Twice speculated that is why they experienced such suffering. She gave birth to ten children; six of them died in the 1930s. She played the organ at St. Agnes Church in Manderson and had strong devotion to St. Therese of Lisieux, the Sacred Heart, and the Virgin Mary.[3]

Her famous father set Looks Twice apart. Black Elk, who became a global icon of Indigenous tradition and revitalization through the 1932 book *Black Elk Speaks*, was in Lucy's lifetime a local Catholic celebrity. Black Elk accepted baptism in 1904. His passion for the faith, ability to memorize scripture, and leadership skills earned him the position of catechist a couple of years later. Black Elk served much like a modern-day permanent deacon: preaching, baptizing, visiting the sick, and catechizing, being called by a Jesuit co-worker a "second St. Paul," and credited with bringing 400 into the Church and being the godfather of 113.[4]

At the age of six, the Black Elk family moved to the Yankton Reservation on the other side of South Dakota. They lived there for about a year. While Black Elk worked as a full-time missionary, Lucy played with the Yankton children and learned the Latin responses to the Mass. The experience marked her: "When I came home, my friends all laughed at me because I talked like a Yankton."[5]

While Catholicism shaped all facets of Looks Twice's life, the Catholicism of the early reservation that Lucy experienced through Black Elk was quite unlike that of later generations. It flowed out of the Ghost Dance, a pan-Native millennial movement that saw an Indian Christ (in Lakota, *Waníkiya*, "He Who Makes Live") as a restorer of the land and Indigenous lifeways. Black Elk had his last major vision while dancing, that of *Waníkiya* before the Sacred Tree, who issued a personal call to Black Elk.[6] This movement served as a conduit of Lakota people into denominational life, particularly Catholicism, where *Waníkiya* was the term used for savior. Communal real-world priorities dominated these early church spaces, in contrast with the individualist, other-worldly tendencies commonly associated with early twentieth-century American Catholicism.[7]

Early reservation Lakota Catholicism was also marked by its relative autonomy and the buffer it provided from US Indian policy. The early Jesuits were made up of German refugees without the default allegiance to the Manifest Destiny ideology of many of the era's American clergy. Most learned Lakota and were relatively tolerant of Lakota tradition. This, combined with the distance of far-flung communities like Manderson from the Jesuit residence, meant a priest might show up once a month, leaving the community in the hand of catechists. Many, like Black Elk, were former medicine men. This is actually quite remarkable: a level of autonomy and lay agency that in many ways is higher than in the contemporary American Catholic Church.

Lakota agency and autonomy in the Catholic circles, though not absolute, meant that many of Looks Twice's generation encountered the content of Christian faith within Lakota culture and not as something forced from the outside. A snapshot (see Figure 3) from Frank Fools Crow (ca. 1890–1989), the last ceremonial chief of the entire Lakota Nation and an important medicine man, illustrates this "internal dynamic."[8] In his autobiography Fools Crow describes how the older Lakota would visit him in the evening and often asked for stories. "The kind of stories they prefer may surprise you, because many people ask me about this extraordinary holy man who lived way back, Jesus Christ. . . . So I tell them stories from the Bible as the priests have told them to me. . . . They are able to sense the greatness of them and to feel their impact on their personal lives."[9]

Looks Twice does not seem to have had much, if any, guidance in Lakota spiritual traditions. She offered some matter-of-fact stories about Black Elk's engagement with traditional practices but does not parse them out, such as diverting a possible tornado by praying with the pipe. When Black Elk was an old man, a big thunderstorm was coming and "looked like it was going to have a tornado in it." He took his pipe to a hill, faced West, and sang to the Thunderbird. "After he was finished, you should have seen those clouds," Looks Twice remembered. "One went off this way, one off that way, and the storm was gone. They must have heard him."[10] She offered no explanation of how this is understood traditionally, nor does she express or indicate that it is problematic to Catholic faith. Outsiders would tend to see this as exotic and foreign to Catholicism, but I suspect Looks Twice, and others of her generation saw it in line with similar stories of Christ and the saints. For better or worse, the rhythms of the church shaped Looks Twice's spiritual life.

Looks Twice, like her father's Catholicism, probably would have remained unknown to the world, a footnote in the literature on Black Elk's early life, if not for a chance encounter. In March 1973, Looks Twice was sitting on a bench outside Red Cloud Indian School, what was formerly named Holy Rosary Mission.[11] The boiler had broken down and students were sent home for the day. Michael F. Steltenkamp, a young Jesuit scholastic (an unordained Jesuit in training discerning his vocation) who taught

NICK BLACK ELK AND FAMILY
CATHOLIC CATECHIST.

FIGURE 3: Lucy Looks Twice, center, with her parents in a family portrait. "Nick Black Elk and family, Catholic catechist," ca. 1890–1910. Photo from Denver Public Library, Western History Collection, Special Collections, X-31818.

in the high school, sat down next to Lucy and began a conversation. He quickened when he learned that Lucy was Black Elk's daughter.

Though in Jesuit formation, Steltenkamp reports that he was more representative of the class of non-Native seekers who began flocking to Pine Ridge about that time. To Steltenkamp, Black Elk's story offered an alternative spirituality untainted by the modern world and institutional religion. Steltenkamp had hoped to fill in more details of Black Elk's spiritual vision by interviewing Black Elk's son Benjamin (1899–1973), who had served as translator in the interviews that became the basis for *Black Elk Speaks* and *The Sacred Pipe*. Like his father, Benjamin became a global showman and ambassador of the Lakota Way. Steltenkamp was crushed when shortly after his arrival Ben died, on February 22, 1973. His passing seemed to end an era.

For Steltenkamp, connecting with Looks Twice unexpectedly reopened a door into Black Elk's vision. Steltenkamp asked Looks Twice if she would speak to his class about her father. She declined but accepted his request to visit her at her home to learn more about Black Elk. The meetings did not go as Steltenkamp planned. Questions about Black Elk's Lakota spirituality led to short answers and long pauses, the kind of silence that non-Natives find so uncomfortable. Finally, feeling that they had reached a dead end, Steltenkamp asked "What did your father talk about?" Looks Twice's unexpected answer, "the Church," opened the floodgates and the stories poured out.

Dutifully, Steltenkamp recorded the stories but was not thrilled. This was not what he had been looking for, and he remembers reaching a kind of breaking point. Steltenkamp returned from Looks Twice's one day and a fellow scholastic asked how it went. "I blurted out an angry exclamation about getting the same darn thing over and over again,—Black Elk's grounding in the Catholic faith!" Steltenkamp remembers. "That's not what I sought."

Yet Steltenkamp continued on, supplementing conversations with Looks Twice with visits with elders that worked as catechists with Black Elk or remembered his ministry. A rich portrait of a dynamic evangelist who never lost his Lakota center emerged and became Steltenkamp's dissertation, published as *Black Elk: Holy Man of the Oglala* in 1993.

Looks Twice's emphasis on the centrality of Black Elk's Catholic faith that came through Steltenkamp's work, along with the publication of the transcripts of the interviews that became *Black Elk Speaks*, which showed

Neihardt's extensive creative shaping of the story and misunderstanding of key Lakota concepts, set off intense academic debate about the nature of Black Elk's identity and spirituality.

A key question in this debate is the difference between Looks Twice's emphasis on Black Elk's Catholic faith and work as a catechist and that of her brother Benjamin Black Elk, who emphasized Black Elk's Lakota spirituality and work for cultural revitalization. Benjamin attended Holy Rosary Mission and Carlisle Indian School. Translating for Black Elk in the Neihardt interviews was Benjamin's first deep engagement with Lakota spirituality and he was quite moved by the elders' stories and his father's vision.[12] Ben began a systematic engagement in Lakota traditions and became an ambassador like his father, earning the name "The Fifth Face of Mount Rushmore."[13] Though an intentional Catholic himself, Ben was less concerned by the omission Black Elk's Catholicism from *Black Elk Speaks* than Looks Twice.

The difference between Looks Twice's and Ben's perspective, I believe, stems from Lakota gender dynamics in the realm of spirituality and ceremonial life and Looks Twice's experience as a lay Catholic woman. Pre-reservation Lakota ceremonial life was primarily a male sphere: conducted by males to give power in activities generally undertaken by men, such as warfare and hunting. Traditionally, only men danced in *Wiwanyag Wachipi*, or the Sun Dance, one explanation being that women shed their blood in childbirth and thus did not need to do so ceremonially.

Catholicism, despite its emphasis on a male savior and all-male clergy, opened up new spiritual opportunities for women in the Lakota world. While men controlled sacramental life, women often took the lead in devotional activities and had autonomous communal spaces, such as the St. Mary's Society, a lay Catholic woman's organization that met on Sundays to pray, sing, catechize, plan church activities, and socialize.[14] Louis J. Goll, S.J. captures the oratory power of the leaders. "The president ("grandmother") would address all present. She, too, would appoint two or four speakers, there being excellent speakers among these Indian women, able to drive home a lesson for men and women alike."[15]

The St. Mary's Society also helped plan the yearly Sioux Indian Congress, a summer gathering of Lakota Catholics from all reservations that incorporated many aspects of the Sun Dance with an important innovation: despite Lakota tradition and original Church policy, women played a prominent role. The 1910 Congress at Standing Rock had a "women's day" where a member of each St. Mary's Sodality addressed the Congress, prompting the Apostolic Delegate who witnessed the speeches, Diomede Falconio, to remark that "In all my life I have never observed women speak with such eloquence and independence, and yet with such modesty." By 1920, women participated fully in the Congresses deliberations.[16]

To be sure, numerous factors limited the voice of Lakota women in Catholic circles. Nevertheless, they had an official voice, which Looks Twice did not have in the Black Elk interviews with Neihardt in 1930. Black Elk set up a ceremonial space, which structured the telling of traditional knowledge to an outsider by creating a kinship relationship with Neihardt. All the participants were men, with the only exception being Neihardt's daughter, who as a stenographer recorded the conversation. As a woman, Looks Twice was part of the support staff that cooked and took care of the children. She had wanted Emil Afraid of Hawk to translate, in part because he was a practicing Catholic and worked as a catechist, but was overruled.[17] Looks Twice, unlike her brother Benjamin, had no direct agency in the interview.

When Looks Twice finally got the opportunity to speak about *Black Elk Speaks* four decades later, she re-centered Black Elk's spirituality and identity on his Lakota Catholicism in part because it was true to her memory, but also because this was the forum that allowed her to speak. For Looks Twice, Catholicism needed to be included because it was a meaningful, vibrant part of her life as a Lakota woman.

Since Steltenkamp published *Holy Man of the Oglala*, academic interpretations tend to pit Looks Twice's and Benjamin's emphases against each other, to assume that one must be correct. A more accurate perspective is to see them as complementary, captured by the increasingly common phrase that Black Elk was comfortable praying with both the pipe and with the rosary.[18]

Yet in the context of complementarity, Looks Twice's quiet agency deserves special attention. There are no official statistics, but my impressions are that Pine Ridge has the highest per capita celebrity religious figures of any reservation. While her father and brother are recognized as being among the most important, we should add Looks Twice to the list. In the context of the Pine Ridge anthropological fishbowl, she quietly redirected the non-Native anthropologist to the missing and in her eyes most important part of the story. Like her father, Looks Twice exercised the Lakota emphasis on relationship in the process of sharing with outsiders, taking Steltenkamp as a *takoja* (grandchild) and initiating ceremony.[19] The summer after being ordained, Looks Twice asked Steltenkamp to say Mass at her house at a gathering of her extended family, both in the tradition of the early Lakota Catholics hosting Mass at their home and the feast Black Elk hosted at the end of Neihardt's visit.[20]

Looks Twice reshaped the whole academic debate, but her greatest impact will be in Black Elk's cause for canonization. Without her testimony and work to shift the public image of Black Elk, it is difficult to envision his cause for sainthood going forward. She is also indirectly connected to the beginning of the cause, which occurred at the St. Kateri Tekakwitha Canonization Mass at the Vatican on October 21, 2012. There, Looks Twice's son George Looks Twice met Marquette archivist Mark Thiel. After conversing about Black Elk, they decided to start a petition to begin his cause for canonization.[21]

Most remarkable of all is that the evidence suggests that Looks Twice did not set out to do any of what we can now see in hindsight: to be a cultural informant and a spiritual leader, or to change the academy and the Church. Looks Twice simply wanted to be true to the memory of her father and her Lakota Catholic faith. Yet she might end up being the midwife of a canonized saint and his vision of the Sacred Tree.

Notes

1. Michael F. Steltenkamp, *Nicholas Black Elk: Medicine Man, Missionary, Mystic* (Norman, OK: University of Oklahoma Press, 2009), 107.

2. Michael F. Steltenkamp, *Black Elk: Holy Man of the Oglala* (Norman, OK: University of Oklahoma Press, 1993), 111.

3. Devotion to Mary was a prominent part of Lakota Catholicism. There was even a reported apparition in the neighboring town of Porcupine. See "Our Lady of the Sioux," in *Shrines to Our Lady Around the World* (Toronto: Ambassador Books, Ltd., 1954), 180–2.

4. Henry Westropp, S.J., quoted in Steltenkamp, *Holy Man of the Oglala*, 65.

5. Steltenkamp, *Holy Man of the Oglala*, 68.

6. *Waníkiya* told Black Elk: "My life is such that all earthly beings that grow belong to me. My father has said this. You must say this." Raymond J. DeMallie, ed., *The Sixth Grandfather: Black Elk's Teachings Given to John G. Neihardt* (Lincoln, NE: University of Nebraska Press, 1985), 263.

7. See Damian Costello, "Black Elk's Vision of *Waníkiya*: the Ghost Dance, Catholic Sacraments, and Lakota Ontology," *Journal of NAIITS: An Indigenous Learning Community*, Vol. 16 (2018): 40–56, and Louis S. Warren, *God's Red Son: The Ghost Dance Religion and the Making of Modern America* (New York: Basic Books, 2017).

8. See Damian Costello, *Black Elk: Colonialism and Lakota Catholicism* (Maryknoll, NY: Orbis, 2005), 80.

9. Thomas E. Mails, *Fools Crow*, with Dallas Chief Eagle (New York: Doubleday, 1979), 174.

10. Steltenkamp, *Holy Man of the Oglala*, 117.

11. This section and the quotations come from an email correspondence with Michael F. Steltenkamp. February 26 and March 8, 2021.

12. DeMallie, *The Sixth Grandfather*, 39.

13. "Dakota Images," *Journal of South Dakota History* 14, no.1 (1984), 92, https://www.sdhspress.com/journal/south-dakota-history-14-1/dakota-images-benjamin-black-elk/vol-14-no-1-dakota-images-benjamin-black-elk.pdf.

14. Steltenkamp, *Medicine Man, Missionary, Mystic*, 98. See Joe Jackson, *Black Elk: The Life of an American Visionary*, (New York: Farrar, Straus, and Giroux, 2016), 352.

15. Louis J. Goll from Steltenkamp, *Holy Man of the Oglala*, 45. See also Mark Thiel, "Catholic Sodalities among the Sioux, 1882–1910," *U.S. Catholic Historian* 16, no. 2 (1998): 56–77 http://www.jstor.org/stable/25154634 and Marie Therese Archambault, "Ben Black Bear, Jr.: A Lakota Deacon and a 'Radical Catholic' Tells His Own Story," *U.S. Catholic Historian* 16, no. 2 (1998): 90–106, http://www.jstor.org/stable/25154636.

16. Ross Enochs, *The Jesuit Mission to the Lakota Sioux: A Study of Pastoral Ministry, 1886–1945* (Kansas City, MO: Sheed and Ward, 1996), 63–4. For the influence of Sun Dance traditions on the Sioux Indian Congress, see Harvey Markowitz, "Converting the Rosebud Sicangu: Lakota Catholicism in the Late Nineteenth Century and Early Twentieth Centuries," *Great Plains Quarterly* 32, no. 1 (Winter 2012), 14–20.

17. Steltenkamp, *Medicine Man, Missionary, Mystic*, 141.

18. For example, see George Looks Twice in "Vatican considers sainthood for Black Elk," *National Catholic Reporter* (August 25, 2018), https://www.ncronline.org/news/people/vatican-considers-sainthood-lakota-sioux-medicine-man.

19. Steltenkamp, *Medicine Man, Missionary, Mystic*, xvi. Black Elk ceremonially adopted both John Neihardt and Joseph Epes Brown, author of *The Sacred Pipe: Black Elk's Account of the Seven Rites of the Oglala Sioux* (Norman, OK: University of Oklahoma Press, 2012). See John G. Neihardt and Philip J. Deloria, *Black Elk Speaks: The Complete Edition* (United States, Bison Books, 2014), 287, 248.

20. Email from Steltenkamp. Another interesting detail is that both Black Elk and Looks Twice gave their interviewers a handcrafted pendant decorated with religious symbols. See DeMallie, *The Sixth Grandfather*, 28 and Steltenkamp, *Medicine Man, Missionary, Mystic*, 124.

21. Damian Costello and Jon Sweeney, "Black Elk, the Lakota medicine man turned Catholic teacher, is promoted for sainthood," America: *The Jesuit Review* (October 1, 1917), https://www.americamagazine.org/faith/ 2017/10/01/ black-elk-lakota-medicine-man-turned-catholic-teacher-promoted-sainthood.

Dolores Huerta Haciendo Más Caras

Navigating a Catholic World Not Scripted for Her

NEOMI DE ANDA

The farmworker activism to which Dolores Huerta dedicated more than six decades of her life has connections to my own life. In preparing for that the first presentation of this work, at the American Catholic Historical Association in 2018, I spent some time talking with my dad and learning some of my own family history connected to farmworkers. My father spent multiple summers of his childhood in the 1950s as a farmworker in the onion fields of New Mexico. He was six years old the first summer Welito (my name for "abuelito"/grandfather) took him and his two siblings—ages 5 and 3—to work in the fields.[1] They would walk about 12 blocks to catch the work truck, which left at five every morning. They did this work to supplement the income Welito made as a welder. Welito was not paid the income due to him because he did not have documents recognized by the US government. (Side note: my dad, Uncle Danny, Aunt Vicki, and Welita were all citizens of the US.)

Dad told me that they would make 15 cents for every two five-gallon buckets of onions. He said that sometimes they would step away from a half-filled bucket and someone would steal the onions. He said, "The hours were long, but I thought it was fun! I was a kid and it gave me something to do. Plus, I knew that our labor was for us to have new clothes and shoes for school. There was a direct link between my labor and my new stuff for school." He continued, "We didn't know anything about social justice. We didn't realize that we were being underpaid. Or that we should have had restroom facilities. My brother and I would go in the bushes. Come to think of it, I still don't know how and where my mom and sister would use the restroom. . . ."

Huerta originated from what is now recognized as the political border between Mexico and the US, and she had what some label "Mexican-American" heritage, ethnicity, and persona. In those regards, Dolores

Huerta and her work—and the work of Gloria Anzaldúa and Chicana feminists—speak very closely to my experience.

This essay explores Huerta's work as a Catholic woman lay leader, through Gloria Anzaldúa's theory of Haciendo Caras. Bringing together interviews, digital archival materials, and personal stories, along with theoretical frameworks from Chicana studies and LatinoXa theologies, the essay delves into understanding Huerta's complex relationship with Catholicism.[2] The essay begins by presenting a discussion of Anzaldúa's notion of Haciendo Caras, where I present an expansion of haciendo más caras to the theory. Next, this essay explores Huerta as raised in a world haciendo caras to discuss her Catholic upbringing and family story. It will then move toward ripping apart the seams and recrafting the interfacing to discuss Huerta's move to a life of solidarity as a community organizer with farm workers. Finally, the chapter will use hacienda más caras to show Huerta's ongoing impact as a Catholic laywoman leader at the age of 91.

Caras, Haciendo Caras, Mascaras, Interface, Mas/caras, Mas caras

Gloria Anzaldúa developed a theory based on caras, the Spanish word for faces. Through various wordplay with both "caras" and "faces," Anzaldúa both swiftly and delicately describes intricacies of working between various identities of domination and oppression to reworking of identities, to living in the world as agents. This theoretical framework, which she named haciendo caras (making faces, making soul) is suggested to manage, negotiate, subvert, and confront dominant structures and ideologies, using "*gestos subversivos*, political subversive gestures, the piercing look that questions and challenges. . . ."[3] Most notably, Anzaldúa points out that a cara is the bodily surface. We are known by our faces because for Anzaldúa writing from the Mexico//US border in Texas and prior to the COVID-19 pandemic, our face is "the most naked, most vulnerable, exposed and significant topography of the body."[4] Social structures inscribe how faces are interpreted. To have face means to have dignity and self-respect.[5]

Haciendo caras is understood as making facial expressions, usually into awkward distortions; "*gestos subversivos*, political subversive gestures."[6] For Anzaldúa, haciendo caras is a metaphor "for constructing one's identity" because to be the shaper of one's flesh is also to be the shaper of one's soul.[7] Haciendo caras is about making faces to make one's soul. The ability to hacer caras shapes one's essence. It is not a superficial gesture meant to be forgotten after a moment. However, cambiar caras, to change faces, is seen as resistance to oppression so as to mask ourselves from many dangers where there are few options for survival, to become chameleons.[8] Based upon the work of Audre Lorde, Anzaldúa claims that sometimes people have been forced to adopt other faces in order to pass for something else as a form of survival.[9]

To adopt other faces through force, Anzaldúa understands as using las mascaras (masks). Because of external forces which bring about the usage of las macaras, they "drive a wedge between our intersubjective personhood and the persona we present to the world."[10] These masks are filled with self-hatred and internalized oppressions. Reflecting on the writings of Dolores Huerta, Stacey Sowards interpolates, "These masks are also *más/caras*, or a type of 'super face' that require extra work to maintain."[11] As women of color, masking roles exact a toll. Therefore, it is important for women of color to strip off the masks imposed on us and to become typographers and agents of our own accord by confronting internalized oppression.[12]

To rip off las mascaras, Anzaldúa turns to interfacing, i.e., the sewing of interface between two fabrics to make an item stronger. Anzaldúa proposes that mestizas need to rip the seams of las mascaras to expose the interface. They then need to remold the interface to crack the mask and form it into our own. Anzaldúa mentions the "left-handed guardian" who does not let the past eat us. So, while Anzaldúa does not spend time describing and developing the notion of the left-handed guardian, it is this guardian who ensures that the ripped seams and the torn fabric of las mascaras will not lead to future demise in the reshaping of the interface into new faces, what I call "más caras"[13]

To continue Anzaldúa's playful and strategic punning on the word "caras," I add an additional layer not presented by Anzaldúa, Chela Sandoval, or Sowards. I call this additional layer "más caras." Through más caras, one is able to recraft the interface to form faces with others. A wisdom figure becomes a face maker. In other words, one engages in the process of hacienda caras / making soul as a face maker. Through the engagement of más caras, one understands the tiny details, moments, and contexts[14] of making faces, haciendo caras, of shaping faces and souls, and also of having one face be read by multiple audiences in different ways.

Anzaldúa discusses haciendo caras as ways of resistance against what has already been written on the faces of Chicana queer women. If Anzaldúa had lived to see how her work has become central to Chicanx studies, I wonder if the volume commemorating the twenty-year publication of *Haciendo Caras* might be called *Interfacing Más Caras*. A part of Anzaldúa's methodology is that she leaves things open, allowing readers to immerse themselves in the writing and make meaning for themselves. Her methodology mirrors her explanation of unmasking through the use and reuse of interfacing. Through this methodology, creation and recreation become natural. Then the world begins to change as we all change ourselves because of engagement in the inter: interfacing, intersections, interconnections. Internalization, therefore, is about attending to the systems which need attention to fight oppression. It is not about internalization of the oppression itself. Internalized oppression is extremely strong in communities and individuals who have been systemically marked for death. Interfacing, intersecting, and interconnecting all lead to internalization of all that is life (including the sinful and messy parts). When systems are internalized for life, they are creative and generative, rather than built on the backs of others and the Earth. Clearly, the previous statement is utopic, as we will never fully arrive at that because sin exists and makes the world a wonderfully messy place.

Applying this all back to Anzaldúa's notion of haciendo caras, those who work for systems of internalization of all that is life and produce más caras, more faces. One who is able to recraft the interface to form faces with others becomes a face maker and engages in the process of hacienda caras: making faces as a face maker while understanding the tiny details, moments, and contexts of shaping faces and souls while also having the wisdom for a cara to be read by multiple audiences in different ways. Wisdom figures also work with each other, so they engage in haciendo caras with an outcome of more faces/more souls—más caras.

This essay will illustrate how Huerta has committed her life to haciendo caras and más caras as a Catholic woman lay leader. Huerta was a young single mother who followed a call and left a stable teaching job to work as an organizer. She has been married and divorced twice. She has children with multiple men. She has never married her latest partner. And these are just the social and Catholic boundaries she has transgressed around marriage and procreation. She has changed her political stance to being pro-choice while she clearly continues to promote an ethic of life. She looks to those who are most marginalized in every situation. She has made a commitment to minister with and to LGBTQ+ persons and their families. And in so many pictures of her, and throughout the film *Dolores*, Catholic symbols persist. Because she has dedicated her life to live and struggle with and among humans marked for death by the mangling systems of domination in the world, she has had to navigate her faith journey in a world not scripted for her. Haciendo caras, she navigates this world as she continues haciendo más caras.

Dolores Clara Fernandez Huerta is considered a national icon in some parts of the USA, yet is largely unknown in other parts. She has, however, greatly increased her visibility through the many webinars she presented during social distancing of the COVID-19 pandemic in 2020 and 2021. She is also largely unknown as a Catholic laywoman leader despite having founded two national organizations and spent a lifetime dedicated to the work of social justice and systemic change rooted in her Catholic faith.

While Huerta does not speak much of the influence her Catholic faith has on her life, so many of her words and actions manifest this reality. Dolores Huerta's commitments to social justice and a lived solidarity are exemplary. As she boldly professes, "Not that we are going to go out there and do things for people but to help teach people how to do things for themselves. They have the power. No one is going to solve these issues for them."[15] The notion of subsidiarity greatly stands out in this quote. For Huerta, people have the power and ability within themselves to create the social change to improve their own communities. She roots the power in the communities, a very grassroots model rather than a model of a savior, colonizer, or empire builder. This way of creating social change also shows wisdom from years of experience.

In addition to the themes of Catholicism that ring through the mission of the Dolores Huerta Foundation (DHF), Dolores Huerta has also spoken about her faith publicly and tied her work to her faith. In 2007, Mario T. Garcia interviewed Huerta on the topic of spirituality. "How important has religion been in your life?" he asked. Huerta's answer: "It has been extremely important in my life. Especially when you start doing things like organizing a union with no money and seven children. Talk about faith. It takes a lot of faith."[16] Partly in response to a later question, she replied, "I always say when people ask me where did you get your values from, I say I got them from religion. Especially in the Southwest where people are very devoted to St. Francis Xavier, to again follow the same values as St. Francis of Assisi about helping others and doing good for other people and not expecting gratification or rewards for what they do; if you see someone in need you should help them, don't wait to be asked. All those core values I did get them from religion."[17] Additional thoughts on her faith from a public conversation at the University of Notre Dame will be presented throughout this essay as well.[18]

Raised in a World of Haciendo Caras

Born in 1930 in Dawson, New Mexico,[19] Huerta and her siblings were all raised devout Catholics.[20] She is a coal miner's daughter who believes in a clean environment.[21] This commitment may come from her father's work; however, she attributes it to her experience of working with farm-workers and seeing their suffering due to being sprayed with pesticides, including children born without brains and limbs.

Her parents divorced during the Great Depression, when Huerta was still a child, and her mother, Alicia St. John Chavez, moved the family to Stockton, California in 1936, when Dolores was six.[22] Now a divorced Catholic laywoman and mother, St. John Chavez was already living in a world hacienda caras, due to patriarchy and the strictures of Catholicism. A very religious woman and a very hard worker, she worked two jobs to keep her children fed.[23]

Raised by her single mother, Dolores learned about women's leadership and entrepreneurship, and about fairness.[24] Their mother would never take anything from welfare—she wouldn't take anything she said was for people who couldn't work. She continued to work two jobs until she saved up enough money to set up a business, and then she opened her own res-taurant. St. John Chavez also took over the hotel of a Japanese friend who was taken to an internment camp during World War II. She also began the first Mexican-American Chamber of Commerce in California.[25]

Although she didn't go to church every Sunday, St. John Chavez made sure her children went to church every Sunday. She would go to church for the holidays and holy days of obligation. She usually had to take her Sundays to catch up on her rest, because she worked days as a server and nights in a cannery.[26] When the family moved to Stockton, California, they went to St. Mary's, where Dolores celebrated her first communion, confirmation, and first marriage. Out of her own volition, Dolores went to confession regularly. She sang in two choirs, one at St. Mary's and one at St. Gertrude's. She also participated in the youth group called Santa Teresita at St. Gertrude's because most of her friends attended that church.[27]

According to Huerta, St. John Chavez was a feminist without the term.[28] She also closely linked charity and justice to Catholicism. St. John Chavez would tell her children that it was their duty to help people if they need help and you can help them.[29] "Don't wait for people to ask you for help; do not expect a reward for the help."[30] "If you demand something in return, you are taking away the grace of that act."[31] Huerta credits her commitment to advocacy, organizing and social justice to her mother, the Catholic church, and her own and her peers' experience of injustice and harassment.[32]

Huerta attended college and earned a teaching degree at the University of the Pacific's Delta College. She worked as an elementary school teacher in Stockton, California, where most of the children in the school were connected to farmworkers and many of them were farmworkers themselves. Huerta found that the children would come to school hungry and with few resources, and she would see students in school with threadbare T-shirts—farmworker children. Huerta petitioned the school principal to let her give the children milk and shoes, but the principal did not allow it. When she visited their homes, she saw that farmworkers had dirt floors and furniture made from cardboard boxes and crates.[33] She believed she could do better for these children as a community organizer trying to change the system to improve their lives rather than by being their teacher. She took her mother's words about helping people to heart, and in her twenties, Huerta formally began her life as an activist. She continues this life, which she considers a calling to today. As she explains in *Dolores*:

> After I had seen the miserable conditions of the farm workers and knowing how to organize people; having achieved these incredible successes on legislation; I decided that's what I needed to do. I felt such a calling. I felt it so strongly that in spite of all of the negatives—despite people saying, "You can't do that! You've got seven kids. You're going

through a divorce." Many people thought I was making a very foolish decision. . . . I did pray that if I was doing the wrong thing, I wanted a sign that I was doing the wrong thing. Making this huge, huge decision to leave my home in Stockton; to come to Delano; not knowing where my next meal was coming from. I was worried how my kids would take the move because they left all of their friends behind and we had a very comfortable home. I left a couple of my younger children behind. I knew that I was doing something that I wanted to do. They had no choice.[34]

As this passage highlights, Dolores as a woman leader has encountered various challenges to her ways of life from society as well as from Catholic circles. One questions whether or not these same challenges would be posed to a man. Stacey Sowards claims, "She is a product of many social forces, related to family, education, religion, social movements of the 1960s and 1970s, particularly the Chicano/a movement, the farmworker movement, the women's rights movement, and collaborative relationships with specific people and organizations."[35] Yet Huerta has managed to make great strides as a co-founder of the United Farm Workers union and many times as the only woman on the leadership board. She always leads in groups to teach others to make great strides for themselves and their communities. According to Luis Valdez, "In the 1950s everyone was fit into a mold. If you were Dolores Huerta, there was no mold."[36]

Interfacing: Crafting and Recrafting

Huerta saw that her students were all farmworkers and that they needed more help than just education. She wanted to help change their conditions through organizing rather than just giving them charity.[37] She met community organizer Fred Ross and saw the work he and others were doing. Because of the harassment she had received as a youth, she wanted to belong to an organization where "you can send police to jail for beating people up."[38] For Huerta organizing was more powerful than classroom teaching because "[t]he main thing about organizing at the grassroots level is to teach people to fight for themselves and that they have the power to do it themselves."[39]

She raised her children in the Catholic faith.[40] Before moving to Delano to organize with farmworkers, she spent much time in prayer discerning the decision. Once they moved to Delano, they were now living off of food from the food surplus commodities (now known as food banks). At one point, her daughter needed shoes for Confirmation. These shoes needed to be white, and the only white shoes the daughter owned were tennis shoes with holes in them. Huerta went to church to pray as to whether or not she had made the right decision for her children. She did not have money to buy the needed new white shoes required for her daughter for her Confirmation. As Dolores was praying, she saw some farmworker children with white tennis shoes with holes. She took that as a sign that she had done the right thing. Huerta grew up rather middle class with nice clothes and dance lessons. Before moving to Delano, she was raising her children in a similar way. About the drastic change in moving to Delano, Huerta reflected, "Being treated like farmworkers was a very good experience."[41]

Because Catholic faith is a very important part of Huerta, she quit being a teacher in the middle of a divorce, with seven children, not knowing where their next meal was coming from. It was a major decision that her family criticized harshly. A compadre told her that her children would be gangsters and druggies. Yet, she did it anyway. Huerta connects her faith to making large sacrifices for important causes.[42]

In partnership with Cesar Chávez, Huerta began the National Farm Workers Association (NFWA) (later accepted into the AFL-CIO as the United Farm Workers union) which was a broad organization that provided a holistic approach to community organizing. Huerta and Chávez were not the first to try to unionize farmworkers. Teamsters and autoworkers had tried to organize the farmworkers, but they were coming from outside and did not understand local needs and culture.[43] Beyond creating an organization for workers to unionize and make demands of employers, the National Farm Workers Association also had a credit union, a faith component, a food bank, a community clothing closet, and worked closely with schools for the education of their children. The employees of the NFWA earned only $5 per week.

In the eponymous documentary film, *Dolores*, Luis Valdez states,

One of the really tragic contradictions about the United States of America is that it has presented itself before the world as a beacon of independence and liberty and human rights. Of course the real stain on this mythology is slavery. And with it the potential for the enslavement of others. This was a real threat for all Mexicans living in California after 1848. It was a continuing threat for everyone who came from China, Japan, the Philippines, and Vietnam. Racism has been endemic to American history. The feudal wage slavery is really just an extension of the attitude that had persisted in the country. The irony is that none of us can live without food. None of us can live without what is produced in our fields. This is life and yet these are the worst paid workers on the planet.[44]

In another account, Rick Rivas, an LGBTQ+ activist articulates, "My grandfather was living on a vineyard in a house owned by the people who employed him. There was . . . this sense of slavery. But you couldn't do anything wrong against your employer because if you did, were they gonna kick out your family? Where were you gonna go? You don't speak the language. You are not even a citizen of the country."[45] Also in *Dolores*, Eloy Martinez, a farmworker, bears witness to the fact that "(t)he women were treated worse than the men. You had no protection. You had a lot of mistreatment and a lot of rape"[46] Huerta understood the strongly woven fabric which created a mascara, the outward face of the US. The work of the farmworker movement with Huerta and Chávez in leadership was about ripping those seams and reworking the interfacing with others while they all claimed their own caras and created más caras.

Cesar Chávez has earned more fame and notoriety because he organized massive hunger strikes to draw attention to the plight of the farmworkers. Chávez died at the age of 62 due to the physical punishment from these hunger strikes. Although Huerta has not worked with the United Farmworkers since the 1990s, she is still often connected to the legacy of Chávez. When asked about their working relationship and its basis in Catholic faith, she moved to astrological signs first by noting they are both Aries, which she attributes to the very difficult discussions between the two. Yet they shared similar philosophy, vision and goals, so that made the commitment to the work easier.[47]

The National Farm Workers Association (NFWA, now the United Farm Workers, or UFW) are best known for the international grape strike which began in 1965. The NFA had made a three-year plan for a strike but decided to move their plan forward to support Filipino workers who went on strike sooner.[48] Huerta claims faith in God, self, and other people as extremely important in creating, joining, and maintaining a movement, especially when one seems to be doing things that are not reasonable, like continuing in the struggle even after seeing people get killed in their fights for justice. Being rooted in her Catholic faith provided a force for her to continue to do something.[49]

Catholic faith was a large part of the NFWA/UFW when Huerta and Chávez were involved. Large Masses of a thousand people were held before every major campaign.[50] Huerta is known to carry a rosary always. She has also used the practice of fasting as an offering for motivation to continue her work. In 2006, at the age of seventy-five, Huerta fasted for the forty days of Lent and ate only one meal per day.[51] Because of Huerta's work through the UFW and the DHF, laws have passed which allow people to vote in Spanish; get a driver's license in one's ethnic language; register voters door to door;[52] provide disability insurance for farmworkers; get public assistance; aid to the blind; attain aid for needy children if they are legal residents (not full citizens) which eventually became federal law that allows legal residents to qualify for the Affordable Care Act.[53] Recently, the Dolores Huerta Foundation led a lawsuit against nine different school districts in the central valley of the state of California which were educating farmworker children because the high schools had suspended African American kids almost 600 times more and Latinx kids 500 times more than white kids. They won the lawsuit and now all employees have to have cultural competency training, implement restorative justice, hold community forums to hear from parents and children, and develop positive behavior intervention systems.[54]

After Cesar Chávez's untimely death, Dolores Huerta left her work with the UFW. She decided to create her own foundation, which engages in broad-based community organizing and education, and the DHF was established in 2003.[55] It is a community service organization, where low-income people organize to change and challenge their communities. The Dolores Huerta Foundation works in communities where most people live on $15,000 or less per year. These communities tend to have no street lights, sidewalks, sewers, and other public services. They tend to be school-to-prison pipelines where students, mostly people of color, begin to be criminalized at a very young age through the education system. As Dolores Huerta says, "It's not a drop-out, it's a push-out."[56]

Layers of Mascaras

This organizing work has not been easy or without cost to Dolores Huerta. She recounts one of the hardest moments of her life,

> There was a time when my mother was dying of cancer and I was in Sacramento and responsible for passing not only that bill but several other bills that I had, like driver's license in Spanish, getting unemployment insurance for farmworkers, disability insurance, I had a whole ton of bills, being able to register voters door-to-door, I had a whole plate of legislation I was carrying, and my mother's dying. I guess my prayers were continual. I would lobby Sacramento and then jump in the car and drive to San Francisco, and then drive back to Sacramento. Then my husband, who I was in the middle of a divorce with, took my kids from the babysitter. I had no idea where my kids were. All of this was going on at the same time. Talk about the need for prayer and faith. It was tested. That's your consolation, that you go there and you have that support.[57]

Huerta claims that she was at first intimidated by being a woman organizer but quickly realized that was all in her head. For those who did not wish to work with a woman organizer, Huerta would continue the work with sincerity and most of the time people were eventually accepting.[58] She claims, "[the] hardest part of going into people's homes is the need to overcome one's own fear, especially of people not accepting us . . . [one has] butterflies when you are doing something new—it's like exercise and your muscles hurt, you are doing the right thing—to come out of our comfort zone and as the work is done more and more, it gets easier; if you do not feel a little nervous—then it is just not important work."[59] She found mothers, abuelas, and tías were more accepting of messages from Dolores Huerta and of farmworker movements. She attributes it to the fact that the conditions in which farmworkers were working and living were so desperate that organizing gave people hope, which went a long way.[60]

In the interweaving of fighting for farmworker's rights among which are women's rights, and environmental justice, Huerta continues to fight battles to even tell her own stories. She does not spend much of her time speaking about her Catholic faith, yet is very rooted in living her beliefs of it. At the age of 91, Huerta works as a full-time, unpaid volunteer for the DHF. She donates more than 95% of the income she receives for her appearances to the DHF, which relies on these funds to support community organizing work. According to the DHF Event and Video Request Form, Huerta is typically offered $20,000 for her appearances.[61] One can see Huerta's commitment to solidarity in the work of social justice. As a lay Catholic woman leader from a historically marginalized ethnic background, Huerta has been able to use her Catholic faith to transform her own world and the world around her, many times through complex and contradicting realities. Sometimes, she has had to use savvy techniques to negotiate her own Catholic perspectives between her own life, official church teaching, and public policy.

Woman Leader Among Women

According to César Chávez, "[o]ne of the things that was very helpful in the beginning, [we] made it alright for the women to be on the picket lines, made it alright for the husbands to permit their wives to be on the picket lines and their daughters and their mothers, and so forth. We found it a tremendous advantage to give women equal participation in the union because what a tremendous resource that we can use."[62]

Huerta does not keep all of the credit of the role of women in the FWU for herself. She remarks, "We had women who ran the clinics. We had women as field directors, women did a lot of clerical work. I remember someone saying to Cesar, 'Why do you have so many women?' and he said, 'Because they do the work.'"[63]

While Huerta was the only woman member when she was on the board of the UFW, she claims that the directors of *Dolores* wanted to increase the drama of the film, so they made it seem like she was pushed out of its leadership when she had actually decided that it was time to move on to different projects more rooted in grassroots organizing.[64] Today, the DHF is majority-women run.[65]

Negotiating with Allies

As part of her strong commitment to solidarity in her work, which is based on Catholic teaching, Huerta needs to work constantly at negotiating with allies, including Catholic allies. Huerta's closest allies who were also faithful practicing Catholics were Cesar and Helen Chávez. Cesar and Dolores were the founders of the United Farmworkers Union, and Helen Chávez played strong roles throughout the movement as well. Cesar Chávez, as the first president of the UFW, has received more international notoriety than Dolores Huerta or Helen Chávez.

Huerta raised her children Catholic. Before the strike, she would attend Sunday Mass with her children and with Helen Chávez. Once the strike broke, the priests with ties to the growers were telling the farmworkers to break the strike and return to work. So, the Chávez family held Mass in their home every Sunday with their own priest.[66] This practice of holding Masses as part of the union no longer exists.[67]

In another example of working with Catholic allies, Huerta discusses how she worked closely with some priests prior to forming the union.[68] For example, prior to working with Cesar Chávez, Huerta worked closely with Father McCullough and Father Dugan to form the AWA, the Agricultural Workers Association. "We were at my mother's house—this was after we had been working together for three or four years—[Fr McCullough] says to me, 'Well, you really should stay home with your children, this is not a good place for women.' Can you believe that? I remember this because I was so close to him. I lived in the housing projects, went to his church every Sunday. I even named one of my kids after him. I was shocked. But luckily my mother said to me, 'Don't pay attention.' She always had really good liquor for company and she pulled out a bottle of tequila and we had a shot of tequila."[69]

She continues, "I didn't see the Father again. We used to talk every day. I didn't see him again until we were doing the boycott in San Francisco. One of my compadres who was also from Stockton said, 'Guess who's at the church across the street from my house, Father McCullough.' I went over there to see him. He was like, 'What can I do for you, do you need any help?' I said 'Yeah, I could use a couple of tires for my car.'"[70] She concludes, "When I was beat up by the police he went to see me in the hospital. He died shortly thereafter."[71]

When asked about the impact Vatican II had on the farmworker's struggle, Huerta recounts how the impact was not immediate. However, in terms of the boycott, the valley in California was controlled by Catholic growers, so the farmworkers' struggle was not central to the hierarchical powers of the Catholic Church. In one example, nuns in Delano asked Huerta to take her kids out of Catholic school because the growers were

Catholic and had their kids in Catholic school. There were two Catholic churches in Delano, "Usually all the growers went to St. Mary's and that was where the school was at. Guadalupe was on the other side of town, on the west side."[72] In another example, Huerta recounts that Cesar Chávez was to take the offering at the Mass with Pope John Paul II in Salinas, California on September 19, 1987. The growers put pressure on the Pope, so at the last minute it was not Cesar, it was a farmworker, while Huerta and Chávez did not attend the Mass.[73]

Among Huerta's most famous Catholic allies was Robert Kennedy. On March 10, 1968, Robert Kennedy spoke to the media about legislation for farmworkers while standing next to Huerta. "We pass the laws that remedy the injustices. That's what we should do. That is what those of us in Washington should do. We shouldn't just deplore the violence and deplore the lawlessness. We should pass the laws of what people are rioting about. We can't have violence in the country but we should also not have these injustices continue."[74] Huerta was standing on the platform next to Robert Kennedy on June 5, 1968, during his acceptance speech upon winning the California Democratic primary for the presidency of the US. After his speech, Huerta was supposed to accompany him to a reception with mariachis, but Kennedy was mortally shot that night.[75]

Popular Religious Practices

Popular religious practices are a central part of Catholicism to many. LatinoXa theologies have taken these practices as central to how these communities do theology. This concept, along with lo cotidiano, or daily lived experience, help to express another Catholic mascara and más cara of Dolores Huerta.

The call and response found both inside and outside of Catholic liturgies is something for which Huerta is famous. She has used this notion of call and response, rooted in practices of psalms, prayers of the faithful, lamentations, etc. to rally, organize, and inspire people. Sometimes, she repeats the same call and response multiple times. Huerta uses call and response brilliantly to raise the energy of a group and motivate people to believe in themselves as agents of social change. For example, in a public interview at the University of Notre Dame in 2018, Dolores finished her time with the group by asking, "Who has the power?" and demanding the response, "We have the power!" And then asking, "What kind of power?" And encouraging the response: "People power!"[76]

Her most famous call and response has become, "Si se puede" which was used by Barak Obama, a former labor organizer, in his 2008 campaign as "Yes We Can." In 2012, when Obama presented Huerta with the Presidential Medal of Freedom,[77] he publicly thanked her for allowing him to "steal" this saying while also praising Huerta for spending her life giving more people a seat at the table. He quoted her, "'Don't wait to be invited', she said, 'step in there.'"[78]

Other popular religious practices in which Huerta has regularly engaged are religious images in the home[79] as well as in organizing,[80] fasting,[81] rosary,[82] and other Catholic rituals. Huerta frequently remarks on the need to pray and ask for grace,[83] pointing out the need to couple prayer with other actions. She recounts,

> I remember when I was lobbying in Sacramento to get the bills passed— we had a bill to get pensions for non-citizens, so people who were legal immigrants would be able to get pensions—because I would go to the capitol to lobby I would go to the cathedral right there by the capitol and I would light all my candles and say my prayers. Then I would go to the legislature hearings. It's really funny because Sal Alvarez who was my assistant later on when I was with the union—I was a lobbyist with CSO[84]—Sal is a deacon and very religious. I would call Sal about people on the committee and he would say, "Well I lit all the candles," and I would say, "No, Sal, that's not going to do it, you have to light the candles and work the committee too. Lighting the candles isn't enough."[85]

Mas caras

Dolores Huerta is an exemplar of the complexities of a Catholic woman's life who is also a strong leader. Through the UFW and long before *Laudato Si'*[86], she made connections between Catholic pro-life teachings and the need to eradicate pesticides in the farm fields because it harms both the land and its inhabitants.[87] Her experience of living a life daily with people in imposed systems of poverty, many of whom were women trying to raise multiple children, as well as her work with the women's movement, has led her to change her political views in supporting legislation which seems to go directly against Catholic teaching. She also critiques the Catholic hierarchy for the sexual abuse that has been perpetuated through official church structures.

On birth control, Huerta remarks,

I've gotten a lot of hate mail on this—someone just sent me an email yesterday comparing me to Lucifer. My feeling is this, I have eleven children and it was my decision to have eleven children. But I don't think I can impose my values on somebody else. That is for some-body else to decide. It's total hypocrisy because if people did not use birth control, like the Church prohibits, everyone would have twenty kids. From day one, even native peoples and indigenous peoples, they always had some way of birth control and abortion. But the bad thing is that if you don't have a safe procedure for women who do need to have an abortion then you put the woman's life in jeopardy. Unless women can control their own bodies then women will always be suppressed.[88]

On abortion it's the same. I don't think any religion or any legislature should be able to dictate to women what they do with their bodies. When you look at the other side of this, what does the Church do? You want women to have a lot of kids, do we provide day care for the children? Do we provide parent classes for families? We really want to make sure that the fetus is born, but what about after they're born? They take these negative positions and even promote people to vote against their own economic interests. The antigay marriage is another thing. How many priests are gay? That's another hypocritical position. Some of my cousins are very devout—I was with them in Colorado recently—these are women who would never miss Mass. On Sunday they don't even want to go to Mass anymore I couldn't believe it. "Why aren't you going to go to Mass?" "Oh, we don't want to give our money to priests who pay off their lawsuits on pedophilia." I was shocked. You find that people are really fed up.[89]

Most recently, Huerta has taken a public stance on euthanasia in sup-port of New Mexico House Bill 47 which was signed into law on April 8, 2021.[90] NMHB47 allows physicians to prescribe self-administered end of life prescriptions to terminally ill patients. Huerta was quoted, "The fact that there is an alternative, and that people can make a choice that they want to end their life in a graceful and a peaceful manner, with their loved ones around them, I think that is something that's very important."[91]

Hopeful Caras y Mas Caras

We, as Catholics, believe in great hope. We believe in life. We have people who believe so deeply that they inspire others to keep believing. Maria Pilar Aquino defines "Empapamiento of Hope" thusly: "*Empapamiento* refers to our ability of 'saturating ourselves,' of 'imbuing ourselves,' of 'permeating ourselves' with hope so that we explore more freely the open possibilities of our reality and bring about the open possibilities of our transforming imagination."[92] Expanding on this concept, I like to tell the following short story in describing this topic to my students. When I was a child, I loved going out to get wet in the rain or in the sprinklers at the park. When I knocked on the door to go back into our house (because I knew I should not enter in my sopping condition), my mother would answer the door with a towel in hand and screech, "¡Estas empapapada!" She would then proceed to help me out of my clothes and dry myself.

This interchange between my mother and I was a ritual of care and made the play in the water all the more fulfilling. It was not until I became an adult that I realized the many reasons why my mother made sure I did not linger in this state of literal empapamiento. When one is soaking wet for an extended period of time, one will begin to smell, may become ill, may develop a rash or other skin issues, and may become fatigued or angry because of these issues. So, if one remains in a state of empapamiento of hope, one knows to expect fatigue, anger, issues to arrive, and not be welcomed by all. The hope of a worker for justice is such hope. Dolores Huerta has exemplified such hope. While Huerta has kept her children close through most of her life and work, Emilio Huerta, one of Dolores' children comments, "We soon recognized that our mother really didn't belong to us."[93] Eliseo Medina, Executive Vice-President of the Service Employees International Union rightly articulates, "She has such a firm belief in what she is doing that she infects you with it. I think she looks deep within you and she understands what you are capable of. That you actually can do more than what you thought was possible."[94]

The Wisdom of Dolores Huerta

In this section, I have created a list of theological and practical wisdom from Huerta to aid along the journey of the struggle for justice.

Theological Wisdom

On Cristologia:

> That was what Christ was about, feeding the poor. All of Christ's life was about that. It's painful to go to Mass sometimes. The priest rants and raves about gay marriage and about abortion, but not one word about farm workers around here not being paid for their work because they're undocumented, or social justice issues. The incarceration rate is going up, the poverty rate is going up. I almost got into a fistfight with a priest on Palm Sunday last year. I was in Northern California and I was putting the foot to the pedal so I could get to Mass on time on Palm Sunday. I finally made it in time and the priest was telling people that Senator Kennedy should be excommunicated. The Kennedy family is one of the most Catholic religious families that exists. He was saying they should be excommunicated because they were talking about the Schivel case. I got mad. He was Latino and to top it all off he was gay. When they were going to give Communion, a nun in a habit—which is a rare thing to see these days—she gets up to go help him to serve Communion and he told her no. Then he goes over to the front row and picks this real *guapo* (handsome), this young Latino dude to come up.[95]

On Liberation Theology

When asked about liberation theologies, Huerta interpreted that liberation theologians are not thinkers but those living into their theology.[96] My interpolation is that Huerta sees faith as a source but sitting around thinking about theology when people have needs is not the primary place to be. Attending to people's needs and working with people to create change in their communities is far more important than writing out long treatises. Theological wisdom comes from living life. Huerta's theological constructs are not based in a university theological education but by the wisdom gathered by living in deep solidarity with some of the poorest of the US.

On Organizing

Huerta claims: (1) Power in one's person is all of the power that one needs. Part of that power is knowing that one cannot do it by oneself. She urges to create systemic change collectively and through nonviolent ways.[97] (2) Organize people beginning in small groups of four to six because in working small it is very possible to create change.[98] (3) When we get angry we shut ourselves down.[99] (4) Sometimes we have to share a message more than once.[100] (5) Respect other people's rights so they may make the choices for themselves and their families that they need to make.[101] (6) Instead of trying to make change alone, organize more people to help create the change, for example, the Dolores Huerta Foundation has organized parents instead of going to the school district.[102]

On Leadership

First, Huerta asserts that (1) leadership is something that cannot only be passed on but lived.[103] (2) Everyone has something to contribute. For example, people who never went to high school or college are sitting on boards to take the power.[104] (3) Teaching other people to organize is sharing power.[105] (4) Teaching people to share the power with others with love, even with people who do not agree with us.[106] (5) Start practical programs like bike shares, a walking school bus, initiatives on health and nutrition, and voter education.[107] (6) Ten percent of corporations own 90% of wealth in the USA; run for office to affect policies for equity.[108] (7) Begin teaching ethnic and women and gender studies long before college.[109] For example, Huerta's life story has been systematically omitted and erased from K–12 educational curriculum in multiple states. (8) Create tools to be easily used by people. Because of Dolores Huerta's life story being systematically omitted from the education curriculum of various states, the Dolores Huerta Foundation has now created a K–12 Dolores Huerta Day Curriculum[110]

Finally, regarding the next generation of leaders, Huerta unites in wisdom with Cesar Chávez and says, "Don't be afraid to take risks." She then continues, leave a legacy of justice; we are on this earth such a short time— what can I do to make the world a better place; no matter how much money you make, you can only wear one outfit a day (or at a time); sharing, cooperation, not domination, not competition; how do we share our resources for everyone?" When asked if it is faith over politics and economics that keeps her going, Huerta responded, "I think so. Because you have so many setbacks in what you're doing."[111]

FIGURE 4: Screening of *Dolores* documentary with Dolores Huerta, seated, at Alamo Drafthouse, El Paso, Texas. October 15, 2017. Photo courtesy of the author.

Más Caras de Huerta and My Interfacing

It was around the same time my dad was working in the onion fields that Dolores Huerta began her work as an organizer. Between 1955 and 1959, she drafted much legislation that was approved in Sacramento. She found great affirmation in seeing policies and laws change, at the age of only twenty-five. (She claims she was very young at the time.)[112] She was also one of the first people to correlate the injustices of race, labor, sex, gender, nationality, and the environment. Long before intersectionality became a vogue term in academia, Dolores Huerta and other activists were using the cruelties of these multiple oppressions to fight for social change.

For a brief time, I was lucky enough to learn community organizing skills from Dolores Huerta in the earliest days of the DHF. In the early 2000s, I worked on the Westside Development Program in San Antonio, Texas, first as an interim director for service learning at St. Mary's University, then as a youth minister at Little Flower Parish on the west side of San Antonio. As I worked full-time, I was also studying at the Oblate School of Theology for a master's degree in theology. It was through this work that I met the sons of another lay Catholic woman community organizer and force of nature, Maria del Rosario "Rosie" Castro. Her sons, Julian and Joaquin, are now local and national political leaders. Inspired by Rosie, I carry a red purse most days as a tribute to the work of women community organizers.

Because of the work of Dolores Huerta, Helen Chávez, Rosie Castro, and so many other Catholic laywomen, many of us have worker's rights that did not exist prior to this work. While I never had to work in the fields as a farmworker, I am so grateful for the work of these women and the many women and men who will forever remain unnamed in our written records. They are the ones who inspire me to do teología and remain en la lucha.

Notes

1. I do not italicize Spanish or Spanglish. I do not differentiate Spanish or Spanglish as foreign or unknown languages. Spanish was the first language used for publication in what is now the USA. In many places found within the borders and territories of the USA, Spanish is used as much as if not more than English still today. Spanglish is a creation of LatinoXas and is commonly used as a way to go between English and Spanish for those who live these realities. Finally, I was raised fully bilingual in the US. I do not understand Spanish as a foreign language. To italicize Spanish, therefore, perpetuates the oppressions of English colonization on LatinaXos. Regarding the term "LatinoXas" see Jeremy Cruz, Neomi De Anda, and Néstor Medina, "Respondiendo a las Demandas Históricas: Analysis of the Transformative Legacy of Samuel Ruiz García of Chiapas, México," *Journal of Hispanic/Latino Theology* 19, no.1 (November 2013): 5.

2. Archival research in the "Dolores Huerta Papers 1970–1995 32 linear feet (32 SB) Accession #1861" collection housed at Reuther Library of Wayne State University was not available due to the COVID-19 pandemic.

3. Stacey Sowards, "Rhetorical Agency as *Haciendo Caras* and Differential Consciousness Through Lens of Gender, Race, Ethnicity, and Class: An Examination of Dolores Huerta's Rhetoric," *Communication Theory* 20 (2010): 228.

4. Gloria Anzaldúa, "Haciendo Caras, Una Entrada" in *Making Face, Making Soul: Haciendo Caras*, ed. Gloria Anzaldúa (San Francisco: Aunt Lute Books, 1990), xv.

5. Anzaldúa, "Haciendo Caras, Una Entrada," xxvii.

6. Anzaldúa, "Haciendo Caras, Una Entrada," xvi.

7. Anzaldúa, "Haciendo Caras, Una Entrada," xvi.

8. Anzaldúa, "Haciendo Caras, Una Entrada," xv.

9. Anzaldúa, "Haciendo Caras, Una Entrada," xv.

10. Anzaldúa, "Haciendo Caras, Una Entrada," xv.

11. Anzaldúa does not use "más/caras" in "Haciendo Caras, Una Entrada," but uses instead "las mascaras." Sowards adds this usage of the term to her article without articulation of what the slash indicates. Sowards, "Rhetorical Agency as *Haciendo Caras*," 228. Sowards argues for what may be called an intersectional approach to rhetorical agency and that for these caras to be employed as rhetorical tools, it should be infused with differential consciousness as developed by Chela Sandoval and a "negotiation of gendered, racial, and classed constraints" toward "reframing and expanded understanding of rhetorical agency." Sowards, "Rhetorical Agency as *Haciendo Caras*," 240. She concludes "that *hacienda caras* functions through differential consciousness and rhetorical styles relating to flexibility, optimism, resistance, and transformation." Sowards, "Rhetorical Agency as *Haciendo Caras*," 228. Sowards states that Huerta employs haciendo caras as a rhetorical device to move among many different groups and cross various boundaries. Sowards further draws upon Gloria Anzaldúa and Chela Sandoval's work to show that *haciendo caras* is a dynamic way of being in the world, especially when needing to transform one's "identity according to the requisites of another oppositional ideology." Sowards, "*Caras*," 228. For more on oppositional ideology, see Chela Sandoval, *Methodology of the Oppressed* (Minneapolis: University of Minneapolis Press, 2000), 60.

12. Anzaldúa, "Haciendo Caras, Una Entrada," xvi.

13. Anzaldúa, "Haciendo Caras, Una Entrada," xvii.

14. See Neomi De Anda, "Together en la Lucha: ACHTUS 2019 Presidential Address," *Journal of Hispanic / Latino Theology* 21, no. 2 (2019):126–132. https://repository.usfca.edu/jhlt/vol21/iss2/2; Neomi De Anda, "Ferramentas para negociar o racismo de fronteiras próximas: Migracoes e a música de Selena," in *Teopoética Mística e Poesia*, eds. María Clara Bingemer and Alex Villas Boas (Rio de Janiero: PUC, 2020), 297–305.

15. "DHF in Action: 15th Anniversary Video," Dolores Huerta Foundation for Community Organizing, last accessed July 7, 2021, http://doloreshuerta.org /dhf-promo-video/.

16. Mario T. García. "Dolores Huerta on Spirituality: Interview with Mario T. García, June 1, 2007" in *A Dolores Huerta Reader,* ed. Mario T. García (Albuquerque: University of New Mexico Press, 2008), 331.

17. García, *A Dolores Huerta Reader,* 332.

18. Dolores Huerta, "On Leadership," interview by Luis Fraga, *Institute for Latino Studies,* University of Notre Dame, February 13, 2018, audio 5:00, https://notredame.app.box.com/s/56ofaesfu9dxqsko 2svdta1j92r1lwv9.

19. "Dolores Huerta," National Women's History Museum, accessed December 3, 2017, https://www.nwhm.org/education-resources/biographies /dolores-huerta.

20. Alex Van Tol, *Voice for the Working Poor* (New York: Crabtree Publishing Company, 2010), 20; García. *A Dolores Huerta Reader,* 332.

21. Huerta, interview, 4:36.

22. Linda Barghoorn, *Dolores Huerta: Advocate for Women and Workers* (New York: Crabtree Publishing Company, 2017): 6.

23. Huerta, interview, 5:36.

24. Alex Van Tol, *Voice for the Working Poor* (New York: Crabtree Publishing Company, 2010), 20; Rebecca Thatcher Murcia, *Dolores Huerta* (Hallandale Beach: Mitchell Lane Pub Inc): 12; Monica Brown, *Side by Side/Lado a Lado: The Story of Dolores Huerta and Cesar Chávez/La historia de Dolores Huerta y Cesar Chávez* (New York: Harper Collins, 2010).

25. Huerta, interview, 7:46.

26. García, *A Dolores Huerta Reader,* 333.

27. García, *A Dolores Huerta Reader,* 333.

28. Huerta, interview, 7:31.

29. Huerta, interview, 10:34.

30. Huerta, interview, 10:50.

31. Huerta, interview, 10:55.

32. As a Latina she received racial harassment from the police coming home from baseball games. She and her friends would be stopped and searched and she knew that was not happening to the "Anglo kids." Huerta, interview, 12:39.

33. Huerta, interview, 9:24.

34. *Dolores,* directed by Peter Bratt (Carlos Santana, 2017), 14:19, https:// www.doloresthemovie.com.

35. Sowards, "Rhetorical Agency as *Haciendo Caras,*" 227.

36. *Dolores,* 5:58.

37. Huerta, interview, 11:11.

38. Huerta, interview, 12:50.

39. Huerta, interview, 16:10.

40. Mario T. Garcia. *A Dolores Huerta Reader* (Albuquerque: University of New Mexico Press, 2008), 334.

41. Huerta, interview, 26:18.

42. Huerta, interview, 26:18.

43. Huerta, interview, 15:39.

44. *Dolores*, 11:17.

45. *Dolores*, 12:56.

46. *Dolores*, 12:46.

47. Huerta, interview, 23:09.

48. Huerta, interview, 18:00.

49. Huerta, interview, 32:32.

50. Huerta, interview, 33:00.

51. García, *A Dolores Huerta Reader*, 338.

52. Huerta, interview, 13:30.

53. Huerta, interview, 14:33.

54. Huerta, interview, 37:52.

55. Huerta, interview, 36:00.

56. Huerta, interview, 39:24.

57. García, *A Dolores Huerta Reader*, 331–332.

58. Huerta, interview, 19:20.

59. Huerta, interview, 21:00.

60. Huerta, interview, 21:55.

61. "Dolores Huerta/DHF Event and Video Request Form," Dolores Huerta Foundation, accessed June 3, 2021, https://docs.google.com/forms/d/e/1FAIpQLSf8hoIntIVrv8_572VLTgathvTOoiNRQoVEwPKXxfe1u-ZqoQ/viewform.

62. *Dolores*, 20:00.

63. *Dolores*, 21:00.

64. Huerta, interview, 35:29.

65. Huerta, interview, 22:30.

66. García, *A Dolores Huerta Reader*, 334.

67. García, *A Dolores Huerta Reader*, 334.

68. García, *A Dolores Huerta Reader*, 334.

69. García, *A Dolores Huerta Reader*, 335.

70. García, *A Dolores Huerta Reader*, 335.

71. García, *A Dolores Huerta Reader*, 335.

72. García, *A Dolores Huerta Reader*, 336.

73. García, *A Dolores Huerta Reader*, 337.

74. "¡Si, Se Puede! (Yes, We Can!): Bobby Kennedy Visits Cesar Chavez-REVISED," Paul Lee, accessed May 20, 2021, https://www.youtube.com/watch?v=qQndvfZyf7w.

75. "Robert F. Kennedy: CBS News—Live Coverage of His Assassination—June 5, 1968," accessed June 8, 2021, https://www.youtube.com/watch?v=QtG4VmIEvpM; "Latinopia Event 1968 Robert Kennedy Assassination," updated September 16, 2013, http://latinopia.com/latino-history/latinopia-event-1968-robert-kennedy-assassination/.

76. Huerta, interview, 1:25:00.

77. "President Obama Honors the Presidential Medal of Freedom Recipients," The Obama White House, last modified May 29, 2012, https://youtu.be/MCAwRkZQM2E?t=1454.

78. "President Obama Honors the Presidential Medal of Freedom Recipients," The Obama White House, last modified May 29, 2012, https://youtu.be/MCAwRkZQM2E?t=557.

79. Dolores Huerta remarks about religious icons in her home growing up such as the Virgin de Guadalupe, crucifixes, the Santo Nino de Atocha. She also references popular religious practices such as Las Posadas and Los Reyes Magos Celebration with family. García, *A Dolores Huerta Reader,* 333–334, 343.

80. Huerta has a special devotion to Our Lady of Guadalupe. García. *A Dolores Huerta Reader,* 338. Catholic symbols suffused her life, the farmworker movement also brilliantly took on the song "De Colores" as their song. *Dolores,* 14:43. This song was already in use as popular religious music, including the Cursillo Movement. It is sung in churches and schools, as the Castillo kids claim on their YouTube channel. "De Colores," The Castillo Kids, last modified June 24, 2010, https://www.youtube.com/watch?v=QWkZ7VzvpSE.

81. Dolores Huerta fasted for 14 days for an immigration bill. Her fast consisted of one meal per day and water. In 2006, she fasted all of Lent, one meal per day as a prayerful offering not to be considered coercive. García, *A Dolores Huerta Reader,* 338.

82. Dolores Huerta prays the rosary on a regular basis and carries one with her. García, *A Dolores Huerta Reader,* 339.

83. Huerta also discusses lighting a candle at the Cathedral when she was unsure how things were going regarding a specific project or part of life. Huerta, interview, 1:27:31.

84. Community Service Organization. Stockton, California chapter co-founded by Fred Ross and Dolores Huerta.

85. García, *A Dolores Huerta Reader,* 331.

86. *Laudato Si',* 18.

87. *Dolores,* 35:05–37:48.

88. García, *A Dolores Huerta Reader,* 340.

89. García, *A Dolores Huerta Reader,* 340–341.

90. "Elizabeth Whitefield End-of-Life Options Act," New Mexico Legislature, last modified April 8, 2021, https://www.nmlegis.gov/Legislation/Legislation?Chamber=H&LegType=B&LegNo=47&year=21.

91. "'End-of-Life Options Act' Heads to New Mexico Senate," Public News Service, last modified March 1, 2021, https://www.publicnewsservice.org/2021-03-01/health/end-of-life-options-act-heads-to-new-mexico-senate/a73350-1?fbclid=IwAR1-ej9JaMiMVgwYJHqhf8O_S3DrvskdeL_b5dqCst52qtfGq1u1qxr2EVA.

92. Maria Pilar Aquino, "Latina Feminist Theology Central Features" in *A Reader in Latina Feminist Theology*, eds. María Pilar Aquino, Daisy Machado, Jeanette Rodriguez, (Austin: University of Texas Press, 2002), 150.

93. *Dolores*, 14:35.

94. *Dolores*, 19:05.

95. García, *A Dolores Huerta Reader*, 341–342.

96. García, *A Dolores Huerta Reader*, 342.

97. Huerta, interview, 19:47.

98. Huerta, interview, 21:22.

99. Huerta, interview, 50:00.

100. Huerta, interview, 50:00.

101. Huerta, interview, 51:47.

102. Huerta, interview, 46:00.

103. Huerta, interview, 35:00.

104. Huerta, interview, 41:23.

105. Huerta, interview, 49:47.

106. Huerta, interview, 50:08.

107. Huerta, interview, 46:47.

108. Huerta, interview, 52:25.

109. Huerta, interview, 46:57.

110. "Dolores Huerta Day Curriculum," Dolores Huerta Foundation for Community Organizing, accessed April 1, 2021, https://doloreshuerta.org/dolores-huerta-day-curriculum/.

111. García, *A Dolores Huerta Reader*, 345.

112. *Dolores*, 8:00.

Catholic Laywomen's Natural Family Planning across Three Generations

KATHERINE DUGAN

In 1968, Paul VI publicly and officially disagreed with a group of Catholic laity, married men and women, who had advised him to reverse the Church's ban on contraception.[1] The encyclical, *Humanae Vitae*, reaffirmed previous Catholic teachings against contraception and emphasized that "each and every marriage act must remain open to the transmission of life." To place the pill or a diaphragm or a condom or a vasectomy in the way of the possibility of life was, the pontiff argued, "intrinsically wrong."[2] The response to *Humanae Vitae* by the Catholic laity in the US was, as historian Leslie Tentler has described it, "incredulity and anger."[3] Theologians disagreed with each other about the arguments, and priests wrung their hands over what to do about the teaching in their parishes.[4] But Catholic laywomen seemed clear in their response: ignore the teaching and continue filling the birth control prescriptions many had been using since the FDA approved the pill in 1960.[5] Patricia Miller has written about the ways some Catholic laywomen actively resisted the teaching.[6] However, alongside these protests and dismissals is another story: Catholic women who took up the charge of *Humanae Vitae* and practice what has come to be known as Natural Family Planning (NFP).[7] Using the same theology of lay leadership that their anti-*Humanae Vitae* peers were using to challenge the teaching, the subculture of NFP-practicing laywomen have created a network of women teaching other women the intricacies of NFP. They teach one another how to track their fertility cycles, pay attention to mucus patterns, and foster intimacy with their spouses outside of sexual contact.

This chapter tracks shifts in how Catholic laywomen across three generations have navigated this practice, as well as the development of their NFP-informed communities. This story is about Catholic women who continue to reach into both Catholic teaching *and* a range of cultural and secular sources about women's health as they articulate what it means to be a Catholic woman. NFP as practiced, developed, and promoted by Catholic laywomen is thoroughly Catholic, of course, but this essay describes how NFP has also been shaped by secular sources on women's health and how NFP has shaped those secular sources.

I begin this story in the 1970s and 1980s with the laywomen who first started teaching one another how to track their fertility cycles by noting basal body temperature and mucus patterns. Their stories of commitment to *Humanae Vitae* are characterized by their personal agreement with Church teaching but also a deep concern about their many, *many* fellow Catholics who were happy to take the pill or use other forms of family planning deemed illicit by papal teaching. I then turn to a middle generation of NFP women who were having children in the 1990s and early 2000s. These women of Generation X tell stories of having used the pill as young women and then discovering NFP in a parish bulletin or through word of mouth at a parish picnic. These women report feeling remorse that they ever took the pill and used condoms, and they feel relief and gratitude over having discovered NFP. They are a particularly enthusiastic generation of women who want younger women to learn from their errors. Finally, I turn to the youngest group of Catholic women practicing NFP: Millennials and Gen Z Catholic women whose relationship with NFP centers on the health benefits of fertility tracking. These women may have discovered NFP through Catholic campus ministry programs, but many others learned it at their yoga studio or at a workshop on women's health sponsored by Planned Parenthood. This generation's NFP looks within but also beyond the Catholic subculture for ways of managing family size without recourse to contraception.

Across these generations, the stories of women's NFP networks illuminate the ways laywomen navigate Catholic teaching within their communities of like-minded women. This is the lived experience of *Humanae Vitae*, through three generations of laywomen's interpretations of how to plan their family size.

The Founders: 1970s and 1980s

In 1971, John and Sheila Kippley founded one of the first organizations in the US committed to teaching NFP: the Couple to Couple League (CCL). Motivated by an earnest concern about what they still refer to as the "theological revolt" against Catholic teaching, John and Sheila see their work in CCL as giving couples the tools necessary to make *Humanae Vitae* live-able.[8]

On a warm Midwestern evening in August 2018, I interviewed these NFP pioneers. They told me about their marriage, their kids and grandkids, and their love of Catholicism. As I listened to John and Sheila's stories about the early days of running CCL from their attic and teaching classes in parish halls around Cincinnati, it became clear that it was Sheila's experience with women's breastfeeding communities that had built the backbone of the work. John has long been the public and theological face of CCL. John promoted a theological vision for Catholic marriages and families with what he calls "covenantal theology." Following *Humanae Vitae*, Kippley has long-argued for openness to life in any sexual act, as well as the necessity to avoid any artificial means of interfering with God's plans for married life.[9] While that theological impetus provides crucial foundations to the work of CCL, it was Sheila's involvement with La Leche League (LLL) that framed the pragmatic work of CCL.

Sheila joined a local chapter of LLL in the 1960s.[10] Committed to breastfeeding during an era when breastfeeding was not the norm, Sheila began to study the relationship between breastfeeding and the often correlated return of fertility.[11] She articulated these ideas in what she calls "ecological breastfeeding," a method of exclusive breastfeeding that involves cosleeping, frequent feedings, and much physical contact between mother and baby. The method naturally delays a woman's postpartum fertility, and Sheila realized that it was another way to space children naturally, without using birth control.[12] In addition, her participation in LLL gave the Kippleys a model for lay Catholics teaching one another how to practice NFP. Sheila explained, "We had four classes because La Leche League had four classes. We had a manual because La Leche League had a manual. We had couples teaching couples because La Leche League had mothers teaching mothers."[13] The Kippleys intentionally chose a doubly lay mode of championing NFP. By relying on women and couples, not doctors or priests, CCL crafted a subculture of sharing knowledge about fertility and family planning. This network relied on formal Catholic teaching, but it was driven by laywomen's shared knowledge about their bodies and babies.

CCL is one of a handful of NFP-teaching organizations that emerged in the wake of *Humane Vitae*. Not long after CCL established its national presence in the 1970s, Dr. Thomas Hilgers and his wife, Sue, a nurse, developed what is known as the "Creighton model" of NFP. This model draws heavily on Hilgers's research into women's fertility, conducted from his post at Creighton University's Medical School and, later, as co-founder (with his wife) of the Pope Paul VI Institute.[14] Hilgers' personality has loomed large, but much of the work of teaching the Creighton method to Catholics across the country has been done by laywomen trained as "practitioners" (the title for those trained to teach the Creighton method). Because the model does not rely on teaching couples and because single women can both teach and learn the method, the ways of sharing the Creighton method between women make it even more explicitly a laywomen's project.

If the Creighton NFP Catholic women's subculture is like a family tree, Kathy Rivet is one of the grandmothers. Before she and her husband settled in New Hampshire, Kathy worked for several years in Omaha, at the Hilgers's Pope Paul VI Institute, where she served as "Education Programs Coordinator." Her commitment, as she told a newspaper reporter in 1995, has always been providing good information to women: "'From my perspective, the most important thing is quality, the quality of education and treatment the institute offers.'"[15] Kathy is currently part of a larger movement in her diocese to make NFP education widely available through the Catholic Medical Center, a local Catholic hospital.[16] While most Creighton model NFP practitioners work out of their home or local libraries or coffee shops around town, Kathy has an office in the hospital. These days, she rarely teaches the method directly to women, rather she teaches and supervises women who are learning how to be Creighton practitioners.

When she and I found a time to connect, I eagerly drove from my home in western Massachusetts to her home in New Hampshire. It was a sunny winter day in February 2020 and, when I arrived, Kathy's husband, Joe, was getting ready to leave for work as a substance abuse counselor. We settled into our interview over fresh mugs of tea that Joe made for us. Kathy told me about the "early days" of working at "the institute" in Omaha and was humble about the number of women she has taught how to use the Creighton method and the number of women she has trained to be Creighton teachers. As she talked, I realized that the reason we had trouble finding a time to meet was that she maintained a hectic schedule of flying around the country to supervise women in the Creighton training programs.

Kathy and Joe were married in 1968, "one month after *Humanae Vitae*," she smiled. They were already committed to not using birth control; like the Kippleys and many other couples in this generation of the NFP sub-culture, it did not cross their minds to start using the pill or condoms. But after Kathy had her first two babies within eleven months of each other, she was exhausted and suspected that there had to be a way to space her children *and* follow Catholic teaching. "The first time I heard about cervical mucus, I thought 'that's it!' The Holy Spirit knew about cervical mucus!"[17] Kathy was in the first class of women who were trained as Creighton practitioners in 1978.

Kathy and Sheila represent just two examples of women who worked to build the first generation of a network of women teaching NFP. Their methods are different, their logistics of exactly how to track fertility signs are different, and their public positions within the subculture are differ-ent. Yet, these women's lives within and around NFP reflect how women shaped the lived experience of *Humanae Vitae*. They were born into a ver-sion of Catholicism that assumed contraception was opposed to Catholic teaching, and they persisted in that belief.

Kathy and Sheila are also two examples of how laywomen's work was overshadowed by the men at the forefront in this generation; John Kip-pley and Thomas Hilgers have a larger public presence in the NFP world. And yet these women saw themselves as more than capable of teaching other women how to manage their family size without contraception. Married laywomen like Sheila and Kathy did the legwork and built the network that made it possible for future generations of Catholic laywomen to step into the landscape.

Building a Community of Gen X Catholic Women: 1990s and 2000s

Sheila and Kathy exemplify a generation of women who were born into a Catholic assumption that the birth control pill was illicit. Yet, as the ma-jority of this generation's daughters came of age, the pill no longer felt il-licit for most women. This second generation of Catholic NFP-practicing laywomen discovered NFP in adulthood. Many in this middle generation of laywomen used the pill and condoms before discovering NFP within their marriage. Their experience of NFP is infused with enthusiasm over the benefits they have experienced but also tinged with sorrow that they have not always practiced NFP.

Early in my research among Catholic NFP laywomen, I met Janet.[18] She is the most local NFP teacher to me and warmly welcomed my questions and conversations. One of her children is roughly the same age as my daughter, so we logged several hours chatting while they played together, running through the empty hallways of her parish's Catholic school and a local playground. Janet loves being Catholic and describes herself as happy to be a "handmaiden of the Lord," which is something she feels particularly while pregnant. She laughed as she told me, "you know, there's always a Marian holiday in there [while I'm pregnant] . . . I love being pregnant because I'm like creating a whole human person that's going to go to heaven someday!"[19]

Janet is a native New Englander who homeschools her five children with a cozy network of homeschooling moms. Janet invited me to join their monthly Friday morning gathering for Mass and "fellowship" at a small-town parish that is roughly equidistant for most members. A retired priest said Mass in a side chapel; the two oldest boys in the group served as altar servers, and Janet was the lector. Behind me in the pew, a mom nursed her young toddler and a couple of the kids wandered the space while the moms prayed together. Sitting among them, chatting over home-packed lunches after Mass, I was struck by the sense of community among these women. Each had between four and six kids with them, ranging from some toddlers up to teenagers, and one baby. Janet told me that ten years prior, the group had decided that one of them should be trained in NFP. They had all been sort of figuring out how to plan their families without contraception but were, collectively, spending a lot of time worrying about it. With a characteristic willingness to jump in when action is needed, Janet took the training for the Billings Ovulation Method.[20] One of her friends described her as their "local guru for all things NFP,"[21] a label that Janet wears humbly but happily.

While a desire to follow Catholic teaching drives Janet's distaste for the pill and invitro fertilization (IVF), her rejection of non-NFP family planning practices is also fueled by cultural norms that oppose medical interventions and by the greening tendencies among the American middle class. Janet self-describes as "crunchy," a label she used to gesture to her tendency to avoid too much medicine, her appreciation for green smoothies, the chickens in her backyard, and other back-to-the-earth impulses. She explained that she and her husband have plans to buy some property where she can keep more chickens and grow a bigger garden. During one of our meetings, she greeted me with me a homemade green smoothie in a mason jar as she told me that nutrition is an important part of doing NFP, tracking her fertility, and being aware of her body. Janet wears long skirts and has grey streaks in her dark hair that is usually piled messily on top of her head. I have never noticed any make-up on her scrubbed-clean face. She told me that she worried about women on the pill whose breasts never fill out fully and whose bodies never become a "grown woman's body with curves!"[22]

During one of the Mass and fellowship Fridays, we were moving Christmas decorations around the church. She told me about the discussions she and her husband were having about whether or not to have a sixth child. In her mid-forties and married for twenty years, she knew that her years of fertility were winding down. But, she confided in a whisper, she hated the infant years and dreaded the idea of having to care for another baby. She also explained that she had hard pregnancies and usually had to spend some time bedridden. But her husband really wanted another baby, and when I asked what happens when you're not on the same page, she smiled and said, "Well, I'm praying a lot. And he's doing a rosary novena."[23] Then she added that she has been talking about it with the woman who first taught her NFP and talking with the women in this group, and, then, she sighed with a small smile, not discontentedly, "I'm coming around to be less afraid." Janet's description here illuminates the tightrope that the women in this NFP generation navigate. Being adept at NFP carries the responsibility of also being open to life. Because Janet and her friends are also immersed in middle-class American norms, she understands the challenges of having a baby. To be "less afraid" is Janet's way of describing God's will, but enacting that, as her comment reveals, requires the help of her community of laywomen.

Janet's generation of NFP laywomen came of age during second-wave feminism and felt some pressure, it seems, to understand themselves in terms of this landscape. These women fit the description of what historian Mary Henold has described as "Catholic (non)feminists." Henold argues that the women who joined the National Catholic Conference of Women (NCCW) were not feminists, but they were not *not* feminists.

Henold posits that women's unwillingness to disregard gender complementarianism and essentialism "was a natural response to the barrage of changes coming at them from multiple quarters. Such prolonged processing made the nature of their feminism more complex and resistant to easy labeling."[24]

A similar engagement with, yet skepticism of, early twenty-first century feminism persists among NFP-practicing laywomen. Janet is not a feminist in the sense that second-wave feminists would recognize her. But she is also not unengaged with the sort of progressive ideas about women's health that emerged around things like the Boston Women's Health Collective and were birthed by LLL. Her tendencies toward ecological awareness and other green practices are informed by increased awareness of women's health and well-being. Her reasons for homeschooling, to protect her children from too much secular influence and to savor being a mom, are found across the spectrum of families who homeschool.[25] Her NFP training came out of her commitment to her community of women and is intertwined with how she mothers her children and cares for other women. Her leadership within parish life and with her group of moms echoes Vatican II's calls for lay leadership. Janet is a Catholic laywoman who has gone within and beyond Catholic sources in an effort to be more fully committed to Catholic practice. Like Henold's laywomen, Janet is not *not* a feminist.

Instead, this middle generation of NFP women articulate an alternative interpretation of feminism. This alternative was perhaps most explicit in how a woman named Paula described her commitment and enthusiasm for NFP.[26] She and her husband John are longtime CCL teachers and are the NFP contacts for their large parish. We met up to attend the 12:10 P.M. Mass in the middle of downtown Cincinnati, so her husband could join us on his lunch break. She used to work as a physicist and then shifted to working as a mom since she and John have eight children. After lunch together, we were headed to our cars when Paula started talking about how the feminist movement has hurt women. She told me that NFP is a way of human flourishing that is about "true femininity." She touched my elbow said, "I just want you to know that NFP *is* true feminism."[27] What she meant here is that NFP is not anti-woman as she (and others in her generation) worry NFP is sometimes caricatured. Paula was framing feminism in terms of what is good for women. And, in her experience of

NFP, motherhood, and building a marriage around eight kids, is good for women. In her effort to frame NFP as feminist, Paula asserted a definition of feminism that not only includes but relies on NFP norms.

Paula's insistence here reflects the larger generational trends of Catholic laywomen who took up NFP in the 1990s and 2000s. She, Janet, and others did so while also having to engage questions about feminism, changing roles of women in the workplace, and shifting definitions of motherhood. Being part of a Catholic network of laywomen practicing NFP has not made these women exempt from cultural norms; instead, it has led to creative interpretations of how to be an NFP-practicing Catholic laywoman. These women grew up in families in the 1970s who either did not know or did not care about *Humanae Vitae*. By 1970, "seventy-eight percent of Catholic married women aged twenty to twenty-four . . . were limiting their families by means other than abstinence or rhythm."[28] They discovered NFP in somewhat haphazard ways ("by God's grace," and the parish bulletin in Paula's case, and "because we needed to know a system," in Janet's case) in the 1990s and early 2000s. Their commitment to teaching NFP to other women is less centered on a desire to be aligned with the hierarchy and more on their positive experiences with it. When Paula pulled my elbow and insisted that NFP is better for women than the pill, she offered a reinterpretation of what women's flourishing looks like. For Paula and Janet, the Catholic network of NFP laywomen offers a rich way to articulate Catholic womanhood, both within and around Catholic teaching.

Setting a Millennial and Gen Z Tone: 2010s and 2020s

If Kathy and Sheila are NFP grandmothers, and Paula and Janet are NFP mothers, then Bridget exemplifies the daughter's approach to NFP. When I interviewed her in late 2019, she was in her mid-twenties, newly married, living in the Minneapolis-St. Paul area, and completing her master's in health communication where she was focused on maternal health and sex education. She graduated from a Catholic high school and was involved with a Catholic campus group at the state university she attended. As we talked about how she got interested in NFP, she told me that it started with her mom, who had introduced her to the idea of tracking her cycle—but without a lot of detail. When she was in college and chatting with girlfriends about fertility and cycles, Bridget began searching out ways to learn how to carefully track her cycle. They were curious about what they could learn from tracking and why it might matter to them. At the time, the most widely available app was the secular app Kindara, which they found easily in the app store.[29] Her group of friends started tracking their cycles, not to avoid pregnancy, but to see what they could learn. Not long after she got the hang of tracking, Bridget was "all in," she told me with a smile. She was "definitely Catholic" at the time, but it was the biology of tracking her fertility that got her excited. The theology of it "came later." She loved "geeking out" over her cycle charts.

Within a few years, she was engaged to her husband and they were trying to learn to do NFP in a more careful way because they wanted to avoid an immediate pregnancy. But, she made a disgusted face, "NFP was presented in such an ugly way during marriage prep . . . some websites are terrible . . . some have *horrendous* stock images of moms in khaki pants with bagged groceries and babies. And that was such a turn-off for me, as an individual who likes to, you know, not wear khaki pants and maybe doesn't want to have groceries on one hip and babies on the other."[30] This did not stop her; she was already invested. Bridget was frustrated, however, by how inaccessible and out of touch NFP felt. She and her fiancé struggled to choose a method and had a hard time sorting out where to learn the science of fertility awareness. And she began to suspect she was not alone in this frustration. Bridget decided to develop what she called a "one-stop shop for learning about NFP." Drawing support from several national Catholic organizations, Bridget launched a website called "Managing Your Fertility" in 2019. Her website is, as she describes it, "aimed at women ages 18–35 trying to track their fertility."[31]

As Bridget both conceived of and developed her website as a resource for women like herself, she told me that she was careful to refer to medical professionals rather than Catholic clerics or Catholic theologians arguing about sexual ethics. The website reflects the very intentional effort by Bridget to work at the intersection of secular science on fertility awareness and Catholic NFP. Other than the fact that a few of her resources link to Catholic sources, her website does not reference the Catholic teaching that really motivates and informs Bridget's approach. When we talked about some of the challenges of her project, the first thing she mentioned was sorting and presenting clear information from doctors and nurses. She said she designed the site's content to walk a line between too much information and giving enough; so women and couples feel like they have enough information to decide which method to use.

Bridget has also been explicit about crafting a Gen-Z aesthetic here. She told me about her frustration with the "ugly" and "old clip art" websites that make it look like they are "from 1987!" In addition to highlighting the science of fertility awareness and the women's health aspects of NFP, Bridget is presenting an aesthetic of NFP that echoes what other have described as "not your grandmother's rhythm method!" What this means is not just that Catholics like Bridget and her website are drawing from secular culture, but they are engaged with non-Catholic sources to reshape the nature of Catholic NFP.

One of the defining features of this generation's NFP is this careful interaction between Catholic and secular medicine, which is reworking the landscape of Catholic family planning. These millennial and Gen Z women are less interested in the project of adherence to Catholic teaching. The rhetoric of NFP is shifting, sometimes expanding, from an emphasis on papal dictates to engagement with the scientific community, adapting language of organic and all-natural, and framing the conversation in terms of women's health. Catholic talk about family planning is being reworked by conversations with non-Catholics.

The Cycle Power Summit exemplifies the kinds of productive interaction between Catholics and secular fertility awareness within this expanding NFP subculture. Over a long weekend in May 2019, an NFP teacher named Anna Saucier hosted an online conference she called "The online conference for women. Period."[32] Over twenty-five speakers spoke on topics regarding what Anna describes as the "charting lifestyle."[33] Cycle Power Summit had two tracks. One was the "Fertility Awareness Track," which focused on using fertility charting to avoid or conceive children. Speakers included NFP-trained doctors, the founder of a digital basal body temperature tracker called TempDrop, a men's health professional, and someone speaking on infertility, among others. The other, "Restorative Reproductive Health Track," promoted fertility tracking as a part of women's health care. Talks argued that a woman's ability (and willingness) to track her fertility can help treat things like PCOS (polycystic ovary syndrome) while also being a more natural form of medical management. These speakers were nurses and naturopaths as well as NFP-certified teachers.

The Catholic roots of this program were quietly coded throughout the program. Anna graduated from the Franciscan University of Steubenville, a Catholic university in Ohio known for its rigid interpretations of what it means to be Catholic. She is also the founder of a subscription-based service for helping NFP teachers run their teaching like a business.[34] Anna and several other speakers have CFCE or FCP after their names, which stand for "Certified FertilityCare Educator" and "FertilityCare Practitioner." Both designations signal that the person has completed a ten-day intensive training in the Creighton method of NFP, as well as a year-long internship under the guidance of another trained educator, like Kathy Rivet. The Creighton training is an explicitly and proudly Catholic training. Under Hilgers and Rivet, future NFP teachers learn the science of tracking a woman's cycle. But they also learn about Catholic teaching from *Humanae Vitae* against the pill. They pray regularly and attend Mass during the trainings. Creighton teachers are expected to instruct their clients not to use condoms or other barrier methods during the fertile period and to abstain during periods of fertility if they are "TTA," i.e., trying to avoid pregnancy. There is an intentionally Catholic ethos within Creighton.

However, Cycle Power Summit was *not* a Catholic event. I did not hear any explicitly Catholic language from any of the speakers. One Creighton teacher, Mandy Cox, gave a presentation on "The sex ed you slept through in sixth grade." When I interviewed her in Denver a few months later, it was clear that she got involved with NFP because of her Catholicism. But her presentation had none of that. She focused on the biology of reproduction. Indeed, the entire summit is an example of how a once explicitly Catholic practice is being repackaged for and with a non-Catholic audience.

On the one hand, Anna's Cycle Power Summit is Catholics capitalizing on the all-natural moment of this cultural milieu. Certainly, there is a marketing aspect to this that is sometimes tinged with evangelical zeal, along the lines of "if we hook them with the science, maybe they'll see that Catholicism is right about other things too!"[35] But there is also something more dynamic at work here. Catholics are learning from non-Catholics about the very methods that they pioneered, which puts NFP Catholics in a partnership with the broader landscape of fertility awareness and is expanding the perspectives of the Catholic NFP worldview. The relationship between the Catholic and secular worlds of avoiding contraception is becoming entangled. The Catholic landscape of NFP has been strengthened by the secular women's health movements. NFP teachers are happy to incorporate women's nutrition, breastfeeding, and education about bodies into their work.

This relationship is not just one-directional. The Catholic NFP world has also been informing and shaping the secular fertility awareness world. A key example of how Catholic laywomen's NFP is reshaping secular models is the newest NFP model, called FEMM: Fertility Education & Medical Management. Officially launched in 2015 as a smartphone app, FEMM is an outgrowth of the World Youth Alliance (an organization that embraces Catholic moral positions) aimed at international efforts, especially at the UN, on maternal and women's health.[36] FEMM positions itself as an advocate of women's health literacy providing access to quality health education for women. An example of its education focus is a 2013 white paper which argues that current medical practices for women's health care, especially in developing countries that do not teach women about their bodies. FEMM insist that it offers "[c]omprehensive education on women's hormonal health . . . at a time when it is evident that women around the world do not understand how their bodies work or the importance of understanding and monitoring their hormones and other reproductive biomarkers."[37] The Catholicism of the original project is papered over with the emphasis on women's health.

Embedded in this focus on education, FEMM insists that the method is neutral and of potential good anywhere. The language frames FEMM as a tool of women's health. The white paper complains about the amount of money being spent on contraception and argues that "FEMM is compatible with all religions and cultures and does not pose any health concerns or potential side effects."[38] This claim asserts that FEMM's agenda is non-religious.

At the same time, FEMM is definitely an organization influenced by Catholicism, and the funding sources are of a particularly conservative bent of Catholicism. The five FEMM teachers that I have interviewed are clearly and proudly Catholic. But there is a flexibility in their Catholic approach that illustrates this generation's approach. One woman teaches FEMM out of a women's holistic health clinic in Brooklyn alongside an acupuncturist and a tarot-card reader. Another is a doctor in the suburbs who teachers her clients how to use FEMM. Though it has not officially received recognition from the US Bishops' NFP office, a member of FEMM leadership told me they are trying to create a version that would be appropriate for Catholic marriage preparation and pre-Cana settings.[39] Anecdotally, I have heard parishes and dioceses using it as such already.[40]

One way to read FEMM is as Catholic teaching coated secular. Their app is easier to use than many other options, especially CCL's and Creighton's, and their promotional materials are warm and attractive to Millennial and Gen Z women. There is a teach-yourself option, clearly targeted to Gen Z women. Yet another interpretation is that FEMM exemplifies Catholic laywomen in dialogue with their cultural context. Catholic women are not the only women who are deciding to go off the pill for reasons that sound like the same reasons they buy organic meat: values around health. A 2018 survey by *Cosmopolitan* of two thousand "young" women found that "seventy percent of women who have used the Pill said they'd stopped taking it or thought about going off it in the past three years."[41] A 2018 commentary in the *New York Post* referenced this survey and then surveyed the many apps and smart technology options for "Fertility Awareness Methods" and suggested that Millennial women are just no longer interested in the birth control pill because "hormonal birth control isn't just unnatural. They are also worried about its long-term effects, from depression and digestive disorders to—on the more extreme end of the spectrum—stroke, blood clots or breast cancer."[42] What this survey suggests is that Catholic FEMM practitioners are part of a larger cultural hesitancy with contraception. It is possible that for the first time since 1968, Catholics are *part* of a reproductive trend, rather than resisting it

The fact that these Millennial and Gen Z Catholic laywomen's organizations are very carefully crafting an aesthetic that appeals to younger women reflects that Catholic laywomen are less entrenched in their NFP worldview. This emphasis on the medical reasons to eschew contraception is most evident in the Cycle Power Summit, but it is an important theme in Managing Your Fertility and FEMM, too. The health focus is an intentional effort to rid NFP of its old links to the rhythm method. Instead, this generation's NFP is framed as women's health. The push here is less about family planning and more about women knowing their bodies. The focus is not entirely new. I have gestured to its presence in Sheila's ecological breastfeeding and Janet's crunchy lifestyle. It is a new emphasis with broader appeal. Millennial and Gen Z NFP is unapologetically Catholic but not staunchly Catholic. These laywomen are reframing a practice born within the context of sacramental Catholic marriages as accessible for single women, for women with irregular cycles, and for women trying to figure out their infertility issues. They are managing to widen the scope of NFP far beyond the original context of *Humanae Vitae*.

Conclusion

This survey of three generations of Catholic NFP laywomen picks up where Leslie Tentler's field-defining *Catholics and Contraception* ends. In the very last two paragraphs of her book, Tentler summarizes the landscape these laywomen have been traversing since the 1970s. Tentler describes early twenty-first century NFP-practicing Catholics as "want[ing] an existential sense of Catholic identity, too, notwithstanding their simultaneous desire to be unambiguously American."[43] Practicing NFP situates these women as outside the majority sentiment of Catholics and Americans. And yet they draw carefully on both Catholic and American sources in crafting the norms of their various NFP subcultures. Across the three generations of NFP women, these laywomen simply do not fit into the available categories. They do tend to be Catholic pro-life voters, but they also promote progressive knowledge of women's bodies and frank conversations about sexual health. They also teach each other about women's orgasms and trade tips on the best baby carriers. They teach one another about how to delay pregnancy through breastfeeding and share ideas about how to grieve miscarriages. Their NFP practices rely on a range of sources about women's bodies, and they use that to articulate what it means to embody lay Catholic womanhood.

At the same time, these twenty-first century Catholic women are not alone in rejecting contraception. Their cultural context is different from the pro-pill atmosphere in which Sheila and Kathy taught NFP. The "all-natural," "organic," and "free-range" health-conscious movement of the past decade has made some secular women nervous about the birth control pill. Planned Parenthood has begun listing what are called "Fertility Awareness Methods" on their website.[44] Furthermore, many Catholic women tell me about the health benefits of charting and going off of the pill. This dual frame, Catholic and secular women's health norms, permeates the contemporary NFP world. The heavily Catholic rhetoric of NFP is being reworked, sometimes softened, but also turned to different audiences in and for a new generation of Catholic women.

These NFP-practicing laywomen are embodying Catholic teaching in careful and creative ways. Their fertility tracking methods, their community-building, and their methods of teaching one another have put life onto the bones of *Humanae Vitae*. Drawing on sources from within and beyond Catholicism, it is laywomen across three generations who have turned a document about avoiding contraception into a practice of Catholic teaching on family planning.

Notes

1. Robert McClory, *Turning Point: The Inside Story of the Papal Birth Control Commission, and How* Humanae Vitae *changed the life of Patty Crowley and the future of the Church* (New York: Crossroad, 1995).

2. Paul VI, *Humanae Vitae*, encyclical letter, Vatican website, July 25, 1968, http://www.vatican.va/content/paul-vi/en/encyclicals/documents/hf_p-vi_enc_25071968_humanae-vitae.html, 14.

3. Leslie Tentler, *Catholics and Contraception: An American History* (Ithaca: Cornell University Press, 2004), 265.

4. Tentler, *Catholics and Contraception*, 268–69.

5. According to the Guttmacher Institute, Catholic use of the pill has not varied from non-Catholic use. Estimates by the Guttmacher Institute find that 96–98% of Catholic women either have been or are on the pill. "Guttmacher Statistics on Catholic Women's Contraceptive Use," February 2012, https://www.guttmacher.org/article/2012/02/guttmacher-statistic-catholic-womens-contraceptive-use. See also Jonathan Eig's *The Birth of the Pill: How Four Crusaders Reinvented Sex and Launched a Revolution* (New York, NY: WW Norton & Company, 2014).

6. Patricia Miller, *Good Catholics: The Battle over Abortion in the Catholic Church* (Berkeley, CA: University of California Press, 2014).

7. There are a range of methods that fall under the category of "Natural Family Planning" (NFP), but all rely on women observing and tracking various biological markers of their fertility cues on their fertility charts. The most common observations tracked are women's "basal body temperature," her mucus pattern, hormone levels, and, less often, the shape of her cervix.

8. James T. McHugh, "A Theological Perspective on Natural Family Planning," Diocesan Development Program for Natural Family Planning (Washington D.C., 1983).

9. John F Kippley, *Sex and the Marriage Covenant: A Basis for Morality*, 2nd ed. (San Francisco, CA: Ignatius Press, 2005), 7.

10. Jule DeJager Ward, *La Leche League: At the Crossroads of Medicine, Feminism, and Religion* (Chapel Hill, NC: University of North Carolina Press, 2000), 11. La Leche League has never been an explicitly Catholic organization, even though all of the founders were Catholic women, and many of them had been involved with the Christian Family Movement and Young Christian Workers of the immediately pre-Vatican II era of 1950s and 1960s Catholicism.

11. Katherine Dugan, "*Humanae Vitae*, Natural Family Planning, and US Catholic Identity: The Founding of the Couple to Couple League," *U.S. Catholic Historian* 39, no. 2 (Spring 2021): 113–32, Project MUSE.

12. Sheila Magen Kippley, *Breastfeeding and Natural Child Spacing: How Ecological Breastfeeding Spaces Babies* (First edition, 1969; Second Edition, New York: Harper and Row Publishers, 1974; 4th edition, Cincinnati, OH: Couple to Couple League International, 1999), 1–2.

13. Sheila Magen Kippley, in interview with the author, August 23, 2018.

14. Pope Paul VI Institute, "The Saint Paul VI Institute for the Study of Human Reproduction was founded in 1985 to answer the call for reproductive health care that fully respects life." https://popepaulvi.com/about/.

15. Jennifer Williams, "At Ten Years: The 'Miracle on Mercy Road' Celebrates," *The Catholic Voice*, September 1, 1995.

16. About Catholic Medical Center, Obstetrics and Gynecology, Manchester, NH, https://www.catholicmedicalcenter.org/care-and-treatment/obstetrics-gynecology.

17. Kathy Rivet, in interview with the author, February 11, 2020.

18. A pseudonym, per Springfield College's Institutional Review Board (IRB) protocols.

19. Janet [pseud.], in interview with the author, August 18, 2018.

20. This method is closely related to the Creighton method, but relies more on sensations than the strict observations of cervical mucus of Hilgers's method. See About Billings Ovulation Method, https://www.boma-usa.org/about.html.

21. Janet [pseud.], in interview with the author, September 20, 2018.

22. Field notes, August 6, 2019.

23. Field notes, February 1, 2019.

24. Mary J. Henold, *The Laywoman Project: Remaking Catholic Womanhood in the Vatican II Era* (Chapel Hill, NC: University of North Carolina Press, 2020), 84.

25. Kate Henley Averett's *The Homeschool Choice: Parents and the Privatization of Education* (New York: NYU Press, 2021), 12, argues that "[h]omeschooling is a social movement that has served as a container for multiple, competing ideological perspectives."

26. Paula is a pseudonym.

27. Interview and field notes, August 23, 2018. Parsing what Paula meant here by feminism and the ongoing work of what is sometimes called "JPII feminism" is an important project that requires sustained attention elsewhere.

28. Tentler, *Catholics and Contraception*, 266. Quoting Charles F. Westoff and Larry Bumpass, "The Revolution in Birth Control Practices of U.S. Roman Catholics," *Science* 179, no. 4068 (5 January 1973): 41, 42.

29. In 2015, Kindara reportedly raised an additional $5.3 million to boost its offerings. As one of the first and most popular apps that was widely accessible, Kindara has retained its powerful position in the fem-tech world. Adita Pai, "Kindara raises $5.3M for fertility tracking app, device," *Mobile Health News*, August 19, 2015, https://www.mobihealthnews.com/46125/kindara-raises-5-3m -for-fertility-tracking-app-device.

30. Claire Swinarski, "Managing Your Fertility," July 25, 2018, in *The Catholic Feminist*, podcast, Accessed January 10, 2024, https://www .thecatholicfeministpodcast.com/shownotes/bridget.

31. "About," Managing your Fertility, Accessed January 10, 2024, https:// www.managingyourfertility.com/

32. Cycle Power Summit, Accessed January 10, 2024, https://go.asaucier.io /cyclepowersummit.

33. Anna Saucier, in interview with the author, May 31, 2019

34. Anna Saucier, in interview with the author, May 31, 2019.

35. Anna Saucier, in interview with the author, May 31, 2019.

36. Unnamed FEMM member interview with the author, July 10, 2019.

37. Megan Grizzle Fischer, "The Case for FEMM," White paper, https:// femmhealth.org/research/femm-whitepaper/, 67.

38. Fischer, "The Case for FEMM," 66.

39. Unnamed FEMM member interview with the author, July 10, 2019.

40. Field notes, November 1, 2019.

41. Julie Vadnal, "Are Young Women Totally Over the Pill?" *Cosmopolitan*, March 12, 2018, https://www.cosmopolitan.com/sex-love/a18930043/are-young -women-over-the-pill/.

42. Raquel Laneri, "Millennials ditch the pill for high-tech pull & pray," *New York Post*, March 19, 2018, https://nypost.com/2018/03/19/why-millennial -women-are-ditching-the-pill/.

43. Tentler, *Catholics and Contraception*, 279.

44. "Fertility Awareness," *Planned Parenthood* website, https://www .plannedparenthood.org/learn/birth-control/fertility-awareness.

Our Lady of the Liturgical Movement?

Rejecting and Reclaiming Marian Devotion by American Catholic Laywomen

KATHARINE E. HARMON

In September 1942, Catholic Worker artist Ade Bethune (1914–2002) offered the following admission:

> I confess that in my childhood I never had any devotion to the Blessed Virgin Mary. I admit experiencing a vague sense of guilt at this heathen lack of devotion. But I couldn't help it. Devotion cannot be forced. And the grayish, slick, holy pictures which I saw, showing a prissy young woman with lilies, all bathed in an ethereal, clammy fog, did not help matters in the least. [. . .] I just couldn't stand her.[1]

Writing for the central English-language journal of the liturgical movement, *Orate Fratres*, Bethune was not alone in her "prejudice" against the Blessed Virgin, particularly when artists projected Our Lady as an insincere-looking glamor girl trapped in "commercial plaster statues and sentimental muddy paintings."[2] Bethune numbered among many American laywomen who took up the mission of the twentieth-century liturgical movement in the US, a social and spiritual movement which called for a reclaiming of active and intelligent participation in liturgical worship as a font for the Christian life.[3] But, like others working to adopt the precepts of the liturgical movement, Bethune found her relationship with traditional Catholic devotions, even Mary herself, to be an uncomfortable fit. In the midst of a powerful Catholic culture which promoted feminine domesticity[4] and Mary's multi-faceted role in the spiritual lives of the faithful, American Catholic laywomen influenced by the Christ-centered spirituality of the liturgical movement needed new visions of Mary. Mary was the Christ-bearer, and the faithful were called to be Christ-bearers in life.[5] With this frame for viewing the Blessed Virgin, liturgical movement advocates both rejected traditional Marian devotions and reclaimed them by placing Mary within the theological narratives guiding the liturgical movement, such as social transformation, the intelligent participation of the faithful, the liturgical year, the unity of the Mystical Body of Christ, and the domestic church.

The following essay will consider this complex context of Marian devotion in the US and highlight lay Catholic women's approaches to reframing the Blessed Virgin Mary in the light of the liturgical movement. While religious women, as well as both lay and clerical men, were involved in this conversation, this essay focuses on laywomen, often working women or mothers, who wrestled with their relationship as advocates of active participation while remaining dutiful daughters of the Blessed Virgin Mother. After a brief account of the development of Marian devotion in the West and the US in particular, this essay looks to American Catholic laywomen to discuss the relationship between the liturgical movement and Marian devotions, especially the rosary; explores some alternative aesthetic visions for Marian art and how these intersected with theologies operative in liturgical renewal, such as the Mystical Body of Christ; describes how some central figures encouraged para-liturgical rituals inspired by Mary to accentuate the moments of the liturgical year within the Christian home; and considers how Mary served as a model not only for women and girls, but also for the domestic church.

Mary's Role in the Lives of the Faithful

The cult of the Virgin Mary has its clearest origins in fourth-century Jerusalem, when visitors to the Holy Land began circulating traditions about Mary's life.[6] Interest in Mary increased significantly after the Council of Ephesus (431), which affirmed her role as *theotokos*. Over the course of the medieval church in the West, a series of Marian feasts began to fill the Christian calendar,[7] and newly compiled liturgical books began including hymns and prayers addressed to Mary, such as the "*Ave Maria* (Hail, Mary)," many of which had their origins in antiphons appearing in the Divine Office.[8]

In the Western church, Marian devotions continued to multiply and diversify as they crossed oceans with missionaries and immigrants, providing an alternative to sacramental practices which required the mediation of scarce sacramental ministers. Mary began appearing in new corners of the globe, making herself as accessible to poor and indigenous peoples as she had been to the European missionaries who brought her with them. As the US organized in the eighteenth century, devotion to Mary formed a significant component in the lives of English-speaking Catholics, whose infrequent visits by clergy required the faithful to rely on devotional materials such as Richard Challoner's (1691–1781) *Garden of the Soul* (1755), which included exercises such as the Office of Our Blessed Lady, a Litany to Our Lady of Loreto, and the fifteen mysteries of the Rosary.[9]

Mary appealed to the faithful as protectress on land and sea, as patroness over fragile young children, and as mediator, bringing prayers to Christ himself. But, unlike Christ, whose tangible presence in the Eucharist could hardly be carried about in the pockets or purses of the faithful, the portable and accessible nature of Marian devotions propelled the frequency of their use.[10] Rosaries, statues, prints, or medals could all be held in the hand and kept in the home. Coinciding with increasing rates of literacy and availability of printed texts during the nineteenth century, the faithful could read and pray their own devotions in private, familial, or more public settings like a parish mission by following a prayer book. Prayer books included, among other things, instructions for the rosary, Marian litanies, prayers for the Sacred Heart of Mary and Our Lady of Seven Dolors, the various Marian hymns that accompanied the liturgical year, and the Little Office of the Blessed Virgin Mary.[11] Pope Pius IX's (1846–1878) 1854 proclamation of the Immaculate Conception as a dogma of faith inspired American pastorals to emphasize the importance of devotion to Mary.[12] Then, in the latter half of the nineteenth century, increased organizational power among American Catholics inspired the rapid establishment of sodalities devoted to Mary and accompanying print journals.[13] In tandem, a proliferation of commercially produced objects allowed not only churches, but also parochial schools, parish centers, and private families to purchase their own devotional items, and, if desired, to construct their own Marian shrines.[14]

Meanwhile, technological advances in communication increased the rapid dissemination of papal directives via Catholic print media. This proved useful for the promotion of the rosary by Leo XIII (1878–1903) who, between 1883 and 1898, composed twelve encyclicals and five apostolic letters encouraging devotion to the rosary.[15] Leo XIII's praise of the rosary not only buoyed its practice with attached indulgences but also encouraged the use of the rosary in public settings and during Mass itself.[16] Already accustomed to reading allegorical meditations during the Mass, the faithful readily embraced rosary-guided meditation on the passion of Christ as a preferred devotion during the Mass.[17]

In addition to papal encouragement, Marian apparitions captured the faithful's attention, and served to globalize local experiences of Mary. Aside from the sixteenth-century vision of Our Lady of Guadalupe, which powerfully impacted the devotional worlds of Latino/a Catholics, the appearance of Mary to children at Lourdes, France in 1858, and at Fatima, Portugal in 1917, inspired the imaginations of American Catholics.[18] Lourdes would be reproduced in shrines and parish dedications across the US. Fatima's Mary, who proclaimed herself "Our Lady of the Rosary," asked not only for the conversion of sinners but also for the conversion of Russia, coinciding with anti-Communist political views of twentieth-century Americans. As Catholic cultures continued to evolve in the post-World War II flight from urban centers, organized Marian devotions served to solidify Catholic identity in the face of increasing assimilation into more "mainstream" American society. Pope Pius XII (1939–1958) called for even greater attention to Mary with the declaration of the Dogma of the Assumption of Mary in 1950, and the proclamation of a Marian year (surprisingly, the first), in 1953–1954. Efforts by American Catholics, such as Patrick Peyton, CSC (1909–1992), and his Rosary Crusade and accompanying productions, further served to popularize and energize both personal and family prayer and worked to normalize more public displays of devotion to Mary with conspicuous communal prayer events, like the "block rosary."[19] Even the American film industry would capitalize on the popularity of the Blessed Mother, with apparitions providing fodder for films produced in the US, including *The Song of Bernadette* (1943) and *The Miracle of Our Lady of Fatima* (1953).[20]

Finally, the Blessed Virgin Mother's popularity extended beyond her role as identity-forming staple of American Catholic devotional life. She served as the model of perfect womanhood for American Catholic women.[21] In the first half of the twentieth century, American Catholics experienced rapid growth in population and infrastructure, as well as improving socioeconomic opportunities and access to education. Accompanying this, a domestic ideology emerged which not only praised but spiritualized women's role in the home and family life and held up Our Lady as its ideal.[22] Catholic publications and ecclesial leaders alike praised womanhood and, particularly, motherhood, while reflecting their contemporary Americans' assumptions about the place of women in both private and public life.

The Rosary and the Liturgical Movement

If the proliferation of Marian devotions, indulgences, literature, mass-produced art, and reproductions of shrines tells us anything, it suggests that Marian devotion was both highly encouraged and frequently practiced by American Catholics. Mary was a truly popular phenomenon, one whose role as mediator in prayer was perhaps more frequently appreciated than Jesus' role as *mediator Dei*. And yet, in the midst of the great Marian revival occurring through the first half of the twentieth century, a parallel liturgical revival emerged that sought to place Christocentric, liturgical prayer at the center of spiritual life.

While the liturgical movement is best understood as a spiritual and social movement aimed toward social regeneration, its practical efforts targeted one specific activity: getting the faithful to pray the Mass. Some liturgical advocates saw the faithful's seeming preference for Marian devotions as evidence of deficient catechesis,[23] while others were more acerbic in their critique of the "monotonous mumbling" of the faithful.[24] Among the sharpest critics would be social worker Ellen Gates Starr (1859–1940) of Chicago. A leading member of the Chicago Calvert Club, Starr promoted liturgical worship in her public lectures, writing, and support for the work of the Liturgical Press and *Orate Fratres*. A convert to Roman Catholicism, Starr had begun corresponding with Virgil Michel, OSB (1890–1938), editor of *Orate Fratres*, about efforts to promote the liturgical movement:

> I have railed formally and privately about doing the rosary at Mass for years—ever since I became a Catholic. I even arise or depart from a church when I see they are about to do it. I even told a sister, leading her flock into church, while I was going in [that I was going to leave if they started praying the rosary.] "You aren't going to miss Mass!" she said, in a horror-struck tone. "No, I'm going to find a church where I shall *not* miss Mass."[25]

For many American Catholics, the Mass, especially the more frequently offered low Mass, provided a context for prayer.[26] In this quiet and relatively brief space created by the presiding priest *sotto voce*, a lay person in the pew (who would not necessarily be sacramentally communicating) could easily hold a rosary, rather than fumble through a missal, and devote a few minutes to uninterrupted prayer. Members of the lay faithful not only gravitated toward the rosary because of encouragement by their popes and pastors; the rosary's invariable prayers could be memorized, said in the vernacular, and allowed meditation on Christ's life. To the average Catholic, this was, perhaps, more efficacious than the effort required to follow along with a missal, or attend a High Mass (usually) sung by a choir, in Latin.[27] Yet Starr, well-educated and distant from an immigrant past, had little patience for such devotional habits which, in her view, were far less sophisticated than liturgical prayer.[28]

Other liturgical movement advocates, such as sociologist (and mother of five) Therese Mueller (1905–2002), pointed out that the supposed "ease" of devotional practices like the rosary required their own kind of challenging concentration.[29] In describing the possibilities of the Breviary as a "prayer in common" for a family, she explained:

> From a psychological point of view, devout praying of the easier Psalms does not require more effort or training than does the rosary, which [the] latter, if it is to be more than a mere mechanical repetition, demands a very considerable amount of concentration in the "double action" of the vocal prayer and the contemplation of the successive "mysteries."[30]

Yet the American Catholic faithful had become accustomed to praying the rosary, not the psalms, as part of routine prayer. Finding the time and resources required (like a hand missal with English translation, let alone learning Latin), and the desire needed to accomplish this goal was challenging, if not impossible, for first-generation immigrants or for members of taxed blue-collar Catholic families, and was met with considerable resistance by many other members of the faithful. Even Pius XII's 1947 encyclical on the liturgy, *Mediator Dei*, praised as the "magna carta" of the liturgical movement, expressly stated that, by reason of necessity, or even inclination, not all could or wished to use a missal—and emphasized that devotions that meditated on the mysteries of Jesus Christ (e.g., the rosary) were effective and harmonious means of participation for the faithful.[31] Liturgical movement advocates found themselves at odds with pastoral arguments for using the rosary instead of a missal, but also at odds with preferences and habitual practices of the lay faithful and their pastors, who were accustomed to low Masses accompanied by silence.

Promoting a Liturgical Vision of Mary

Aside from continual recommendation to redirect liturgical prayer to the texts of the liturgy itself, liturgically minded advocates also sought to redefine how the faithful imagined Mary. The images of Mary made popular through cheap mass production had created a Blessed Virgin who synchronized well with traditional pedestalizations of the feminine but not as easily with the notions of social action and intelligent participation that had sharpened the worldviews of most liturgical movement advocates. This tension was well articulated by artist and art patron Elizabeth Howard Ward Perkins (1873–1954) of Boston Massachusetts.[32] Perkins observed, "Many of our people have seen only one type of a picture and statues commercially turned out in quantity . . . . The people are tied to one type of image and their thought is often 'Our Lady looked like that.'" Instead, Perkins argued, the "adventure of variety" was needed, with "good reproductions or originals" from all the "ages of faith," so that one could be "carried back to the thought that Our Lady is all things to all men at all times." She cited images created in "the foreign mission fields" as strong examples, where "the idiom of the country is used," with images of "Our Lord and His disciples in Chinese or Indian dress," as rightly befitting a universality. Mary should be allowed to project such a reality, rather than her image being mass-produced with the hope of provoking "sentimental" emotions.[33] Perkins' encouragement of Catholics to look beyond the nineteenth-century West for models resonated with the *ressourcement* method employed more widely in liturgical movement circles, including discussions of liturgical symbolism, retrieval of scripture, and the revisiting of more ancient liturgical sources beyond the medieval Latin West.[34]

Other liturgical movement advocates saw traditional Marian images as limiting the sacramental imagination regarding who Mary was, what she could do, and how she could be perceived as a model for socially oriented Christian life and community. Reflecting in an essay on the significance of artistic integrity (c. 1950),[35] Ade Bethune critiqued how an (unnamed) artist depicted a group of young children encircling Mary. Bethune recounted:

> But, when it comes to the Blessed Virgin, oh dear, look what happens. Suppose I hadn't told you this is the Blessed Virgin, would you trust such a woman with your child, your cat, your dog or your canary? Not on your life. What do you suppose happened to that artist? Why is it that he can draw his children, his lamb, everything else quite decently, but when it comes to a sacred subject he falls down upon the worst sort of thing.[36]

Bethune evaluated this disparity as displaying a lack of ability or comfort with religion: "Religion is not a reality to [such artists], not having anything to account for it, they simply substitute some sort of sentimentality and let it go at that. [. . .] The lack of sincerity is immediately transferred to the quality of the work."[37] Bethune's critique resonated with that of Elizabeth Perkins: both artists and lay Catholics had a limited vision not only of what Mary might look like, but also of how she might serve as inspiration for the American Catholic faithful.

Bethune herself struggled with how to develop images of the Blessed Mother over the course of her artistic career,[38] a difficulty she overcame only with a complete reframing of Mary from that unreal glamor girl to one who was startingly ordinary. In 1935, Bethune drew the holy family at work, with Joseph and Jesus bending over their carpenter's tools and Mary bent over her sewing. In "Our Lady of Homework," a print created ca. 1937, Mary knelt over a soapy bucket, scrubbing a tiled floor with a brush.[39] In 1940, Bethune depicted Mary holding the baby Jesus, surrounded by eleven children of diverse ages and ethnicities. And, in 1942, Bethune created a print which appeared in the *Catholic Worker*, titled "Our Lady of Chickens." Bethune had embraced the claims of the liturgical movement: that the liturgy invited the formation of the whole human person, and that becoming the Body of Christ shaped one's everyday actions, and one's work. For Bethune, good work and social interaction, not rosy cheeks and piously lifted eyes, symbolically reflected a life fed by Christ. And so, a picture of Mary feeding the chickens said more about the Virgin Mother than a commercial print of Our Lady of Fatima.

FIGURE 5: "Our Lady of Chickens," by Ade Bethune. Image courtesy of Archives and Special Collections, St. Catherine University, St. Paul, Minnesota.

Inviting Mary into the Liturgical Home

Resonating with mid-twentieth century American culture, which privileged female domesticity, liturgical movement advocates also turned to
traditionally feminine spaces and activities as arenas of the liturgical
movement. One such visionary, Florence Berger (1909–1983), who lived
with her family of six children on the outskirts of Cincinnati, Ohio, was
an active member of both the Grail (in nearby Loveland, Ohio) and the
National Catholic Rural Life Conference (NCRLC).[40] Inspired by these
organizations to connect her family's life to the liturgy, Berger began
compiling recipes associated with the liturgical calendar of feasts and
seasons, and was invited to publish her collection under the auspices of
the NCRLC in 1949.[41] The volume, *Cooking for Christ: Your Kitchen Prayer-
book*, taught families about the liturgical year, cultural Catholic practices,
and the social implications of carefully using resources in an age of "mal-
distribution."[42] But, while the mid-century American Grail movement held
up Mary as an active apostle for God's work in the world, it also tended to
emphasize a highly gendered view of womanhood and a preference for
Mary as one who accepted sacrifice.[43] While influenced by the Grail,
and even though Berger was writing a cookbook, she took a different approach. This domestic resource did not emphasize the role of Mary as a
model for Christian women. It emphasized Christ, starting in the kitchen:

> Cook, you may call [the woman in the kitchen]. I prefer to call her
> "Christian in Action." She herself is Christ-centered because she
> brings Christ home to her kitchen and, in corollary, her kitchen re-
> flects the Christ within her.[44]

Despite this framing, it is still surprising that Berger makes so little mention
of Mary, in the face of the cultural popularity of Marian devotions for Catholic families and women in mid-century. But Berger focused principally on
major liturgical seasons (Advent, Christmastide, Septuagesima, Lent, Pas-
chaltide, and the time after Pentecost) rather than saints. The saints she did
include were almost exclusively male, and mostly associated with cults
popular in Germany or the British Isles.[45] Only two feast days associated
with Mary were named as specific points of celebration and supplied
with accompanying recipes: the Assumption (August 15—which Berger

admitted to almost forgetting![46]) and the Annunciation (March 25). Other solemnities, like the Immaculate Conception on December 8, received passing mention, placed within a wider discussion of Christmas cookies. With something of a stretch, Berger suggested baking Moravian gingerbread cookies on December 7, because Mary, too, "gave forth a sweet smell like cinnamon and aromatic balm and yielded a sweet odor like the best myrrh."[47]

While Berger was somewhat unique in her remarkable lack of attention to Marian feasts, a number of subsequent liturgical movement advocates devoted more space to the celebration of Marian-centered feast days throughout the course of the liturgical year. Interestingly, some liturgical movement advocates called for moving Marian devotions and para-liturgical practices *back* to the home (instead of encouraging devotions to be celebrated in public spaces, as Leo XIII or Patrick Peyton, CSC, had). For such advocates, Mass and, to a lesser extent, the Divine Office, were to occupy public spaces for worship. In this strain, liturgical movement advocate and mother of seven Mary Reed Newland (1916–1989) of Monson, Massachusetts, readily integrated Marian devotions within her volume on the liturgical year, *The Year and Our Children: Planning the Family Activities for the Church Year* (1956). In Advent, Newland included a reflection on the Immaculate Conception and a Novena to the Infant Jesus.[48] For Candlemas, Newland recommended constructing a family project, a shadow-box theater with Mary, Joseph, the Baby Jesus, Anna, and Simeon as "an especially easy medium for learning the mysteries of the Rosary [. . .]."[49] Newland suggested saying the Joyful mysteries while meditating on a constructed scene, followed by a family procession with lighted candles around the house, an adult reading the antiphon for the day, and everyone joining in songs such as the chant, *Salve Regina* (in English), or hymns like *O Sanctissima* and "Hail, Holy Queen."[50]

Newland's description of a Marian-inspired para-liturgical ritual with the family might seem idyllic, but Newland helpfully grounded such activities in a dose of reality. She admitted:

I have never been terribly enthusiastic about transforming my house into a shrine. [. . .] People light cigarettes uneasily in the presence of

too many vigil lights, and an ordinary family fracas about playing allies on the living-room floor, with small boys to be hauled apart and
given a word or two about wrestling in the house, seems far more sac-
rilegious than the occasion merits when performed in front of an altar. That, it seemed to me, was not the purpose of shrines: to make
everyone uncomfortable.[51]

To this end, Newland suggested keeping family projects simple. Employ-
ing recycled materials, like baby cereal boxes, socks, or old towels, and
encouraging kids to take part in the creation of home-devotional objects
and space, reflected a sensible use of resources and drew the family together. Mass-produced sentimental pictures were not the order of the
day when Mary was made out of clay or cardboard. As Newland described: "There is a great difference between [buying a plastic statue
made by a machine] and taking the clay in your own hands, thinking
about what you will make, praying to the Holy Spirit for help, and then
lovingly shaping it this way and that [. . .] until you have a creation of
your own."[52]

Newland also recognized that Mary, the mother of Jesus, was a mother
and protectress of all, thus providing another impetus for the Christian
to recognize Christ in others, even if the "other" might be the communist enemy, or be standing on the other side of the color line. To highlight
this, her family's home shrine rotation included a reproduction icon of *Our
Lady, Mother of the Russians*, to remind her family to pray that the Russians
might "find God," and a white china statue remodeled as a home-made
"black Madonna" to honor *Our Lady of Africa*.[53] Looking to Mary as a model
of diversity could teach children that all were one in Christ, as Newland
recounted in 1959:

> Now, if [seeing our brothers and sisters in Christ] is true of the Christ
> life, it is true of the mysteries of Mary's life also; we must know the
> mysteries of her life and identify them as we see them in the lives of
> the people around us. It can help our children, the children we teach
> and the children we live with and know, as well as all our adult fellows,
> to see life in this fashion.[54]

This viewpoint had clear resonance with Mystical Body of Christ theology, foundational for liturgical movement advocates.[55]

Another notable liturgical movement advocate is found in Liturgical Press author Helen McLoughlin, and her volume, *My Nameday, Come for Dessert* (1962).[56] This text devotes more than fifty pages to Marian-related celebrations, including twenty-one feasts, liturgically inspired home celebrations, Marian hymns, and decorations. True to the title of McLoughlin's book, dessert recipes combined traditional Marian symbols with the conveniences of modern cooking, such as the "Rose Petal Coconut Cake," made from an instant white cake mix, for Blessed Virgin Mary of the Rosary (October 7); "Snow Hearts," with lemon-flavored gelatin for Our Lady of the Snow (August 5); and an "Assumption Day Fruit Medley," which made use of the quintessentially mid-century "melon ball" among recommended fruit combinations (August 15).[57]

Supporting her compatriots who sought to provide higher-quality images for Marian devotion, McLoughlin provided contact information for purchasing art by noted liturgical artists, such as Ade Bethune.[58] Not only art but also music caught McLoughlin's attention, and she admitted how many popular Marian hymns were made up of "pseudo-religious words superimposed on sentimental ballads."[59] As alternatives, she recommended a number of sources for Marian music, including the Trapp Family Singers' Yuletide songs collection, songs produced by the Grail women of Loveland, Ohio, and the volume *Our Parish Prays and Sings*, published by Liturgical Press.[60]

In describing various feasts, McLoughlin highlighted the celebration of the Immaculate Conception of Mary on December 8 as "one of the most popular Marian devotions."[61] Instead of a novena or rosary, as Newland had suggested, McLoughlin recommended throwing a private family party utilizing the "lily of the valley" as a symbol to decorate paper plates, place cards, or cupcakes crowned with white frosting. She recommended some sources from which to procure "ready-made" lilies for icing but noted "it's a great satisfaction to make one's own and gives a mother a chance to use her talents."[62] But, alongside the aesthetic and culinary practices, McLoughlin recommended family prayers—not the rosary, but a home-based liturgy, comprised of a mash-up of texts drawn from the breviary and missal. In McLoughlin's ritual text, both mothers and fathers were assigned roles in praying the collects and reading homily excerpts, though fathers more frequently were assigned a leadership role. All persons (assumedly, children or other family or friends present) were involved in the responses.

Theological Alternatives, Mary, and the Domestic Church

Unlike her contemporaries, liturgical movement pioneer and catechetical advocate Mary Perkins Ryan (1912–1993) sharply critiqued the adoption of aesthetic and culinary components into one's life as a chief means of living a liturgical life.[63] She asked,

> [T]hink of the picture conjured up by the phrase "celebrating the feasts and seasons of the Church." Isn't it that of a congregation crowding out of a church, singing snatches of Gregorian chant (or a Gelineau psalm or some old French or German hymn tune), going home to say a special grace around "liturgically" decorated tables spread with "traditional" dishes, and looking forward to returning to church to take part in Vespers or some para-liturgical service and to ending the day with a festivity including songs, games, and square dancing, followed by Compline?[64]

With a note of exasperation, Ryan concluded, "Where does such a picture come from, and why has it come to be more or less accepted as the liturgical ideal?"[65] In this essay published in 1963, Ryan cast a skeptical eye on what she saw as an "unrealistic" life centered in the liturgy which had been promoted by liturgical pioneers over the last decade—and perhaps was aware of the dimming hold of such imported domestic traditions on a rapidly evolving American Catholic lay faithful of the unfolding 1960s. Ryan claimed how various practices projected the "nostalgia of various European origins" which was several generations old and severely limited in its cultural scope. Such a projection was attractive, as it recalled "a way of life remembered as more integrally religious, more in touch with the realities of the faith, than is our chaotic, secular, materialistic American culture," but it did not reflect the realities of life or an appropriate appreciation of the liturgical movement's true aims.[66] For Ryan, such assumptions about how to live a liturgical life perpetuated a long-standing issue for understanding the liturgy: just as liturgical reformers fought to have the liturgy understood as more than "rubrics," now liturgical reformers had to fight to have the liturgy understood as more than external aesthetics, be they "liturgical vestments" and "liturgical altars," or "liturgical customs" parading through one's home.

Ryan, wife and mother of two boys, took a different view as to how one might integrate faith and catechesis with family life. Rather than decorating one's table, Ryan recommended a theological, relational model as touchstone for a family's living of the liturgical life, the holy family. She had dedicated her 1955 volume, *Beginning at Home*, to "the holy family— Joseph, Mary, Jesus—in whose home the divine ideal of family life found perfect fulfillment."[67] Rejecting aesthetic means of understanding the liturgy or highlighting Mary's role within salvation history, Ryan looked to Mary and Joseph together as models for a "Christian and sacramental pattern" for family life. Ryan suggested that parents teach their children about the dynamics of the holy family, where "our Lord obeyed our Lady and St. Joseph when He was a boy on earth." God gave children obedience to Father and Mother as an opportunity to "practice" obeying God when they grew up.[68] Avoiding gender binaries, both boys and girls were given the pattern of Jesus' behavior, and Mary and Joseph were named together as models for parents. Likewise, Ryan was not interested in reclaiming traditionally feminine spaces or activities as suitable avenues for the liturgical life. Rather, as Ryan described:

> If we train our children to sacramental thinking, in sacramental living, we shall, certainly, be educating them along truly traditional Christian lines. Moreover, children so educated should be able to see, far more clearly than we do now, how modern life can and may be made holy, re-oriented to Christ.[69]

Ryan not only adopted the liturgical movement's emphasis upon the social character of the Church as Christ's body but adopted a social model for the home, emphasizing the domestic church as a community of persons, training for Christian life.[70]

Conclusions

If Mary and her accompanying devotions caused some tensions for American Catholic laywomen invested in liturgical renewal in the middle of the twentieth century, she would cause even greater consternation for a rising tide of second-wave Catholic feminists. As Rosemary Radford Reuther, in 1967, remarked, "the idealization of Mary goes very well with the contempt for the question of women."[71] Marian devotion dropped significantly in the decade following the Council, with fewer devotional offerings in parishes, less use in parochial and secondary schools, and flagging interest displayed by an American Catholic faithful who were increasingly moving beyond the "Catholic ghetto."[72] Examining how laywomen accepted, rejected, and re-visioned Mary and her intersection with liturgical renewal provides some insight into changing patterns of Marian devotion, even prior to more definitively observable shifts in practice which would be evidenced more broadly by the Catholic faithful in the US after the Council. A turn toward eucharistic reception and participation in the text of the Mass itself, made inescapable by the reformed liturgy in the vernacular, further propelled the move of Marian devotions from the church into the home. Likewise, *Sacrosanctum Concilium* itself described devotions as leading to, and flowing from Mass, necessarily moving devotional practices, including those addressed to Mary, into private spaces rather than public ones.[73]

Aside from this, liturgical movement advocates preferred a more broadly social understanding of Mary, rather than an individualized relationship. Even within accounts which were more "domestically" oriented, Mary was emphasized in terms of her role within the archetypal family, as universal mother with no bounds of ethnicity, place, or race, and as inviting contemplation of salvation history. Mary portrayed the Church, understood as the Mystical Body of Christ, as one who was appropriately living the Christ-life. As Bethune concluded, in her 1942 essay on Mary:

> When I had fallen in love with the Church it was only one step to realizing that the Blessed Virgin and the Church are the same thing, that she is the type of all Christ-bearers who are the Church, that she is the image of the life of the Church, that, in her acceptance of the Christ-life and in her bearing it and in her giving birth to it, we find the direction for ourselves the Church, who continue her, in many ages and lands, even to this here and now.[74]

In short, mid-century Roman Catholic American laywomen advocates of the liturgical movement did not outright reject Mary as part of an "unusable past;"[75] but they tended to articulate a liturgical spirituality which placed Mary within a more complex theological landscape: as icon of active participation, located firmly in the unfolding salvation history of the liturgical year, as model of living out the mystical body, and as inspiration for communal prayer and unified family life. Mary was undoubtedly lifted up as inspiration, guide, and protectress. But liturgical movement women turned the tables on traditional Marian devotions. Rather than looking through Mary as a scope for Jesus, they contemplated Mary through the lens of Christ.

Notes

1. Ade Bethune, "On the Blessed Virgin," *Orate Fratres* 16, no. 7 (1942), 294–298, here at 294.

2. Ade Bethune, "On the Blessed Virgin," 296.

3. For general histories that focus on aspects and leaders in the liturgical movement, see, among others: Ernst Koenker, *The Liturgical Renaissance in the Roman Catholic Church* (Chicago: Chicago University Press, 1954); Massey Hamilton Shepherd, *The Reform of Liturgical Worship: Perspectives and Prospects* (New York: Oxford University Press, 1961); R. K. Fenwick and Brian D. Spinks, *Worship in Transition: Highlights of the Liturgical Movement* (Edinburgh: T. and T. Clark, 1995); Keith Pecklers, *The Unread Vision: The Liturgical Movement in the United States of America: 1926–1955* (Collegeville, MN: The Liturgical Press, 1998); and Katharine E. Harmon, *There Were Also Many Women There: Lay Women in the Liturgical Movement in the United States: 1926–1959* (Collegeville, MN: The Liturgical Press, 2013).

4. For more discussion on Marian devotion and gender, see Tine Van Osselaer, "Marian Piety and Gender: Marian Devotion and the 'Feminization' of Religion," in *The Oxford Handbook of Mary*, ed. Chris Maunder (New York: Oxford University Press, 2018), 579–591.

5. Bethune, "On the Blessed Virgin," 298.

6. Miri Rubin, *Mother of God: A History of the Virgin Mary* (New Haven: Yale University Press, 2009), 20. Resources for general information on Marian devotion include: Marina Warner, *Alone of All Her Sex: The Myth and Cult of the Virgin Mary* (New York: Random House, 1976); Elizabeth Johnson, "Marian Devotion in the Western Church," in *Christian Spirituality: High Middle Ages and Reformation: An Encyclopedic History of the Religious Quest*, ed. Jill Raitt (New York: Crossroad, 1986), 392–440; and Stephen J. Shoemaker, *Mary in Early Christian Faith and Devotion* (New Haven: Yale University Press, 2016).

7. See P. Jounel, "The Veneration of Mary," in *The Liturgy and Time*, ed. Aimé Georges Martimort, vol. 4, new edition, *The Church at Prayer*, eds. Irénée Henri Dalmais, Pierre Jounel, and Aimé Georges Martimort (Collegeville, MN: The Liturgical Press, 1985), 130–150; and Kilian McDonnell, "The Marian Liturgical Tradition," in *Between Memory and Hope: Readings on the Liturgical Year*, ed. Maxwell E. Johnson, (Collegeville, MN: The Liturgical Press, 2000), 385–400.

8. For a more robust treatment of the development of Marian hymnody, see Jounel, "The Veneration of Mary," 142–143; and Thomas A. Thompson, "The Virgin Mary in the Hymns of the Catholic Church," in *The Oxford Handbook of Mary*, ed. Chris Maunder (New York: Oxford University Press, 2019), 247–264.

9. Richard Challoner, *Garden of the Soul: A Manual of Spiritual Exercises and Instructions for Christians who, Living in the World, Aspire to Devotion* (London: n.p., 1775).

10. Leo XIII, *Augustissimae Virginis Mariae* [Encyclical on the Confraternity of the Holy Rosary], Vatican Website, https://www.vatican.va/content/leo-xiii /en/encyclicals/documents/hf_l-xiii_enc_12091897_augustissimae-virginis -mariae.html, September 12, 1897, sec. 7–8. Joseph J. Casino, "From Sanctuary to Involvement: A History of the Catholic Parish in the Northeast," in *The American Catholic Parish: A History from 1850 to the Present* (Mahwah, NJ: Paulist Press, 1987), 7–116, here at 53. For some responses regarding the importance of the rosary in Catholic devotion and how its use was encouraged among the lay faithful, see "The Rosary Confraternity," *Kentucky Irish American* (Louisville, KY), October 3, 1903, p. 3; and "Devotion of the Rosary," *Catholic Union and Times* (Buffalo, NY), November 15, 1900, p. 8.

11. Ann Taves, *The Household of Faith: Roman Catholic Devotions in Mid-Nineteenth-Century America*, Notre Dame Studies in American Catholicism ser., (Notre Dame: University of Notre Dame Press, 1986), 36.

12. Joseph P. Chinnici, *Living Stones: The History and Structure of Catholic Spiritual Life in the United States*, The Bicentennial History of the Catholic Church in America, ed. Christopher J. Kauffman (New York: Macmillan Publishing Company, 1989), 83; Taves, *The Household of Faith*, 36–39.

13. James Hennessy, *American Catholics: A History of the Roman Catholic Community in the United States* (New York: Oxford University Press, 1981), 177. A few Marian periodicals include: *Ave Maria*, founded in 1865 by Edward Sorin, CSC (1814–1893), *The Queen's Work*, founded by Edward Garesché, SJ (1876–1960) in 1914, and *The Rosary* magazine begun by Dominican friars in 1891.

14. See Elisha McIntyre, "Rescuing God from Bad Taste: Religious Kitsch in Theory and Practice," *Literature & Aesthetics* 23, no. 2 (2014): 83–108; David Morgan, *Images at Work: The Material Culture of Enchantment* (Oxford: Oxford University Press, 2018); and Deirdre De La Cruz, "Mary and Modern Catholic Material Culture," in *The Oxford Handbook of Mary*, ed. Chris Maunder (New York: Oxford University Press, 2019), 635–647.

15. For more on the development of rosary devotions, see John Desmond Miller, *Beads and Prayers: The Rosary in History and Devotion* (London: Burns & Oates, 2002); Nathan D. Mitchell, *The Mystery of the Rosary: Marian Devotion and the Reinvention of Catholicism* (New York: New York University Press,

2009); and Hilda Graef and Thomas A. Thompson, *Mary: A History of Doctrine and Devotion* (Notre Dame: Ave Maria Press, 2009).

16. Leo XIII, *Supremi Apostolatus Officio* [On Devotion of the Rosary], Vatican Website https://www.vatican.va/content/leo-xiii/en/encyclicals /documents/hf_l-xiii_enc_01091883_supremi-apostolatus-officio.html, 1 September 1883, sec. 8. Indulgences associated with the rosary can be found in the many editions of the *Raccolta*—for example, the 1910 edition includes the "Rosary of Our Lord," instructing that 200 years might be taken off one's purgation each time one went to confession, or simply expressed the "firm resolution" to confess (*The Raccolta, or Collection of Indulgenced Prayers and Good Works*, ed. Ambrose St. John, [New York: Benziger Bros., 1910], 35.) For some commentary on and interpretation of the issue of Leo XIII's encouragement of the rosary at Mass, see "The Rosary at Mass," in "The Apostolate," *Orate Fratres* 4, no. (1930): 327–329.

17. See Joseph J. Casino, "From Sanctuary to Involvement: A History of the Catholic Parish in the Northeast," in *The American Catholic Parish: A History from 1850 to the Present* (Mahwah, NJ: Paulist Press, 1987), 7–116, here at 53. See also, Nathan D. Mitchell, *Cult and Controversy: The Worship of the Eucharist Outside Mass* (Collegeville, MN: The Liturgical Press, 1982), 49–62.

18. For some studies focusing on Marian apparitions, see Sandra L. Zimdars-Swartz, *Encountering Mary: From La Salette to Medjugorje* (Princeton, NJ: Princeton University Press, 1991); and Chris Maunder, *Our Lady of the Nations: Apparitions of Mary in Twentieth-Century Catholic Europe* (Oxford: Oxford University Press, 2016).

19. See James P. McCartin, *Prayers of the Faithful: The Shifting Spiritual Life of American Catholics* (Cambridge, MA: Harvard University Press, 2010), 71–99.

20. See Catherine O'Brien, "Symbol, Vision, Mother: Mary in Film," in *The Oxford Handbook of Mary*, ed. Chris Maunder (New York: Oxford University Press, 2018), 546–558.

21. The very existence of such a narrative suggests that some women were defying it. Such assumptions that respectable females did not work (whether married or unmarried) ignored the socioeconomic realities faced by significant numbers of American women, particularly women of color. Historical and feminist analyses of Catholic women, and their relationship with Mary, include: Clarissa W. Atkinson, Constance H. Buchanan, and Margaret R. Miles, eds., *Immaculate and Powerful: The Female in Sacred Image and Social Reality* (Boston, MA: Beacon Press, 1985); Marina Warner, *Alone of All Her Sex: The Myth and Cult of the Virgin Mary* (New York: Random House, 1976); Mary J. Henold, *Catholic and Feminist: The Surprising History of the American Catholic Feminist Movement* (Chapel Hill: The University of North Carolina Press, 2008); and Elizabeth Hayes Alvarez, *The Valiant Woman: The Virgin Mary in*

Nineteenth-Century American Culture, (Chapel Hill: University of North Carolina Press, 2016).

22. See Colleen McDannell, Catholic Domesticity, 1860–1960," in *American Catholic Women: A Historical Exploration*, ed. Karen Kennelly, The Bicentennial History of the Catholic Church in America, ser., ed. Christopher J. Kauffman (New York: Macmillan Publishing Co., 1989), 48–80.

23. Virgil Michel, quoted in Paul B. Marx, *Virgil Michel and the Liturgical Movement* (Collegeville, MN: The Liturgical Press, 1957), 65. Michel's statement comes from p. 13 of a document, "Liturgy and the Catholic Life," published posthumously in parts between 1939–1941 in *Orate Fratres*.

24. William M. Cashin, "Pray Brethren," in "The Apostolate," *Orate Fratres* 21, no. 8 (1947): 370–371, here at 370.

25. Ellen Gates Starr to Virgil Michel, January 20, 1930, The Virgil Michel Papers Z 28: 1, Saint John's Abbey Archives, Collegeville, Minnesota.

26. For some witness to pre-Conciliar experiences of Mass, see "Our High Masses" in "The Apostolate," *Orate Fratres* 11, no. 9 (1937): 416–419; and Martin B. Hellriegel, "Merely Suggesting," *Orate Fratres* 15, no. 9 (1941): 390–397.

27. For some critique and discussion of this issue, see Hans Anscar Reinhold, "Are We Losing Our Identity?" *Orate Fratres* 19, no. 6 (1945): 273–278; and Sister M. Albert [no surname given], O.P. "II. Its Complementary Role" [extracts from "The Rosary and the Liturgy," in Feb-Mar issue of *Doctrine and Life*] reprinted in "The Rosary," in "The Apostolate," *Worship* 27, no. 6 (1953): 311–314.

28. The liturgical movement has been critiqued as being the domain of the Catholic intellectual elite; see Keith Pecklers, *Unread Vision*, 14.

29. For more information on Therese Mueller, see Harmon, *There Were Also Many Women There*, 255–272.

30. Therese Mueller, "The Christian Family and the Liturgy," *1941 National Liturgical Week Proceedings* (Newark, NJ: Benedictine Liturgical Conference, 1942), 162–171, here at 165–166.

31. See Pius XII, *Mediator Dei* [Encyclical On the Sacred Liturgy], Vatican Website https://www.vatican.va/content/pius-xii/en/encyclicals/documents/hf_p-xii_enc_20111947_mediator-dei.html, November 20, 1947, sec. 108.

32. Elizabeth Howard Ward Perkins was the mother of Mary Perkins Ryan, also discussed in this chapter.

33. Mrs. Charles B. [Elizabeth] Perkins, "The Perennial Art of the Liturgy," *National Liturgical Week Proceedings 1945* (Elsberry, MO: The Liturgical Conference, 1946), 99–105, here at 104. While not as appropriately sensitive as a twenty-first-century mind might desire, these attempts at inclusivity and global awareness are breakthroughs for "white" mid-century lay Catholics.

34. Some sources include: Brian Daley, "The *Nouvelle Théologie* and the Patristic Revival: Sources, Symbols, and the Science of Theology," *International Journal of Scholastic Theology* 7, no. 4 (2005): 362–382; and Gabriel Flynn and Paul D. Murray, eds., *Ressourcement: A Movement for Renewal in Twentieth-Century Catholic Theology*, (Oxford: Oxford University Press, 2012).

35. Ade Bethune, "The Importance of Personal and Artistic Integrity," (und. manuscript, c. 1950), Box 14, p. 1. Ade Bethune Collection, University of St. Catherine Library, St. Paul, MN 55105.

36. Bethune, "The Importance of Personal and Artistic Integrity."

37. Bethune, "The Importance of Personal and Artistic Integrity."

38. For more on Bethune, see Harmon, *There Were Also Many Women There*, 191–221; and Judith Stoughton, *Proud Donkey of Schaerbeek: Adé Bethune: Catholic Worker Artist* (St. Cloud, MN: North Star Press of St. Cloud, 1988).

39. While the print has no date, the coding of Bethune's work done by Blue Cloud Abbey in South Dakota is 3715, which suggests the work was done in 1937. Email exchange with Amy Shaw, Head of Archives and Special Collections, St. Catherine University Library, St. Paul, MN, March 10, 2021.

40. The American Grail and the NCRLC (now Catholic Rural Life) frequently intersected; selected resources which explore one or both of these movements include: Alden V. Brown, *The Grail Movement and American Catholicism, 1940–1975*, Notre Dame Studies in American Catholicism (Notre Dame, IN: University of Notre Dame Press, 1989); Janet Kalven and Grail Members, "Living the Liturgy: Keystone of the Grail Vision," *U.S. Catholic Historian* 11, no. 4 (1993): 29–38; Mary Jo Weaver, "Still Feisty at Fifty: The Grailville Lay Apostolate for Women," *U.S. Catholic Historian* 2, no. 4 (1993): 3–12; Michael J. Woods, *Cultivating Soil and Soul: Twentieth-Century Catholic Agrarians Embrace the Liturgical Movement* (Collegeville, MN: The Liturgical Press, 2009); Jeffrey Marlett, *Saving the Heartland: Catholic Missionaries in Rural America, 1920–1960* (DeKalb: Northern Illinois University Press, 2002); and Davis S. Bovee, *The Church and the Land: The National Catholic Rural Life Conference and American Society, 1923–2007* (Washington, D.C.: The Catholic University of America Press, 2010).

41. For more on Berger, see Harmon, *There Were Also Many Women There*, 300–324.

42. Florence Berger, *Cooking for Christ: Your Kitchen Prayer Book* (1949; repr., Des Moines, IA: National Catholic Rural Life Conference, 1996), 76–77. See also Debra Campbell, "Both Sides Now: Another Look at the Grail in the Postwar Era," *U.S. Catholic Historian* 11, no. 4 (1993): 13–27.

43. See Brown, *The Grail Movement and American Catholicism 1940–1975*, 103–113. The vision of women first espoused by founders Lydwine Van Kersbergen and Janet Kalven was eventually rejected by the Grail and does not

describe its approach at present. See Janet Kalven, "Grailville in the Seventies and Eighties: Structural Changes and Feminist Consciousness," *U.S. Catholic Historian* 11, no. 4 (1993): 45–57; and Janet Kalven, *Women Breaking Boundaries: A Grail Journey, 1940–1965* (Albany, NY: State University of New York Press, 1999).

44. Berger, *Cooking for Christ*, Introduction.

45. In fact, only one female saint, St. Lucy, appears. Like many of Berger's colleagues in the North American liturgical movement, most examples and experiences reflect northern and western European ethnic heritages.

46. Berger, *Cooking for Christ*, 102–106, here at 104.

47. Berger, *Cooking for Christ*, 8. Mary is named, but the cookies, cut into heart shapes and decorated with icing, are interpreted as "an expression of love in honor of Him who loved man most" (Berger, 9).

48. Mary Reed Newland, *The Year and Our Children: Planning the Family Activities for the Church Year* (New York: P. J. Kenedy & Sons, 1956), 59.

49. Newland, *The Year and Our Children*, 105.

50. Newland, *The Year and Our Children*, 106.

51. Newland, *The Year and Our Children*, 219.

52. Newland, *The Year and Our Children*, 55.

53. Newland, *The Year and Our Children*, 218–220.

54. Mary Reed Newland, "St. Bernadette and Our Lady," (1959). Marian Reprints. Paper 50. http://ecommons.udayton.edu/marian_reprints/50.

55. See, for example, Francis A. Brunner, "Mary, Mother of Christ's Mystical Body," *National Liturgical Week Proceedings 1954* (Elsberry, MO: The Liturgical Conference, 1955), 56–72, here at 56.

56. Additional biographical information about this well-versed writer and lecturer continues to be sought by the author of this chapter. Some valuable details about McLoughlin's life appear in *My Nameday: Come for Dessert* (Collegeville: Liturgical Press, 1962), in which she discusses her neighborhood and parish (Our Lady of the Scapular of Mount Carmel in Manhattan, New York City).

57. Fruits were associated with Assumption day due to the practice of gathering garden produce, herbs, and/or flowers to bring to church for a blessing.

58. A complete list of sources for publishers, artisans, and institutes referenced in the volume is given on McLoughlin, *My Nameday*, 7–9.

59. McLoughlin, *My Nameday*, 88.

60. McLoughlin, *My Nameday*, 89–90.

61. McLoughlin, *My Nameday*, 41.

62. McLoughlin, *My Nameday*, 42.

63. For more on Mary Perkins Ryan, see Harmon, *There Were Also Many Women There*, 272–300.

64. Mary Perkins Ryan, "Liturgical Piety for American Catholics?" in *Liturgy for the People: Essays in Honor of Gerald Ellard, S.J. 1894–1963*, ed. William J. Leonard (Milwaukee: The Bruce Publishing Co., 1963), 215–243, here at 217–218.

65. Ryan, "Liturgical Piety for American Catholics," 218.

66. Ryan, "Liturgical Piety for American Catholics," 217–218.

67. Mary Perkins Ryan, *Beginning at Home*, Popular Liturgical Library, ser., (Collegeville: Liturgical Press, 1955), front matter.

68. Ryan, *Beginning at Home*, 28–29.

69. Ryan, *Beginning at Home*, 9.

70. Ryan, *Beginning at Home*, 65.

71. "The Woman Intellectual and the Church: A Commonweal Symposium," *Commonweal* 85 (1967): 446–56, here at 448. Cited in Henold, *Catholic and Feminist*, 51.

72. Paula M. Kane addresses the decline in Marian devotions in "Marian Devotion Since 1940," 89–129.

See also John C. Cavadini and Danielle M. Peters, eds., *Mary on the Eve of the Second Vatican Council* (Notre Dame: University of Notre Dame Press, 2017).

73. Second Vatican Council, Sacrosanctum Concilium [Constitution on the Sacred Liturgy], Vatican Website, https://www.vatican.va/archive/hist_councils/ii_vatican_council/documents/vat-ii_const_19631204_sacrosanctum-concilium_en.html, December 4, 1963, sec. 13.

74. Bethune, "On the Blessed Virgin," 298.

75. Henold, *Catholic and Feminist*, 51–52.

The Catholic Novel

Book Reviews in Katherine Burton's 'Woman to Woman' Columns, 1933–1942

ANNIE HUEY

Katherine Kurz Burton (1887–1969) converted to Roman Catholicism on September 8, 1930, and soon became one of the most prolific Catholic writers of her time. She was recognized both for her monthly column "Woman to Woman" in *The Sign* magazine, and her forty-five biographies of modern Catholic men, women, and religious orders. Though the quantity of her work is quite impressive, the quality made her a household name. Her "Woman to Woman" column, which she wrote for thirty-six years, was the third or fourth most popular column in *The Sign*, and by 1964, *The Sign* itself had become the fourth most popular Catholic magazine in the country.[1] Her biographies were regularly reviewed in reputable periodicals like *America*, *Commonweal*, *Catholic World*, and the *New York Times*. She had books chosen for the "Catholic Book of the Month,"[2] for book clubs' selections,[3] and recommended reading and must-have Christmas lists.[4]

It may seem strange that such a well-known Catholic laywoman writer has essentially vanished from recent scholarship of mid-twentieth century US Catholicism. However, this disappearance is not altogether surprising. The daily faith life of Catholic laywomen is a topic that scholars have only recently begun to unearth, and Burton, though once a well-known figure, is a challenging one to unearth since she did not belong to a community still in existence today. She was not a vowed religious or a member of a social community such as the Catholic Worker, which meant her papers were not kept, and her story was not passed down. Burton has also remained forgotten because she truly was a woman who wrote about and for her time. Her columns included her opinions about current events, books, movies, fashion, child-rearing techniques, and cooking fads. Her columns are fascinating insights into her world, but many of today's Catholics would not find her writing relevant to their own lives. Her biographies, though reviewed in well-established periodicals, were written in a particular style[5] that often did not meet academic requirements for historians of her (or the present) day. This style was appreciated by many of her readers and reviewers because it made the stories of the holy figures more "interesting," but some of her reviewers were dismayed that, even though Burton clearly utilized primary sources to write her biographies, she never included footnotes and rarely included a bibliography.[6] The subjects of Burton's biographies are still being researched and written about today (Isaac Hecker, Elizabeth Seton, Pope Pius XII, Katherine Drexel, to name a few), but modern historians rarely cite Burton's biographies because she didn't follow scholarly conventions.

Burton has not entirely disappeared, however. Basic biographical information can still be found in compilations of Catholic Women writers, Catholic converts, and Catholic women, but these entries just skim the surface.[7] A more complete recovery of Katherine Burton is significant to the study of US Catholicism because she presented the Catholic[8] faith as a woman to other women, especially in her monthly column. The fact that her writing career existed for several decades at a time of enormous changes in women's lives and in Catholic life makes her a unique and invaluable resource

A more extensive study is needed to explore how Burton's interpretation of Catholicism shifted in the four decades of her writing, but this particular essay starts at the beginning. At the beginning and the end, Burton was a writer. Her close friend, Catholic journalist, pacifist, and active member of Catholic Relief Services Eileen Egan said of Burton, "She was a writer, not just a woman writer, it was the warp and woof of her life. She had a typewriter in her dining room and went to work."[9] Though her passion for writing and her belief in its importance began pre-conversion and lasted until she died in 1969, this essay examines the period of 1933–1942 because this was when much of her life and work focused on the very topic of literature and its importance. During this period, Burton was regularly invited to give speeches about various literary topics for secular and Catholic groups, and she wrote extensively about literature in her "Woman to Woman" column and other articles. Though her speeches tended to revolve around writing techniques and tips,[10] her "Woman to Woman" column, and especially in the book reviews included in this column, strongly argued that literature was powerful and transformative and that Catholicism must utilize it as a tool to spread Catholic principles and values to the entire world. This argument for the importance of literature was not unique to Burton and, instead, places her within a larger community of Catholics who were part of the mid-twentieth century Catholic Literary Revival.

Burton believed, along with many Catholic lay intellectuals of her time, that lay Catholics had a responsibility to spread the universal and timeless message of Catholicism and speak of its ability to moor the untethered and disillusioned world recently torn asunder by depression, war, materialism, modernism, and Communism.[11] They believed "in the existence of a moral law built into the nature of the universe by God" that was stabilizing and "available to 'all people of good will.'"[12] Since Catholics already knew these laws, they "had an obligation to collaborate with their fellow citizens in protecting the moral good" by disseminating Catholic teaching. One particularly effective means to disseminate this message was through literature.

Catholic print culture grew at an unprecedented rate during the mid-twentieth century. The literacy rate among Catholics increased, leading to an increase in Catholic periodicals, publishing houses, and bookstores. This Catholic Literary Revival encouraged authors to take their role as "lyricists of Christ"[13] seriously and make it their mission to write Catholic stories that would show the Truth of Catholicism and entice those outside the Church to join the "True Fold."[14]

The Gallery of Living Catholic Authors were key facilitators of the Catholic Literary Revival. The Gallery of Living Catholic Authors was founded in 1932 by Sister Mary Joseph, of the Sisters of Loretto at the Foot of the Cross, as "an effective, constructive and intelligent instrument for the promotion of the greatest of the lay apostolates-The Apostolate of Catholic Letters."[15] In her 1942 speech given at the 10th anniversary celebration of the Gallery, Sister Mary Joseph praised the authors for "brilliantly refuting the atheistic, communistic and materialistic arguments of a sin-seared world" and called the authors "powerful penmen mirroring morality." She compared the work of modern Catholic authors to that of the apostles at Pentecost who were asked to "spread[. . .] the spirit of Christ throughout the world" and "fearlessly proclaim[. . .] the words of Christ in a pagan-threatened world." For Sr. Mary Joseph, as well as for those involved in the Catholic Literary Revival more generally, "Catholic literature [was] truly the handmaid of the Church."

Sr. Mary Joseph was not the only speaker at this anniversary celebration; other speakers included famous names such as Francis X. Talbot, S.J.,

Peter Guilday, James M. Gillis, C.S.P., Padraic Colum, Jacques Maritain, Sigrid Undset, and Katherine Burton. By 1942, Burton found herself at the center of the Catholic literary circle, an achievement she took very seriously, and she expected other authors to do the same. If other authors fell short, she was not afraid to call them out in the book reviews often included in her monthly "Woman to Woman" column.

An examination of her book reviews not only reveals a list of books that Burton encouraged her readers to read, or not to read, but it also reveals the Catholicism that Burton disseminated to her readers. For Burton, "good" books were "Catholic" books[16] which did not necessarily mean they were written by a Catholic author or about Catholic people, but instead that they were imbued with Catholic teachings and principles and the inevitable consequences when those teachings and principles were rejected.[17] Before examining her book reviews, let us first learn a bit more about this Burton herself, and to understand why a strict adherence to Catholic teachings was vital to her.

Brief Biographical Sketch

Katherine George Kurz Burton was born in Cleveland, Ohio, on March 12, 1887, to Jacob and Louise Buttner Kurz. Throughout her life, Burton was an avid reader and writer. In her youth, this love of literature led to her being placed on a "literary diet" by her parents and the librarian, who all thought she was spending too much time reading.[18] In her senior year high school yearbook, Burton is listed as a member of the editorial board for the yearbook, the class president, and the poet for the senior class. The yearbook also includes several poems and other writing samples of hers (significantly more than her peers). Her quote in this yearbook is also quite revealing: "Heavens! Was I born for nothing but to write?"[19] During her years at the College for Women of Western Reserve University, Burton was the class historian and, in her graduating year of 1909, won the Holden Prize for the best English essay written by a senior or junior. It is no surprise then that when Burton did decide to marry, she married a fellow literary enthusiast, Cleveland journalist Harry Burton. In 1910, the two married and, depending on the location of Harry's job, became part of the literary circles in New York, Cleveland, and Chicago. In 1921, Harry became editor of *McCall's*, and the couple, with their three young children,

FIGURE 6: Katherine Burton image from the book jacket of *The Golden Door: The Life of Katharine Drexel*, (New York: P.J. Kenedy & Sons, 1957).

moved to the posh neighborhood of Garden City, NY, where they owned a large house, a swimming pool, a tennis court, a horse, and a pony.[20] Throughout this time, Burton continued to write verse and to assist Harry in some of his work as a journalist and editor, even playing a role in the selection of serialized fiction for *McCall's*.

Though Burton glowingly remembered their time in Garden City and continually complimented Harry for being a terrific editor,[21] there were already undercurrents of distress within the Burton family. From the time Katherine met Harry, she knew that Harry was often sickly and constantly seeking a remedy for his racing thoughts and his troublesome digestion. Harry's mental anxiety continued, and by 1926, he had moved out of the family's house in Garden City and into an apartment in New York City to evade his most prevalent stressors.[22]

In writing about this troubling time, Katherine claimed it "was an unhappy and uneasy life" which "ended in the complete collapse of our home."[23] One evening, Katherine took a walk and passed a Roman Catholic church and felt pulled to enter even though she had been apathetic toward religion for most of her life.[24] Following those around her, she knelt and became "aware of a new sensation." "For weeks and weeks," Burton wrote, "I had had the feeling of falling, and falling nowhere. Now, of a sudden, something seemed to be holding me up [. . .] Somehow I had been caught and lifted high above my own pain and loss. They were still there, still heartbreakingly real, but the sense of being alone with them was gone."[25] Though it was a Roman Catholic church that first gave her this sense of connection and security, Burton chose to become a member of an Anglo-Catholic church due to the friendships she already had with members of this denomination and her belief that Anglicanism could be the uniting force between Protestants and Roman Catholics.[26]

When his move to the city did not ease Harry's problems, it was decided that he, Katherine, and their eldest son should take a trip to Europe so that Harry could see Dr. Rank, a famous psychoanalyst in Paris. Katherine stayed with Harry in Paris until Dr. Rank suggested that she take a break and tour around Europe for a while. After returning from her travels, Katherine knew that she was no longer of any use to Harry, so she and her son returned home to a life in complete disarray. Since Harry was no longer employed, Katherine had to sell their house in Garden City, send their two older kids to boarding schools, send their five-year-old to her in-laws in Cleveland, and seek employment to support her family and eventually bring them back home together. Due to her connections with the magazine, in late 1927 Burton procured an assistant editor position at *McCall's* and rented a small apartment in New York City. In late 1928, she happily brought all her kids back home to an apartment she rented in Bronxville, New York, a small village outside of the city known for its high population of women authors and poets.[27] During the 1930s, Burton was actively involved in the Bronxville Women's Club, especially its Literary

Department, and was often asked to give talks on various literary topics and to judge the club's annual literary contest.[28]

In 1930, Burton became assistant editor of *Redbook* and managed its literary organ, *Spirit*. This same year, Burton decided to leave her Anglo-Catholic church and convert to Roman Catholicism. This was not the abrupt departure that it may seem to be, for her particular Anglo-Catholic parish was extremely High Church, and she had fallen in love with the benediction, the altar light denoting the Real Presence, and many other ritualistic elements of their liturgical celebrations. The sticking point for Burton was deciphering which of these Churches (Anglican or Roman Catholic) was the primitive Church. She had found solace in the beliefs of the apostolic succession and the continuity of the doctrines and had been taught that those beliefs originated in the Anglican Church. With sustained reading and discussions on these topics with both Anglicans and Roman Catholics, Burton gradually came to see the Roman Catholic Church as the only tradition able to draw a clear line from its present leaders back to Jesus Christ. After realizing this, it was not long before Burton was baptized at Our Lady of Lourdes Roman Catholic Church in New York City. Even at her baptism, Burton had her hesitations and was worried that she was making a mistake. During these doubts, Burton's baptismal sponsor pointed to a statue of Jesus with his arms outstretched, and "from that moment on," Burton recalled, "I knew no doubts. After all, if one is born in a certain house and there are witnesses to attest the matter, there can be no doubts about one's birthplace. And so with me, for in that Home [sic] I was born."[29]

After her conversion, Burton continued writing in secular magazines and began writing in Catholic periodicals such as *Commonweal, Catholic World, America*, and *The Sign*. In 1933, Burton was approached by Father Harold Purcell and asked if she would like to write a monthly column entitled "Woman to Woman" for the Passionists' periodical, *The Sign*. Like most Catholic journalism of the time, *The Sign* aimed to be "informative for the ordinary Catholic and informative not only in the religious sphere but also in the sphere of current events."[30] Purcell wanted Burton to write her column to *The Sign*'s middle-class female readers and convey a Catholic perspective on various modern issues. And for the thirty-six years that her column ran, Burton did just that. She chose to discuss topics such as the rhythm method, the need for women in politics and the church, charitable organizations, current events, modern educational theories, child-rearing methods, prayers for peace, books, and occasional recipes. Her later columns of the 1950s–1960s, often focused on one event or issue, but in her earlier columns, Burton addressed several topics each month. For each topic, Burton provided her readers with a bit of background information and concluded with her own opinion. Burton was given independence by *The Sign*, and because she was a "prudent person with her topics," the editors always approved her columns. That is not to say that her columns were without controversy, for Burton often mentioned and responded to critical letters she received from her readers.

By 1933, Harry was appointed editor of *Cosmopolitan* and regularly sent Burton money, allowing her to quit her job at *Redbook* and become a freelance writer. Burton continued contributing to Catholic periodicals and began her most lucrative writing enterprise, writing Catholic biographies. During her conversion to Roman Catholicism, Burton desired to read biographies of modern Catholic converts but was dismayed by the lack of "good" biographies of Catholic converts. According to Burton, those that did exist were "encumbered with pious utterances," and the subject's "spiritual struggles were minimized."[31] For Burton, biographies about converts needed to include the real and sometimes difficult struggles that converts faced on their journey to the faith. Unlike the biographies that Burton read during her conversion, compelling biographies needed to connect with the modern reader to the point where the reader could see themselves in the subject's journey.[32] From 1937 to 1969, Burton published forty-five biographies of individuals and religious orders. Though her reviewers sometimes bemoaned a lack of scholarly conventions in her biographies (i.e., no footnotes, indexes, and completed bibliographies), most praised her biographies for creating truthful depictions of her subjects and assisting converts along their own journeys into the Church.[33]

But what of Harry and the Burton household? In her autobiography, Burton mentions Harry only briefly after she leaves him in Europe with Dr. Rank. After their first year living in Bronxville, Katherine and the kids took a trip to Connecticut, where they "ran into Harry one day."[34] Based on this phraseology and family letters from this time, there seems to have been little if any contact between Harry and the family up to that point.[35] Following that meeting, Harry became a more present figure in the family's life, but Burton makes it clear that she was glad for his visits, letters, and phone calls for the *children* "for they had always been devoted to him, and he to them." In the few correspondences that still exist between Katherine and Harry, it appears that Katherine reached out to him if she or the children needed money, if he had done something to upset the children, or if his health was particularly concerning to her.[36] Though Harry and Katherine remained legally married until his death by suicide in 1952, the couple lived separate lives; she with the children in Bronxville and he on a farm in Connecticut. The topic of divorce was discussed, but Katherine was always against the idea.[37] Though she never explicitly stated why she didn't want to get divorced, examining her book reviews provides insight into some possible reasons.

Book Reviews

Burton reviewed more than fifty books in her "Woman to Woman" column from 1933–1942. Compared to the rest of her writing career, she wrote significantly more reviews and was more engaged in larger conversations about literature during this period. Most of the books Burton reviewed were written by women, and Catholics wrote about half of them. Burton chose to review these particular books for many reasons; some were very popular, some were sent to her by friends/readers, some made her joyous, and others made her furious. She did not stick to any set format in her reviews, and rarely gave a complete synopsis of the book. Her reviews were relatively short (often just one topic in a multi-topic column), merely focusing on the element or two that distinguished it as or prevented it from being a Catholic book. Her reviews not only provided her readers with a list of quality Catholic books, but they also revealed a popular interpretation of Catholic teachings and principles of the time. By exploring Burton's reviews today, particularly noting whom she says can write Catholic books, the purpose of these books, and their content, modern scholars are given a glimpse into how Catholicism was being presented by a Catholic woman for her large Catholic women readership.

Authors of Catholic Books

According to Burton, for a book to be Catholic, it did not need to be written by a practicing Catholic. Burton purposely made a point of recognizing

Catholic books written by non-Catholic writers. She praised Margery Sharp's *The Flowering Thorn* saying, "here is a really good book, an excellent story, carrying the ethics of the Church even though there is no obvious religious element in it. Its moral is inserted with great deftness and it has realism of the right sort."[38] Similarly, Burton spoke highly of Elizabeth Cambridge's *The Sycamore Tree*; "in these days of cheap writing and definite scouring of moral values, here is a book which points out the true values of life, shows how to keep them and use them, and does it so entertainingly that it is an excellent volume to put into the hands of our younger folks who are filling up on dreadful trash."[39] Burton emphasized in these two reviews that a good book needed to promote specific moral values and principles. However, she also highlighted that writing such a book was possible without being religious and, more specifically, without being Catholic.

It was crucial for Burton to make this claim because she believed that "many, both in the Church and outside, have very limiting notions as to just what a Catholic novel [. . .] is."[40] For Burton, the arts (especially literature) could be "a very effective instrument for the Faith." The arts must present Catholicism, not in the narrow sense of its exterior trappings (i.e., stories only about priests, nuns, Catholic schools, and parishes), but present it as the ancient and intact Faith comprised of universal values and principles. By praising Catholic works of art created by non-Catholics, Burton desired to "show how much of the morality—nay, all of it—of the Western world is built on this Catholic basis" and accessible and salvific for all people.

The Book's Purpose

Burton disapproved of late nineteenth and early twentieth century modernist literature, which emphasized nihilism, irrationality, and a break with the traditional.[41] She regularly scoffed at the idea of "art for art's sake" and criticized stories written with characters that remained sinful from start to finish.[42] Burton reviewed Edna Ferber's short story "Keep It Holy," which tells of a small-town young woman who moves to New York City. The young woman fills her Sundays with trips to the Battery, the Aquarium, the Metropolitan Museum, and restaurants but remains lonely and unhappy. Burton thought this was an unrealistic story because if the heroine was as intelligent as Ferber writes her, the young woman would find plenty of places for good conversation (hospitals and Welfare Island, to name a few). Burton knew, though, that the woman visiting these other locations would lead to a more satisfying conclusion to Ferber's story, and a happy ending "is not allowed in this modern analytical writing." Art may never be "for life's sake, and never, by any possible chance, art for God's sake."[43]

Reviewers who dismissed books for being too moralistic angered Burton because she believed literature should have a purpose: bringing readers closer to God. That did not mean that the books should be dripping with pious utterings, but rather that the stories be led by values and principles, even specifically religious ones. When writing about Catholic Press Month, Burton argued that just as an apple a day can keep the doctor away, "then a Catholic book a month and a Catholic magazine and paper once a month or once a week can do the same by the devil [. . .]If we could only put across Catholic books and periodicals so well that Catholics would be thoroughly imbued with their teaching, then surely the philosophy and truth in them would begin to spill over to Protestants and pagans of our land as well."[44] For Burton, Catholic writers had the responsibility to "translate principles of [the] Faith into a literature that [would] be accepted by non-Catholics as well as Catholics"[45] and there was plenty of room "in the magazine field for articles written by those who have faith and who do not write merely for art's sake."[46]

Though it was not mandatory for her, Burton believed that Catholic books could have a strong Catholic presence and was annoyed when other reviewers made disparaging remarks about this characteristic. In her May 1935 column, Burton discussed several novels that had a "Catholic background and foreground," which were also all written by women. "Now, as long as one writes of Catholic backgrounds," Burton wrote, "all is well with the secular book reviewers. But as soon as you bring Catholicism up to date and show it as a working force in a modern world the book critics get annoyed."[47] Though Burton herself was judgmental of books that were overly pious and sweet, comparing them to opiates and soothing syrups that lulled readers to sleep,[48] realistic religion could be a present force in good Catholic books.[49] For example, Eleanor Chilton's *Follow the Furies* tells "the story of what happens to the children of a man who marries a Catholic, deliberately undermines her faith, and brings up his children in the belief there is no God."[50] The mother eventually returns to her faith, but her children are left to live untethered and unhappy lives. Burton thought that this was "a brave, true book, with no palliation, no pleasant ending because there could be none." Other reviewers were not as moved by this story. Secular reviewers thought that it was a beautiful and well-written plot, however, they did not know what to do with the ending, which "shows clearly that the greatest loss of the people in the story is their lack of religion." Religious reviewers were disturbed by the sinfulness and the late, or absent, reconciliation in the story, but Burton praised this book as "a straightforward examination into the troubled minds of many of our young people."

The Content of a Catholic Book

As noted above, a Catholic book did not need to have specific Catholic content; however, it always had to be "in conformity with the Ten Commandments," and not "make fun of the facts of the Faith or seek to undermine them."[51] For example, Burton did not like the book *Holy Ireland* by Nora Hoult even though there were priests and nuns and the Catholic characters were often praying. Burton observed that "the author never miss[ed] a chance to let you know how childish all this sort of thing [was]," driving home its central message that "Catholicism makes everybody mean or stupid."[52] Similarly, Burton also disparaged Pearl Buck's 1942 story about a missionary priest, writing that "the language used in this story, show[s] utter ignorance of Catholic phraseology."[53]For Burton, the characters and the story itself were unrealistic because of Buck's known "distaste for priests and for spirituality" and her unfamiliarity with the topic. According to Burton, erroneous information about Catholicism, such as was present in these books, would not assist in the proclamation of the faith but, instead, might lead readers down false paths.

The stories and characters then must be realistic in Catholic books. Creating realistic characters meant more than including prosaic details and quirks; it meant depicting flaws and struggles. Quoting a letter from her friend and mentor, Selden Delaney, Burton wrote, "writers and artists who tell us of this world cannot be expected to give us always what is pious and pleasant. They must often paint a picture that is revolting, stark, cruel, and diabolical. The true artist is one who gives it to us in all its hideous reality—vile, dreadful, hopeless."[54] For Catholics, "belief in creation and incarnation mean[t] that all created reality and all human experience potentially revealed the presence of God," even "things distinct from Catholic doctrine and practice,"[55] and therefore, all reality could and should be included in Catholic stories. As such, most Catholic reviewers agreed that authors should create realistic depictions of the human experience, however, there was quite a bit of divergence on what that looked like in practice.[56] How real was too real?

In her reviews, Burton enthusiastically praised authors who brought their characters to life. Though Burton had qualms about some of Kathleen Norris's books, Burton was quick to praise Norris' "uncanny gift for making her people real . . . three dimensional and true."[57] Burton also commended Sigrid Undset's ability to make people "come to life on her pages"[58] even though some religious reviewers critiqued Undset and shouted "naturalism" at her inclusion of "vice and its transient loveliness."[59] Burton, however, was not dismayed by the presence of sin in Undset's writing because Burton believed that "sin is often beautiful. Its guises are as fair as sunshine. Why deny it? Its results are usually hideous. Together they show life."[60] This is a critical differentiating point between Modernist and Catholic writing for Burton; though they both claimed realism as their foundation, the former showed sin for sin's sake, the latter showed sin for God's sake. As long as the characters faced consequences for their sinful behaviors, Burton praised stories that other Catholic reviewers critiqued as being too immoral.

This presence of the cycle of sin and redemption was an essential Catholic principle for Burton, and, for Burton, Undset was a master at it. "Here is a writer," Burton stated, "who is making at least a fair bid for eternity, who states truthfully the vice and its transient loveliness, but who always rounds out her story with its inevitable result of misery as the consequence of a fall."[61] Those reviewers who disparaged the attractive sin in Undset's stories did not see how sin was just part of the story, a genuine part, but just the beginning. Moreover, they did not see how including a fall was "an excellent way of learning and being warned." For example, Burton praised Undset's *Images in a Mirror* even though some Catholic reviewers were "taciturn, grumpy, or at most faintly polite" about it. Burton saw Undset's book as a parable or homily about a young woman with a husband and four small children at home who had grown dissatisfied with life. Her husband sent her out to a mountain resort for some relaxation, and there she ran into an old fling who gave her much attention. The woman and this man spent a lot of time together at the resort and, finding that their homes were also near one another, continued meeting after their vacations. A few months later, "her thoughts clear, she sees how silly she has been and the story, after giving a dramatic scene between husband and wife, with a complete reconciliation, ends with her tucking her baby in bed."[62] According to Burton, there was not a true love affair between the man and woman, only an infatuation and, as such, not a complete "fall" (like "the story of Eden"), only a mental one. But the elements, i.e., "the great cycle of innocence and sin and repentance and punishment,"[63] were present, making it a "very good tale."[64]

Just as Burton praised books based on this "great cycle," she harshly criticized those that lacked it, especially Daphne du Maurier's best-seller *Rebecca*. Burton admitted that it was a beautifully written book, "poetical at times," but she was appalled by its bad ethics.[65] The story is of a man who killed his first wife because she was unbearable and pregnant with another man's child. The murder itself was not the issue for Burton; it was the lack of remorse of the murderer. There was no sense of reparation for breaking this Commandment. When it was revealed that he was the murderer, he and the rest of the characters maintained a "served the woman right" attitude. Though some of her readers agreed with Burton's critique of *Rebecca*, many others wrote to Burton, disagreeing with her analysis and pointing to the fact that the novel was on "a Catholic white list."[66] Burton responded to these letters with dismay, saying that "such a book should bring a storm of protest for it is the most dangerous kind of all" for it was "a charming personal setting in novel form, contradicting basic tenets of Christian doctrine."[67]

Burton's readers continued to write about *Rebecca*, both in agreement and disagreement with Burton. Those who disagreed with Burton's analysis of the novel pointed to the Cardinal Hayes Literature Committee's so-called White List, which stated that *Rebecca* was a "very presentable novel—well written and at times rather spooky."[68] Burton remained stalwart in her convictions and instead believed that the committee "should put a little paragraph in their next bulletin and do a nice little *mea culpa*."[69] This Catholic approval of *Rebecca* was not a minor concern for Burton; instead, it pointed to a much larger issue, "an appalling misunderstanding or lack of teaching of Catholic doctrine." "Catholic ethics goes like this," writes Burton, "you do wrong, you repent, you make reparation. Of this triangle, the hero of the book carried out only one angle: he did wrong."[70] After several months of debates, Burton refused to continue this discussion with her readers unless a priest joined in and proclaimed the book ethical. Since this did not happen, the matter was mainly laid to rest.[71]

Just as breaking the divine commandment and killing without reparation makes for a non-Catholic book, so does breaking Church teaching about marriage and divorce. During the mid-twentieth century, "public support was growing for legalizing divorce and contraception" and "these changing standards provoked a new level of literary debate in which the moral criterion was central."[72] For Burton, the main culprit of this crime was famed Catholic novelist Kathleen Norris. Burton was not always a critic of Norris and, in fact, loved her earlier novels *Mother* and *Little Ships* because of their lifelike characters and adherence to Catholic values.[73] However, from the mid-1930s to the early 1940s, Burton wrote harsh reviews of three of Norris' stories that positively portrayed divorce and remarriage. Burton accepted that stories of divorce and remarriage were trendy and sold well but was angered that Norris, a Catholic who knew Church teaching, was not utilizing her popularity to "enlighten the women of America on the beautiful doctrines of our Faith."[74] In all three of these stories, the female protagonists were divorced, and remarriage either occurred or was mentioned as a future possibility.[75] One of these stories is titled *You Can't Have Everything*, and the plot centers on a man and woman who marry and have children, divorce, remarry, and have more children with their new spouses. Burton did not understand this title since "according to the worldly hearts of her characters, they do get everything in the world—everything, that is, except those tiresome Christian commandments that Mrs. Norris drops lightly overboard when her craft needs lightening."[76] Burton truly could not comprehend how Norris could "reconcile her conscience" to these sorts of plots, especially since Norris had previously written about the sanctity of marriage[77] as well as more ethical stories where a death or invalid marriage provided a clear path for a lovers' betrothal.[78] Burton then likened Norris to Judas Iscariot, saying that just as he betrayed Jesus for a handful of silver, Norris betrayed her faith for "a handful of huge checks."[79]

Burton received many letters from readers regarding her judgment of Norris. Some of her readers agreed with Burton, hoping that "God will forgive [Norris] for the mischief she has done,"[80] and others thought that Burton must be "ignorant or jealous."[81] Burton did not budge on her condemnation of Norris, but hoped that Norris would use her knowledge of the faith and her authorial gifts to once again place "Catholic ideals and principles before the general reading public."[82] Just as in *Rebecca*, it was not the presence of the sin or even the attractiveness of the sin which prevented Norris from being a good Catholic author; it was that there was no acknowledgment of or reconciliation for the sin.[83]

Conclusion

The book reviews in Burton's "Woman to Woman" column provide a glimpse into how Burton, and many of those involved in the Catholic Literary Revival, interpreted Catholicism for their readers. The many letters she received from her readers point to the diversity and complexity within the Catholic Church and the presence of active lay engagement in theological discussions defining Catholicism. Though there were divergent opinions on the topic, many of her readers still agreed with Burton, revealing a widespread understanding of Catholic books and Catholicism more generally. Like the Catholic faith, a Catholic book was not solely for or about Roman Catholics; it was for and, therefore, should be about everyone. Catholicism did not exist in a separate realm but was on Earth and found among the muck and strife of everyday life. Furthermore, Catholic books, which had the practical purpose of assisting readers through everyday life, must include mundane details and hardships to be helpful guides.

Catholic books, like Catholicism itself, must also be based on the central cycle of sin and reparation. There are fundamental laws that govern the world, and there are consequences when those laws are broken. In literature, Catholic writers who are devoted "to fundamental and eternal fact and truths" feel called to depict these laws.[84] Burton and those involved in the Catholic Literary Revival believed that adhering to Catholic doctrine provided a sense of stability in the unmoored and fragmented mid-twentieth century.

On a more personal level, these eternal and absolute Laws provided Burton a lifeline when she felt untethered after Harry departed from the family.[85] The life she had known had ended. Her husband was sick and gone; she sent her children away from her; she worked a full-time job as an associate editor; her extended family lived in Cleveland; and she sold her house and many belongings to start anew. Catholicism not only grounded her, but it also saved her and gave her a new life.[86] Burton then felt called, not only because of her faith but also because of her personal experiences, to share Catholicism with her readers, hoping that it may bring life to someone drowning in the modern, broken world. And it is no surprise that the Catholic teaching about divorce and remarriage was of particular interest to Burton. Not only was the topic trendy in stories, but it was also a choice that Burton faced and refuted, despite Harry and other family members at times pushing for a divorce.[87] If the Church that had saved her condemned it, then Burton condemned it as well, despite the broken marriage it left her.[88] In the end, she felt it was her duty and gift to live and spread the message: "How vast and free is the world for him who is obedient to the law of the Church which was our Lord's gift to his people."[89]

Notes

1. Claire Foy, "Unnamed Interview," interview by Robert E. Carbonneau, March 13, 1987, Cliffside Park, NJ. This interview was included in Carbonneau's unpublished article on Katherine Burton, which he sent to the author. Claire Foy was a staff member at *The Sign* from 1934 to 1981.

2. "Literary Department Program Presented," *Bronxville Review-Press* (October 28, 1937): 2; "100 Books Placed on Cardinal Hayes Literature Committee," *New York Times* (June 22, 1940); "Cardinal Hayes Literature Committee's Book Recommendations," *New York Times* (October 10, 1942).

3. "Reading Circle of Literary Department of Bronxville Women's Club," *Bronxville Press* (April 2, 1939); Daniel M O'Connell, SJ, review of *In No Strange Land*, by Katherine Burton, *America* (June 6, 1942).

4. "Christmas Check List" Longmans, Green & Co ad, *America* (November 26, 1938); "A Memo for Your Christmas Buying: Noted Books from Longmans, Green & Co." *America* (December 2, 1939); "Holy Lives for Lenten Reading," Longmans, Green & Co. *America* (March 1, 1941); "Longmans Books for Your Easter Book Buying," *America* (March 21, 1942); "For Christmas: Longmans, Green &Co." *America* (November 28, 1942).

5. Annie Huey, "'Be Interesting but Tell the Truth at All Times': Katherine Burton's Fictional-Narrative Approach to Biographical Writing," *American Catholic Studies* 131, no. 1 (Spring 2020): 57–78.

6. John A. Lyons, review of *No Shadow of Turning: The Life of James Kent Stone*, by Katherine Burton, *Catholic Historical Review* 31 (April 1945): 92–93; Vincent F. Holden, review of *Celestial Homespun* by Katherine Burton, *Catholic Historical Review* 29 (October 1943): 372–373.

7. Robert Carbonneau, "'Woman to Woman': Katherine Kurz Burton and the Quest for a Feminine Catholic Identity in *Sign* Magazine (1933–1969)," *The Passionist* 27 (1994): 49–69; "Rebecca L. Kroeger, "Katherine Burton," in *Catholic Women Writers: A Bio-Bibliographical Sourcebook*, ed. Mary R. Reichardt (Westport, CT: Greenwood Press, 2001), 20–22; Arlene Anderson Swidler, "Katherine Kurz Burton," in *American Women Writers: A Critical Reference Guide from Colonial Times to the Present*, ed. Lina Mainiero, vol. 1 (New York: Frederick Ungar Publishing Co., 1979), 279–281.

8. I am not suggesting a monolithic interpretation of Catholicism. Since Burton was a popular writer, her interpretation of Catholicism would have been disseminated to her readers and therefore would have influenced a large population.

9. Eileen Egan, "Unnamed Interview," interview by Robert E. Carbonneau, March 13, 1987, New York City. This interview was included in Carbonneau's unpublished article on Katherine Burton, which he sent to the author.

10. "Freelance Questions Answered from the Editor's and Publisher's Point of View," "Assembling a Book," "Increasing Demand for Satire and Realism in Propaganda Stories," "Plenty of Room in Magazine World for Those Who Have Faith," "Columnist's Scope," "How Judges Judge," "Writing of the Article," "The Power of Good Literature in Individual and National Life," Topics of Talks taken from the *Bronxville Press* and *Bronxville Review Press*, 1933–1942.

11. Una M. Cadegan, *All Good Books Are Catholic Books: Print Culture, Censorship and Modernity in Twentieth-Century America* (Ithaca, NY: Cornell University Press, 2013), 14; Arnold Sparr, *To Promote, Defend and Redeem: The Catholic Literary Revival and the Cultural Transformation of American Catholicism, 1920–1960* (Westport, CT: Greenwood Press, 1990), 113.

12. Cadegan, *All Good Books*, 31–32.

13. Sr. Mary Joseph, S.L. "Speech at 10th Anniversary of Gallery of Living Catholic Authors," May 24, 1942 Gallery of Living Catholic Authors, Box 73, Folder 15, Georgetown Archives, Washington, DC.

14. Neil Boyton, "Review of *No Shadow of Turning*," *America* 72, no. 12 (Dec 23, 1944): 237. In reviewing one of Burton's biographies, Boyton argues that this biography will lead others into the "True Fold."

15. Sr. Mary Joseph, S.L. "Speech at 10th Anniversary of Gallery of Living Catholic Authors," in *To Promote, Defend, and Redeem*, 41.

16. Cadegan, *All Good Books*.

17. Katherine Burton, "Woman to Woman," *The Sign* (July 1934); "Woman to Woman," June 1936; "Woman to Woman," October 1941.

18. Katherine Burton, *The Next Thing: Autobiography & Reminiscences* (New York: Longmans, Green and Co., 1949), 15–16.

19. Lakewood High School, *The High School Annual*. Lakewood, OH: 1904. Elizabeth Burton Kelly Collection.

20. Burton, *The Next Thing*, 89.

21. Burton, *The Next Thing*, 80–81.

22. Burton, *The Next Thing*, 96.

23. Burton, *The Next Thing*, 96.

24. Burton, *The Next Thing*, 64.

25. Burton, *The Next Thing*, 98.

26. Burton, *The Next Thing*, 93.

27. Eloise L. Morgan, editor. *Building a Suburban Village: Bronxville, New York, 1898–1998*. (Bronxville, NY: Bronxville Centennial Celebration, Inc., 1998), 24–28.

28. Issues of *Bronxville Press* and *Bronxville Review-Press* (1933–1942).

29. Burton, *The Next Thing*, 142.

30. Claire Foy, Interview with Robert Carbonneau.

31. Burton, *The Next Thing*, 192–193.

32. Huey, "Be Interesting," 70–71.

33. Theodore Roemer, "Review of *In No Strange Land: Some American Catholic Converts*," *Catholic Historical Review* 28, no. 2 (July 1942): 251–252.

34. Burton, *The Next Thing*, 115.

35. Minnie Burton to Harry Burton, December 18, 1928, Elizabeth Burton Kelly collection.

36. Letters from Katherine Burton to Harry Burton, c. Spring 1937; Spring 1938; February 27, 1939; Spring 1942; Elizabeth Burton Kelly collection.

37. Letter from Wed Burton to Harry Burton, July 7, 1942, and Letter from Katherine Burton to Beatrice Morgan, c. 1932, Elizabeth Burton Kelly collection.

38. "Woman to Woman," July 34.

39. "Woman to Woman," Aug 34.

40. Katherine Burton, "What is Catholic Theatre," *Ave Maria*, Feb 1938.

41. Burton critiqued modern art in her "'Dada' or 'Gaga,'" *Catholic Digest* 1:46–47, October 1937.

42. "Woman to Woman," June 1936.

43. "Woman to Woman," Aug 1933.

44. "Woman to Woman," March 1942.

45. "Catholic Authors," *Catholic Telegraph*, July 17, 1942. Gallery of Living Catholic Authors. Georgetown Archives. Box 73, folder 20.

46. A part of a speech that Burton gave at the Bronxville Women's Club's Literary Department meeting. *Bronxville-Press*. October 25, 1935.

47. "Woman to Woman," May 1935.

48. "Woman to Woman," February 1936, regarding Mary Pickford's *Why Not Try God?*; Burton also mentioned her dislike of preachy and pious books in "Woman to Woman," October 1935.

49. Another book that Burton disagreed with the reviews on is Ethel Cook Eliot's book, *Angel's Mirth*. Burton liked that it "insists on involving Catholicism in everyday modern life" and critiqued reviews that thought it was too religious. Burton believed that if it were a different religion and not Christianity, secular reviewers would not be as quick to criticize. "Woman to Woman," March 1937.

50. "Woman to Woman," May 1935; Burton also reviewed this book in "Woman to Woman," April 1935, remarking the critiques it had received for being too Catholic.

51. Katherine Burton, "What is Catholic Theatre?" *Ave Maria*, (February 1938).

52. "Woman to Woman," June 1936.

53. "Woman to Woman," June 1942.

54. "Woman to Woman," June 1936.

55. Cadegan, *All Good Books*, 33.

56. Cadegan, *All Good Books*, 30.

57. "Woman to Woman," August 1935.

58. "Woman to Woman," October 1935.

59. "Woman to Woman," October 1933.

60. "Woman to Woman," October 1933.

61. "Woman to Woman," October 1933.

62. "Woman to Woman," April 1939.

63. "Woman to Woman," October 1935.

64. "Woman to Woman," April 1939.

65. "Woman to Woman," May 1939.

66. "Woman to Woman," July 1939.

67. "Woman to Woman," July 1939.

68. "Woman to Woman," Aug 1939.

69. "Woman to Woman," Aug 1939.

70. "Woman to Woman," Sept 1939.

71. Burton briefly mentions *Rebecca* in her "Woman to Woman," October 1939 and "Woman to Woman," March 1940 columns.

72. Cadegan, *All Good Books*, 30.

73. "Woman to Woman," November 1941.

74. "Woman to Woman," October 1935.

75. "Woman to Woman," Aug 1935; November 1937; November 1941.

76. "Woman to Woman," November 1937.

77. "Woman to Woman," January 1942, referring to a piece that Norris wrote in *Catholic World* in 1925.

78. "Woman to Woman," November 1937; November 1941.

79. "Woman to Woman," November 1937; November 1941.

80. "Woman to Woman," January 1942.

81. "Woman to Woman," June 1942.

82. "Woman to Woman," January 1942.

83. Murder and Divorce/ Remarriage are not the only sins that Burton harps on in her reviews. She also condemns the harmful effects of a negative portrayal of childbirth (November 1941); Communism (March 1941- Anne Lindbergh's the *Wave of the Future*); abortion (October 1941, unnamed author, "Marriage is a Private Affair"); making an impure/ sinful act look attractive (July 1940, in *Kitty Foyle*), (March 1942, *All That Glitters* by Frances Parkinson Keyes).

84. Harold C. Gardiner, "Unity of Catholic Literary Ideas," *America* 67 (June 6, 1942).

85. Burton, *The Next Thing* 98, 121, 124.

86. Burton, *The Next Thing*, 142.

87. Letter from Wed Burton to Harry Burton, July 7, 1942; Letter from Katherine Burton to Beatrice Morgan, c. 1932, Elizabeth Burton Kelly collection.

88. It is worth noting that Katherine was also receiving money from Harry monthly, which allowed her to keep her large apartment in Bronxville and provide for her and her children's care, though I'm not sure how much of this figured into her desire to stay married to Harry.

89. Katherine Burton, "The Arms Outstretched That Would Welcome Them," *America* 61 (July 29, 1939).

"We Are Not Here to Convict but to Convince"

A Catholic Laywoman's Witness to Anti-Racism in Twentieth-Century Philadelphia

MAUREEN H. O'CONNELL

Anna McGarry does not fit the mold of a heroine, particularly one on the front lines in the struggle for racial justice. She had a sturdy character, but she was also of average height and a bit pillowy. She wore practical dresses with subtle floral prints, sensible shoes, and jaunty hats on special occasions. She belly-laughed and liked to play pinochle. She worked a desk job in city government. She was a mother, a young widow, and a doting grandmother. Ultimately, Anna McGarry was a nice white lady. A nice white, *Catholic* lady. A nice white Catholic lady of *pre-Vatican II Catholicism* and pre-civil rights *Philadelphia*, no less. In other words, she hailed from an ecclesially conservative southern-most northern city. Anna McGarry also possessed a mundane super power: the holy racket of her typewriters. She had one on her desk in the city's Fair Employment Practice Commission and the other at home on the 800 block of Perkiomen Street in the Jesuit parish, Church of the Gesu, in North Philadelphia. Clatter and dings drowned out her white neighbors' silences, particularly white Catholic silences about the conflicts swirling around them: the violence that accompanied attempts to integrate neighborhoods and parishes, unequal access to jobs and education, blackface public pageantry. Still, typewritten letters of introduction and recommendation, meeting minutes and budget reports, opinion columns and strategic plans are hardly the stuff of heroines.

With all of her ordinariness, as well as her limited contextual and personal capacities to be anti-racist (a term that would have been totally unfamiliar to her ear), Anna McGarry might be exactly the heroine white Catholic women need right now. Over the course of her 84-year lifetime, all but her final years spent in her beloved Gesu parish and neighborhood, McGarry fine-tuned her recipe for turning her nice white Catholic ladyness into a no nonsense lifelong commitment to racial justice and equity: don't hide behind your whiteness, insist on the full humanity of all people

FIGURE 7: Anna McGarry with Sylvester McCook. Photo courtesy of Anna M. McGarry collection at the Villiger Archives of St. Joseph's Preparatory School.

wherever, whenever, and with whomever you can, find the work to be done and just keep inviting people to do it with you.

I first learned about Anna McGarry in *Urban Trinity*, a documentary about Philadelphia Catholicism produced just in time for Pope Francis's visit to Philadelphia in September of 2015.[1] Her story came toward the end of film, as nostalgia for the golden age of American Catholicism in the middle of the twentieth century yielded to the pain and anger of looming parish closures and the sexual abuse crisis. Her three-minute segment did a significant amount of work for the documentary in terms of white Catholics' amnesia about the Archdiocese's role in redlining and white flight to the suburbs. As a white Catholic woman of Philadelphia myself,

I wondered why I had never heard about McGarry. So I went looking for the details of her story. The heroism I discovered has much to teach white Catholic laywomen today.

The Fundamentals of McGarry's Witness: Chronology and Method

By 1960, those involved in the Catholic Interracial Council (CIC) movement called Anna McGarry the First Lady of the Interracial Apostolate. A review of her *bona fides* suggests she deserved that mantle. In her late sixties by then, McGarry had done much to confirm her early-in-life inclination that "the world had something in mind for [her] besides having a family."[2] McGarry was an early member of the West Philadelphia Interracial Forum in St. Ignatius parish in West Philadelphia in 1936. Within a year, she helped grow it into Philadelphia's CIC chapter as she attempted to evangelize the Jesuits and parishioners at her own Gesu in CIC methods, most notably through informal conversations among Black and white parishioners in her home and open forums with invited speakers. Her home on Perkiomen Street became the unofficial headquarters of Philadelphia's CIC, as well as an intercollegiate chapter for six Philadelphia colleges that she helped to found in 1943. In that same year John LaFarge, S.J., leader of the national CIC movement, tapped her for a national leadership role and she dedicated the next two decades of her life to that work. There she oversaw the work of a variety of national committees by the mid-1960s. "Her warm, friendly manner and her transparent honesty have been among her most effective weapons," read the citation upon her receipt of the Hoey Award by the National CIC in 1948. By 1963 the National Catholic Council for Interracial Justice (NCCIJ) boasted forty chapters in twenty states, with forty-nine Bishops making financial contributions.

On the home front, McGarry served on the executive committee of the Gesu Parish Improvement Association in the 1930s, supported transit workers in the Philadelphia Transit Corporation strike in 1944, wrote a regular column for Philadelphia's leading Black newspaper, *The Tribune*, from 1940 to 1945, and hosted a radio show on the Catholic WJMJ radio network. She was formally employed in the first Fair Employment Practices Commission (FEPC) of the City of Philadelphia in 1948 and served as Supervisor of Community Relations when the FEPC morphed into the

Philadelphia Commission on Human Relations in 1952. She retired from that role at age sixty-five in 1959. McGarry was part of the founding of the St. Elizabeth's Parish credit union in the 1930s, the Philadelphia Fellowship Commission in the 1940s, the Philadelphia Catholic Housing Council in the 1950s, and the Gesu Home and Family Service Guild after her retirement in 1959. During her lifetime she conspired with priests and nuns, Black and white parishioners, college students and cardinals, newspaper editors and Catholic college presidents to tackle racism in housing, education, employment and within the Church itself. She earned recognition from the association of Afro-American Newspapers for "superior public service without personal gain" in 1952; and the Brotherhood Award from the Philadelphia Chapter of the National Conference of Christians and Jews in 1967; and posthumously received the LaFarge Award from the national NCCIJ in 1981.[3] On receiving that final recognition on behalf of her mother, Mary (McGarry) Kane said, "Whether with the backing of the law and the authority of the City of Philadelphia or simply on her own conviction, Anna McGarry came on larger than life in everything she put her hand to."[4]

It's tempting, especially for white Catholics, to think that McGarry's heroism lies in all of her interracial industriousness, in *what* she did. If we pay attention instead to *how* McGarry approached her work, white Catholics can learn that racial justice is more than the busyness of the work itself. McGarry's own description of her approach to racial justice is prescient of contemporary scholar Ibram Kendi's claim that racism and anti-racism arise from ideas about Black people—either their inherent inferiority to other people (racism) because there is something wrong with or about them; or their inherent equality with other people (anti-racism) because there is nothing wrong with or about them.[5] Decades before Kendi, McGarry sensed that ideas shape policies that either perpetuate racism or anti-racism, and then these policies form our ideas about ourselves and other people. McGarry worked to debunk myths, mostly about Black inferiority, which is the first step of anti-racism. She wrote occasional columns in mainstream Philadelphia newspapers about racially charged descriptions of crime or segregated neighborhoods, and letters to key city officials and power brokers about alternatives to anti-Blackness in everything from hiring practices to Philadelphia's legendary mummers parades. "My technique, if you can call it that," McGarry explained in an undated letter, "was based on a realization that racial prejudice was not a personal thing, but the result of a historical situation that has left many people conditioned to think that way. In approaching these people I have made allowances for the fact that they may not have had the opportunity to learn the truth, and so I would rather explain than criticize."[6]

While McGarry understood that racism is much more than personal prejudice or even interpersonal interactions, she nevertheless insisted that solving structural racism entailed a mixture of policy change and personal engagement among people most affected by the pain of racism and with those limited by their racial prejudices. Certainly, this relational approach to responding to racism reflects her connection to the CIC movement and LaFarge's approach to addressing racism. In a 1950 newsletter put out by the College Interracial Monthly, one of the fruits of her labor among Catholic college students in Philadelphia, LaFarge couched interracial justice primarily as a virtue, and not merely an expression of protest. "Interracial justice looks to the establishment of permanent relations of cordiality, cooperation, genuine affection, and mutual esteem between the members of different racial groups," he wrote.[7] The *why* behind McGarry's commitment to racial justice is even more important than how she worked. We turn to those dimensions of her witness to racial justice now.

Stay Vulnerable: "Don't Put It in a Package and Forget It"

At some point in the early 1950s McGarry called upon the pastor of St. Columba's at Lehigh and Judson Streets in North Philadelphia. The parish was about as old as she was, so young by Philadelphia standards. Parishioners were white-knuckling the growing presence of Black families within the parish boundaries. McGarry's nephew, John Bloh, who drove her to the meeting because she did not drive, recalls that the point of her meeting was simple: to introduce the pastor to interracial justice as a possible method he could use to turn conflict within his parish into opportunities for parishioners' growth. To her mind, the pastor was in the ideal position to call for engagement across the color line, rather than permitting it to be defended. "I don't see a need for me to get involved," Bloh recalls the pastor saying, after McGarry made her case. "Just look out your window," his aunt insisted. "They are picketing a family up the street—a Catholic family." The pastor got up from his seat and closed the blinds.[8]

McGarry's attempt to call attention to racial injustice and offer one solution rooted in dialogical encounters reveals the first of three features of her commitment to anti-racism with import for today's white Catholics: allow yourself to become undone by the dissonance, pain, and recrimination of racism. In other words, don't pull down the blinds. I contend McGarry couldn't turn a blind eye to injustice because she knew scarcity in Philadelphia as a child and young adult. This is evident in two ingredients of her approach to social change: empathy for those who are disadvantaged and insider knowledge about systems that create such disadvantage.

McGarry was the third of seven children and born on St. Patrick's Day in 1894. When she was ten, her father was killed in a traffic accident, the first of several tragic incidents that would claim the lives of people she loved. As the primary breadwinner in a large young family, McGarry's mother, Sara McGinley, moved her children into a two-room apartment and worked at a shirtwaist factory. Even then, childcare was an issue for single mothers. The cost of inadequate care for the youngest members of the McGinley family forced Sara to place them under her oldest daughter's supervision. Anna dropped out of school twice in order to assume this responsibility. She recalled that her mother was "dogged" by a truant officer "who took her to court for neglecting our education" and by co-workers at the factory who balked at special privileges the foreman afforded her in doing some of her work from home.[9] Sara supplemented her income with odd jobs, "but there wasn't enough to make up the difference," McGarry recalled to her sister, Alice, "so the old grind started all over again, only worse by the fact that acute rheumatism set in and the obstacles to a good solution were just too great."[10] Although a strong personality who taught McGarry never to be "cowed by anybody" and to "above all things stand for your rights," Sara's grief, stress, and health complications led to hospitalization, although she told no one.[11] She made arrangements for the children to be dispersed among a variety of Catholic organizations. McGarry and her youngest brother, James, were sent to St. Vincent's Orphans Asylum in northeast Philadelphia. Ultimately, Sara grew stronger and with the help of an inheritance from her brother-in-law, she was able to get the children back under one roof.

At fifteen, McGarry got a job as a receptionist in a beauty parlor that paid $3.50 a week. She walked both ways to work in order to save on car fare "though it must have worn out shoe leather."[12] Not long after that, she accepted a position at Bell Telephone that paid $4.95 for a 12-hours a day, six-day work week. While she helped keep her family afloat, her work meant she was no longer enmeshed in its daily goings on. "I seldom ate with the family except on my day off on Sunday," she noted to Alice, and she went more regularly to Confession and Mass at the Gesu Parish, only two blocks from work, than her home parish of St. Malachy's, on the other side of Philadelphia's iconic Broad Street. At eighteen she went to a business school in order to be credentialled as a secretary, which she eventually became with the National Label Company. Sara died in 1917, at the age of fifty-one, the same year that McGarry married her husband, Frank.

There are elements of McGarry's childhood that she never quite put behind her. "Life has its own goals and I look back with both regret and satisfaction mixed," she said toward the close of a 1969 letter to her sister.[13] Perhaps a source of her satisfaction was her determination to keep her regrettable childhood and adolescent entanglements with structural inequality in the forefront of her mind. She was intimately familiar with the stress economic precarity places on families, especially the women and children in them: counting pennies, needing to depend on others, being manipulated by those on whom you depend. She knew the shame of not being able to meet family obligations and needing to rely on the charity of individuals and institutions. She recognized that while necessary, charity alone is far from ideal. She learned the value of stable and affordable housing, as well as the social capital that comes with being embedded in the fabric of a neighborhood. She knew personally the integrity that comes with meaningful work and the importance of wages that can sustain families.

While she didn't frame her 1969 recollections of the McGinley family struggles through the lens of racism, it is clear that these experiences of injustice served as McGarry's touchstones for creating a prosperous common ground between racially segregated Catholics rather than as justifications for segregation. They didn't make her callous to others' pain but rather made her more attentive to it. For example, her own experiences with housing insecurity gave her the courage to remove barriers to Black wealth through homeownership rather than embrace the redlining impulse that gripped fellow parishioners. Her mother's struggles for a living wage emboldened her to reject the notion that race should be a factor in determining a laborer's pay. Her experiences of being pulled out of school in order to take care of younger children compelled her to propose an employment program around "homemakers services" to the President of the Board of Education, highlighting the impact of women's lack of stable work on school-aged children.[14] The emotional boost she experienced when connected to Catholic parish communities in the midst of her struggles allowed her to see more clearly that "the Irish and the Italians and the Poles had the Church to support them in their efforts to win first-class citizenship"[15] while Black Catholics did not.

McGarry's willingness to embrace shared vulnerabilities rather than defend against them is the foundation of her approach to racial justice. She learned this lesson again in the midst of being undone by the pain of losing her husband, Frank McGinley. They married a month after Frank was drafted. Anna had their only child, Mary, while he was in France. He returned in July 1919, but carried back with him lung damage from the mustard gas he inhaled at the battle of Argonne. In 1921 he suffered an electrical shock while doing home repairs, which proved too much for his weakened respiratory system. McGarry became a widow and single mother only four years into their marriage.

To manage her grief, she became active in the American Legion. Here, in a network of financial and emotional support anchored in the common experience of loss in the context of service to the country, which she called "a great outlet for what could have been smothering grief," Anna received gifts that changed the trajectory of her life. First, she acquired "organizational work and skills" and exposure to an "ecumenical spirit" that became the cornerstones of her ministry.[16] Second, she encountered in the American Legion "animosity based purely on race," which she found unreasonable, unpatriotic, and unchristian.[17] White families balked at the prospect of Black families joining a tour of the battlefields where their fathers, brothers, or sons had been killed. McGarry could not understand how anyone could think that Black veterans were less deserving of respect and access to the freedoms for which Frank too had fought. Rather than dismiss or explain away this shocking incongruence, McGarry used it to help her see racial prejudice everywhere.

"I believed my husband had given his life to protect democracy," she said in an undated letter to a Jesuit friend at the Gesu. "But here in my own neighborhood I saw actions that nullified his sacrifice."[18] She recalled Black families being forced to double- and triple-up in houses in the Seventh

Ward because landlords had raised the rent on the properties, something her own landlord threatened to do in 1923 before she bought her property outright. Two friends of the family, Josephite priests who ministered to parishes in the Deep South, invited Anna for a visit. It became painfully clear to her on that tour that the Catholic Church was not immune to the problem of racism. It quickly became a problem that she could not tolerate. "It seems as if the Lord had given me a vivid illustration of injustice," she went on to confess to her friend about that Southern trip. "I could not put it in a package and forget it."[19]

Philosopher George Yancy suggests that white people like McGarry face a choice when confronted with Black suffering. We can remain intact and un-suffering by consciously calling upon familiar tropes that justify harm to Black people: that their bodies are marked as dangerous, as hypersexual, as criminal, as lazy, etc. and therefore deserving of the treatment they receive. Yancy calls this a "sutured" response: one in which in the name of self-preservation white people keep sewn tightly shut with the needle and thread of white supremacy. Another option when confronted by Black pain, Yancy contends, is to become undone, open-wounded, un-sutured. He calls this an "enlarging" stance, as it invites us to "look again, to wonder, and to stand in awe of [our] shared humanity;" it also confronts us with uncomfortable truths about our whiteness as a weighty problem for others.[20] Yancy also suggests being un-sutured is an ongoing disposition through which we constantly tarry with our histories, our frames of references, our ways of moving through our days and the world with an attention to resisting whiteness that denies the full humanity of others.

To my mind, McGarry was proposing that fellow white Catholics become un-sutured themselves in order to hone their commitments to equity. McGarry's refusal to "put it in a package and forget it" took effort, given the proclivity for that response to racism all around her, was in fact countercultural. Dennis Clark, a Catholic historian and one of McGarry's co-conspirators in Catholic housing reform, noted in a 1978 article about her in the National Catholic Reporter: "She addressed racial attitudes based on her own experience. She shared the laughter and heartaches of her black neighbors, opening up educational opportunities for dozens of local children, getting jobs for men and women, and struggling to form neighborhood groups through which people could act for themselves to improve housing and public services."[21]

Stay Grounded in the Personal, Address the Structural: "We Have a Greater Scope of Action"

In one of her Sunday addresses in 1957 on WJMJ, the Catholic radio station in Philadelphia, McGarry shared a personal story that to my mind captures the interplay of the personal and structural in her approach to racial justice. "One evening," began McGarry in a fireside chat fashion, "in an ordinary room in an ordinary house on an ordinary street in the kind of neighborhood that is often referred to as congested, over-populated, run-down, and many other terms that are used in discussing our communities in Philadelphia a little group of women sat around a dining room table."[22] The hostess, McGarry explained, had just moved into the block with her family of nine children and invited her neighbors in for an hour of prayer—of thanksgiving and hope, as well as for protection. "I was fortunate to have been one of those friends," McGarry said. They agreed that the time spent together brought the eight women—and they were only women—"a real sense of being neighbors in the way that Christ has used the term." They decided to meet monthly and to call themselves "The Claver Club."

In addition to meeting regularly, they simply looked out for each other: caring for children or sick family members, arranging for birthday celebrations, organizing a chess club for the teenagers and outings to the park for kids during the summer. Two years later, their number had tripled. The benefits: "We don't ever feel alone any more . . . And as the little Claver Club began to grow in unity and in strength as well as in numbers, it has reached out into the neighborhood as well and began to talk about neighborhood improvement." This brought them in contact with block organizations who, with the Claver Club's help, began to recognize the relationship between the emotional and physical well-being of the neighborhood. A sense of cooperation emerged and pulled the group beyond their living rooms into collective efforts: summer camps, beautification programs. "Today there is a neighborhood alive with new spirit, people interested in using their talents to make life better for themselves and for those around them . . . people who come together for civic meetings or for family gatherings or for religious motives. . . ."[23]

Even she seemed to be struck by the fact that all of this neighborhood empowerment stemmed from an interracial group of women gathering in each other's homes with the sole intent of friendship. Her home was one of the hubs. When a community clothing closet at the Jesuit high school in the neighborhood closed, McGarry's "dining room and sitting room both became small-sized department stores."[24] Upon the dedication of a memorial at the Gesu in her honor in 1982, a Jesuit noted "Mrs. McGarry's home . . . was always open. I met Dorothy Day there. Members of the Catholic Interracial Council met there. Whomever came to her never went away empty whether it was food, money, ideas, hopes, dreams, consolation, companionship. . . . She shared all."[25]

When the doors to diocesan-wide efforts around interracial justice were closed to her, as we will see in the next section, the Claver Club served as the blueprint for the Gesu Home and Family Service Guild, a subsidiarity-based approach to responding to the impact of three decades of government and ecclesial redlining in what had been one of the toniest of Philadelphia's parishes. The GHFSC reflected a moral agency sustained by interracial relationships in the midst of a deeply segregated city and church. Some of their activities—a 4-H club, garden contests, a preschool and tutoring program, a home visitation program, and work crews that tackled blight—reflected a missionary mindset constitutive of a "missionary" parish in the eyes of the Archdiocese (one that was not financially self-sustaining).[26] In and of themselves, these were hardly anti-racist initiatives. And yet, McGarry embodied an awareness of structural, cultural, and even ecclesial obstacles to integration. For example, an undated and mimeographed Venn diagram of the Neighbors Association that met monthly at the Gesu visually depicted the organization in a circle at the center, bounded by four streets that formed its geographical boundaries at the periphery, and oriented toward four poles of "God and country," home, school, and community. The group's activities aligned with the appropriate pole, suggesting an attention to working within systems at the structural level such as the parents association in the schools, block leaders councils, and committees for health.[27]

Perhaps more importantly, McGarry named the responsibilities that white people like her needed to address in light of the privilege and power afforded them in our racialized society. She partnered with block leaders and the other neighborhood associations to pass fair housing legislation through petitions to state legislatures and visits to their offices in Harrisburg. She wrote letters to public officials about more effective ways of delivering public services, she worked with the pastor in proposing to the archdiocese a home health aide employment service that would link women in mission parishes like the Gesu with "more self-sustaining parishes who need the kind of domestic help of practical nursing care which women in parishes like ours are in a position to render."[28] McGarry acknowledged that this employment program "may seem at first reading a reintroduction of the age-old system of Negro women serving 'white ladies'" but insisted that "bringing women together over racial lines with a Christian motivation" could "[help] present the church as a guide to a fuller life both spiritually and economically."[29] She was unapologetic in identifying white people as a problem. "There are, of course, many things lacking in the background of many of our families, not the least of which is the experience of true and personal concern on the part of those with whom they have dealings, either through necessity or other circumstances," she wrote in an undated letter to a friend. "Because of this, we are hopeful that any contacts which are created through our Gesu Human & Family Service Guild and through those Catholic schools from which the students are coming, shall be such as to create a true spirit of friendship," what she considered "the truly Christian personal relationships which are warm and sincere rather than condescending and paternalistic."[30]

McGarry's comfortability in receiving and offering hospitality allowed her to move in and through intimate spaces—both Catholic and civic—in order to cultivate relationships of mutuality and accountability. In other words, relational intimacy was not a posture she opted in and out of, but rather one fueled by her seemingly endless energy for racial equity. It speaks to her accountability to communities of color with whom and for whom she worked. "Because we have, by the grace of God, been given deeper insights than most of our Catholic brethren (if we judge by the analysis of support herewith)," she wrote to her fellow NCCIJ Board members in 1963, "we also have a greater scope of action by which to bring about some solutions to the various sorespots [sic] which are in existence."[31] She embodied the opposite of a self-protectionist status that we can certainly recognize in the Church then, and that we see in the Church now, which prioritized property values and investments in ecclesial infrastructure over people. She was also willing to challenge the white people with whom she was affiliated. To that end, she recognized that relationships, while good in and of themselves, were also to be leveraged for structural change. She recognized relationship as a form of power. She was not only aware of advantages afforded her as a white woman from a very large and distinguished parish and with time and flexibility afforded her by virtue of her unmarried status, but she also used those advantages to the benefit of those with fewer resources to bring about change in employment and housing practices and policies. She used her power with other white people in positions of power, both within Philadelphia's municipal government and its ecclesial Catholic hierarchy, to call in and privately point out if not publicly call out their individual racism and the racist policies they endorsed.

For example, in 1940–1941, she counseled one of the priests at her Gesu Parish involved in an ecumenical scheme to keep a Black congregation from buying a recently vacated church property within the Church bounds. Later, in 1943, she contacted the Philadelphia Transit Corporation to demand employment equity for Black workers. She later became a field representative in the City's Fair Employment Practices Commission, the first of its kind. When that office evolved into the City's Commission on Human Relations in 1952, she was placed in charge of education, housing, and community service. In that capacity, she worked to develop a program for "leaders in racially changing neighborhoods" that included educating residents, presumably white residents, through a 20-minute film strip they had created called "The House Across the Street." It dispelled myths about racial integration, and discussed "steps to prevent panic."[32] Black parishioners recognized her efforts in influencing other white people in positions of power. A fellow Gesu parishioner put it this way in a letter to her: "You are truly a tower of strength to all of us," wrote Helen A. "God is surely with us in this challenging adventure of building an inter-racial parish. Having the founder of the Interracial Council right across the street is surely an encouragement to Fr. Michaleman."[33]

Perhaps what made McGarry successful is what racial justice activists and educators today name as the distinction between call-out and call-in culture.[34] Rather than shame white people, she relentlessly gave them the benefit of the doubt and invited them to the work. "If you assume at the outset that the other fellow wants to do the right thing," she went on, "you are well on your way to getting him to do it."[35] McGarry's attention to the personal while working to transform the structural is perhaps best captured in an observation a good friend made at her retirement party from the City's Human Relations Commission after a decade. "I thought it was particularly significant that a relatively large number of Negroes [sic] turned out. One can put on a front and fool white people who pretty much don't know what the score is anyway," wrote Robert Callaghan. In a way that points to what we today would recognize as superficial virtue signaling or performance, he noted, "but you cannot kid the Negro [sic]. He can spot a phony a mile away."[36]

Let Go of Agendas, Hold on to Relationships: "Carry On Is the Watchword"

In 1966 the *National Catholic Reporter* ran a feature story about McGarry, which opened with the following: "For most of the past 43 years the Catholic presence in Philadelphia race relations has been a widow who plugged ahead despite the apathy of her neighbors and official archdiocesan disapproval."[37] McGarry was only too aware of resistance and inertia to racial justice work: within herself and among other white Catholic collaborators. "I feel like a piker, having done so little for or with the Conference," she confessed to a friend in 1962,

> but I know what we are doing in the parish is of real value to the overall aims of the Conference because we are in a position to dig deeply into somethings that have not been touched before in a parish, or at lease [sic] not in the same way. And if we lose our present Pastor, who can say whether what we are doing will continue in the same degree. So, we make hay while the sun shines—and incidentally when the countenances of the powers that be do not shine on us so brightly.[38]

That fickle clerical countenance proved to be her biggest obstacle. Changes in Catholic leadership, nationally and locally, brought with it changing commitments to racial justice. McGarry navigated the first half of her racial justice apostolate under the authoritarian eye of Philadelphia's Cardinal Dennis Dougherty, who quietly afforded her leeway in establishing and growing Philadelphia's CIC. Rather than rail against the lukewarm reception she encountered at the parish level, McGarry pivoted in a potentially more impactful direction and sought Dougherty's permission to launch an intercollegiate CIC chapter in Philadelphia in 1937, the first of its kind according to her. He approved and by the early 1940s the six participating chapters sponsored "their own meetings monthly to study and learn more of the difficulties of Negro life and the means which are at our disposal to relieve those difficulties." Campus chapters sent delegates to bi-monthly meetings of the whole "for exchange of ideas and experiences" as well as "contact with leaders of the Negro community at large" who served as speakers and discussion leaders."[39] In her estimation, "when matters of grave importance to the community were involved a large segment of our population were prepared to meet [Black people] with a truly Catholic point of view and to choose between true and false standards."[40]

However, she had less hierarchical support for the latter half of her apostolate. Dougherty's successor, John O'Hara, had a different approach to racial justice. To McGarry's mind, O'Hara placed all of his racial integration eggs into the education basket, assuming that integrating Catholic schools was sufficient. "Accordingly," she recounted to the *National Catholic Reporter*, "there was a complete failure to recognize the everyday problem of Negro life in the city, such as poverty and discrimination in housing, employment, and recreation facilities. Little by little, barriers were put up to block lay efforts in this area. Laymen who attempted to do something as Catholics faced unquestioning disapproval."[41] McGarry encountered O'Hara's first road block in August 1957 in the midst of riots in Levittown, just miles from the city's northern limit but still within the bounds of the Archdiocese.[42] A Black family, William Myers, a World War II veteran, his wife, Daisy, and their three children, had moved into the white-only planned community of more than 15,000 homes built by Bill and Alfred Levitt in 1951, just one example of post-World War II *de jure* segregation in Philadelphia. The Myers were immediately confronted by a mob of residents, at times 300-strong, outraged by their arrival. For nine days rioters blasted the National Anthem, threw rocks, and disregarded a court order to disperse, which the local police enforced with lukewarm enthusiasm. Nearly 1,000 cars a day drove by the property, a cross was burned in the yard of the development's public school, and a "Levittown Betterment Committee" was thrown together to explore legal options in a series of meetings and outdoor rallies. McGarry suspected that Catholics made up a sizeable percentage of the crowds, as well as the police who failed to intervene.

As Vice President of Philadelphia's CIC, McGarry attempted to assist O'Hara to respond by drafting a public statement that articulated the principles of Catholic interracial justice and offered Philadelphia's CIC as a resource for finding a peaceful resolution to the situation. It also offered some immediate action steps: learn the facts, discuss with fellow Catholics the moral implications of racial segregation, facilitate public forums to debunk the myths about residential integration. "To deny an individual any basic right because of his race or color, is to deny both the teachings of the Church and the basic tenets of our American form of government," McGarry's statement declared. Assuming that the Cardinal's under-secretary's approval was sufficient, she went public with the statement, which was printed in South Jersey's *Catholic Star Herald* on August 30 and was picked up by other mainstream local papers that quoted its most central message: "We urge Catholic families to exercise clear judgment and to promote through prayer and through example a spirit of true Christian neighborliness in their community. The only possible solution for the previous social disorders arising from racial differences lies in the application of Christ's teachings. Catholics have a special responsibility to live by these teachings."[43]

McGarry faced hierarchical backlash. O'Hara removed his imprimatur from Philadelphia's CIC. He refused to renew the prelate from the Chancery who served as its chaplain. He pulled his support from an annual Communion breakfast. "Cardinal O'Hara was against the whole prospect of emphasizing race," she told an interviewer. "He encouraged Catholics to move out to the suburbs and to bring colored [people] into cities and become Catholic."[44] O'Hara's replacement, John Krol, then replaced the CIC with a Human Relations Commission and conspicuously refused to appoint McGarry to it despite the fact that she was one of the leading field officers for an office in Philadelphia municipal government with a similar name. Krol commissioned them to make progress, not waves. From this point on, the Catholic hierarchy steered the Archdiocese of Philadelphia away from racial justice as the CIC had understood it, i.e., naming and addressing structural inequality that specifically targeted communities of color, and toward charity offered by suburban white Catholics toward peoples of color contained within specific neighborhoods whose government-drawn redlines the Church helped to reinforce.

To her credit, friend and Catholic historian Dennis Clark notes, Mc-Garry's relationships with Church leadership could be "strained but never acrimonious." He went on to say, "Anna McGarry has one very Irish quality that is invaluable to interracial work, she won't give up and the more you oppose her, the stronger she presses her campaign."[45] Rather than get bogged down, McGarry revised her agenda yet again. Since Krol's "Commission on Human Relations was doing 'charitable work,' but not real change,"[46] she turned her attention to the CIC's national organization, where real change was still possible.[47] After nearly two decades of work coordinating local CIC chapters at the national level, she spearheaded a cadre of CIC chapter leaders from across the country who decided there was a need for a "national voice" to "reach into the hearts and minds of Catholic America" in order to contend with the fact that despite progress in anti-lynching laws, fair employment, and even *Brown v. Board*, "the 'pursuit of happiness' by the Negro was being thwarted on every side by myriad ways and means and countless bonds which he could not break."[48] In August 1963, the first national assembly of the NCCIJ gathered. In preparation materials for that meeting, and in her capacity as secretary, Mc-Garry called all involved to a higher level of commitment and practical action: "I remind you that we should produce some very practical yet far-reaching resolutions as a result of our deliberations, stimulated by an earnest evaluation of the circumstances in our own localities."[49] As chair of the NCCIJ's Resolutions Committee, McGarry's comprehensive report of the organization's activities included: increased number of chapters, with spiritual and financial support of bishops; a "Southern field office"; semi-annual board meetings; bi-annual conventions; and regional institutes. McGarry was also the secretary of the NCCIJ's Housing working group, whose aim was to develop plans for "Catholic individuals, groups, and the institutional Church to improve housing quality" and create "an open market" for housing.

Perhaps most notable is the pivot toward engagement with the bishops as a collective whole, and not simply with individual local ordinaries sympathetic to the cause of racial justice. The NCCIJ drew up an undated working document (sometime after 1963) calling for the US bishops to make a more definitive statement about racism. Despite being well received by Black people and Catholics already onboard with interracial justice, "[interracial justice] has not become a platform for action by Catholics to the extent that is necessary in America . . ." In short, NCCIJ named the "failure of Catholics to respond wholeheartedly" to racism as well as Catholic-specific root causes of the American moral code that failed to dismantle the color line: "the extensive system of Catholic education" as a "factor in maintaining a separateness in educational institutions on both religious and racial lines"; Catholics schools in "'mission areas' conform to the 'prevailing pattern of racial separation established by political and or economic practices'"; racially segregated religious orders; and priests that "feel unprepared to meet the Negro on his own merits even if willing to do so."[50] It is unclear how much of a hand McGarry had in creating this draft, but certainly, her on-the-ground wisdom is evident in its recommendations: incorporate the immorality of segregation into the teaching and training of Catholics "from elementary through seminary educational systems," particularly through regular sermons and textbooks; convene conferences and seminars for religious educators; pair missionary "endeavors and educational opportunities" with an "awareness of the crucial struggle in which the Negro is involved today;" and cooperate with other faith traditions "who are committed to the public penance of participation in 'direct action' techniques." The NCCIJ's concluding prediction is chilling to read in our post–January 6, 2021, America. Catholics, they note, are often quite visible by their "religious emblems" at anti-Negro demonstrations, whose impact is "irreparable." "They are influenced by false propaganda and submit young children to exposure to racial hatred, blasphemous and dangerous exhibitions of anger and physical attack against Negros which will live on in these children long after the original cause has been faded from their memory."[51]

It is unclear whether NCIJJ finalized the draft and delivered it to the bishops, or if they failed to act on recommendations. What is clear, however, is that they released their next statement, *Brothers and Sisters to Us*, at least a decade later, in 1979. By that time, McGarry had long ago pivoted one final time, focusing her racial equity efforts in her life's final decade on the place where they had begun: her North Philadelphia parish. "Enough of that," she concluded in an undated letter to a friend updating her on ongoing work back in the parish, "except you can see we share a bit in the trials and disappointments of the Laiety [sic] in the Apostolate, just as we always did. So, carry on is the watchword."[52]

To Be Sure

Certainly there was room for growth in McGarry's prophetic interracial justice work. In fact, acknowledging that fact is an essential capability white Catholics need to develop in our own ongoing processes of becoming anti-racist. For example, her lack of awareness of the limitations of the CIC approach to interracial justice in light of the movement's history of co-opting Black Catholic leadership and power in the Federated Colored Catholic movement that predates it, points to the inherent anti-Blackness of CIC initiatives and McGarry's unwitting participation in it.[53] Even if in Lafarge's estimation the Philadelphia chapter was more engaged in actual social justice work than others, the fact that Black leaders of this movement remain unnamed or invisible even in McGarry's thorough recordkeeping points to an implicit and or unconscious anti-Blackness in McGarry's own public ministry. Moreover, the CIC's early default to dialogue among Black and white Catholics, rather than on direct actions to dismantle racial inequity within the Church itself, reflect a "race relations" response to racism that too often leaves root causes of inequity intact. Moreover, while the Anti-Defamation League and NAACP sent her congratulatory notes on the occasion of her retirement from Philadelphia's Commission on Human Relations, even these groups are wrestling at this point in their histories about which strategy was more effective: reform via dialogue and assimilation or revolution via Black power and separatism.[54] Clearly, McGarry's efforts emphasized the former. This was not merely due to the relatively small numbers of Black Catholics in the Catholic contexts where she attempted to do her work—colleges, parishes, the NCCIJ. She herself was late in realizing that racial injustice is not simply lack of consciousness about Black worth on the part of white people, but actually white people's persistent belief in their own superiority. Consider, for example, the paternalist tone of the two-fold purpose of the Gesu Home and Family Service Guild (GHFSG), which she chaired: "We are improving our neighborhood outside of our homes and more important, we are building standards within our homes and within our families."[55] Focusing on personal betterment, according to white standards, as a solution to exclusion from the common good reflects a racist tendency to think that there is something wrong with Black people, Black families.

Also, despite her thorough understanding of structural racism, and her comfortability with naming it for people in positions of power, whether in city government or the Church, McGarry was reluctant to do so in her public ministry among everyday white people. She mostly couched her call-in to interracial justice and her call-out stance about racism in the language of ignorance that leads to interpersonal decisions and behaviors. In some ways, her glass half-full approach with whites reflects the "conversion of hearts and minds" approach to ending racism that characterizes just about every public statement from the US Catholic bishops on racism and fails to redress racism deeply embedded in systems and structures. However, I think we see in McGarry far more evidence of working to identify historical conditions that give rise to racist ideas, particularly conditions within the Church itself. Listening to the stories of Black people, whether in interracial forums or through the Fair Employment Office— helped McGarry better see the contours of structural racism.

If she was reluctant to speak in structural terms with the average white person, she did so compellingly with Black people. In her *Tribune* columns she informs Blacks of things they already know, which reflects a desire to be seen as one of the "good" white people by communities of color without risking becoming seen as one of the "bad" white people by other whites. I don't suspect that stems from any kind of white fragility on McGarry's part. She dealt with recalcitrant white employers on a daily basis as a field officer in the City's fair employment office. Rather, it reflected the influence of the Archdiocese's problematic strategies around evangelization and mission-based charity when it came to engaging Black people. The Archdiocese's posturing and actions indicated that its ecclesial social capital was to be spent on assimilation rather than integration and multiculturalism. For example, in sharing the work of the Interracial Councils with Black audiences, McGarry believed she was convincing Black people, including Black Catholics, that it was safe to be Catholic. But in truth, evangelization was a road block to racial justice, since assimilation worked hand in hand with containment strategies that Church leadership hoped would sustain urban parishes and schools with dwindling numbers of white Catholics. To that end, through her own work to evangelize Black people about Catholic interracial justice, McGarry may have unknowingly undermined the very integration she hoped to catalyze. Moreover, even with her awareness of structural injustices, much of her public ministry among Black Catholics reflected a missionary impulse that is thoroughly embedded in and embodied by American white Catholics. She was not impervious to the needs that structural racism created among her neighbors, but in collaborating with them to meet those needs she often worked within the confines of broken systems—civic and ecclesial.

Anna McGarry's Catholic Critical Race Tradition

"We're here to convince not convict," Anna McGarry liked to say. This stance can sound soft, especially in our current climate where convictions that lead to justice for Black people, whether in the court of law or of public opinion, are still so hard to come by, and white people's comfort levels still set the limits for racial justice.[56] Robin Di Angelo also questions the effectiveness of white niceness in dismantling structural racism, noting that it is not enough to simply be kind to the people we encounter as we move through daily lives practically predetermined by the forces of race.[57] And yet, McGarry's convincing had teeth, and not simply because she herself didn't need to be convinced that racism was operative in just about every aspect of American life, including the American Catholic Church. To that end, she predates Camara Phyllis Jones, whose fundamental approach to anti-racism is not to ask *whether* racism is operative in any given situation or system but rather *how* is it at work.[58] Her convincing had teeth because it came from a devout Catholic laywoman who was not afraid to use the Church's resources for racial equity while naming it as a driving cause of them. To that end, she offers us, particularly white Catholic women, resources for what I call a "Catholic Critical Race Tradition."

First, McGarry rooted herself in Catholic Social Teaching (CST), which was still in its nascent stages. It's important to remember that she did much of her life's work in the area of racial justice in the decades prior to Vatican II and its commitment to the role of the laity, fervor for dignity of persons, and openings toward what would become the preferential option for the poor. Through McGarry's witness, I find resonances between Catholic Social Teaching and some of the fundamentals of critical race theory. Unlike many white Catholics who have engaged Catholic social teaching in the twentieth and twenty-first centuries, McGarry saw racism as a *primary* concern that the tradition should and could address. It was not an ancillary issue for her, but at the heart of most injustices, particularly in housing, employment, and education. Granted, she often embodied a missionary impulse when it came to ministering to Black Catholics, which remained a big part of her social imagination. Nevertheless, she did not stop at direct service or charitable giving when it came to her public ministry.

Second, she operated with an awareness of power at the heart of racism. She knew first-hand how racism disempowered some in order to protect the power of others, how racism can be undone when using the privileges a racist system affords white people to dismantle it, how the collective power of people can be stoked for ill or for good. McGarry's interactions with the hierarchy amplify the intersectional dimensions of abuse of power, or more specifically, of white supremacy. She tangled simultaneously with the dynamics of sexism, clericalism, Christian-supremacy, and anti-Blackness. Her struggle reveals the barriers to collective agency when pastors or bishops or cardinals intentionally create conditions that prioritize a protectionist rather than a racially just stance, many of which are operative today: relationships that lack mutuality and accountability, policies that either separate or enforce ecclesial assimilation, preference for remaining invulnerable through inaction rather than risking vulnerability through truthful speech and public witness.

Finally, she relentlessly named wrongs and suggested alternatives. She oriented herself toward a vision of what could be rather than operate within the parameters of what was. This took a particular kind of moral imagination, courage, and fortitude. When met with obstacles or resistance, McGarry didn't bemoan what wasn't possible but rather searched for new avenues toward what could be possible. Moreover, her commitment to converting hearts and minds *as well as* changing systems, offers an example of what racial justice activist adrienne maree brown calls "transformative justice" or "justice practices that go all the way to the root of the problem and generate solutions and healing there, such that the conditions that create injustice are transformed."[59]

In 1946, as she was hitting her interracial justice stride, McGarry punched out a note on her typewriter in her home on Perkiomen Street to Fr. James Gibbons, pastor of St. Joseph's in Malvern, a well-heeled parish in suburban Philadelphia. From her unapologetic assessment of the situation, I got the sense that she was following up on a previous conversation about the challenges Black Americans faced in residential integration.

She highlighted "habits and customs derived from the mistaken notion" that Black people are not "fitted to be inhabitants of this or that neighborhood," or "Catholic real estate men" reflecting the stance about Black buyers that "prevails in other circles," or excessive costs and resentment Black families faced in trying to own or even rent homes. One of her closing thoughts reflects her classic "we're here to convince not to convict" style and offers us the moral encouragement we need to hear today. "It will require the court to change such customs," she wrote, acknowledging both the structural realities of racism and the need to change systems that sustain it. "But with our spiritual resources Catholics can change them and will, we trust lead the way. Housing problems today, of course, are practically unsurmountable, but *there is never a wrong time to begin to see right.*"

Notes

1. Andrew Ferrett, *Urban Trinity: The Story of Catholic Philadelphia* (Philadelphia, History Makers Productions, 2015).

2. Anna McGarry, oral history, Margaret Sigmund, January 1976, Anna McGarry Papers (hereafter AMP), Series 2, Box 1, Marquette University Archives (hereafter "MUA").

3. Walter Fox, "Brotherhood & Mrs. McGarry," June 8, 1966, *National Catholic Reporter*, Anna M. McGarry Collection, Villiger Archives, St. Joseph's Preparatory School (hereafter "SJPS").

4. Mary (McGarry) Kane, comments on occasion of the LaFarge Award, May 8, 1981, John Bloh papers.

5. Ibram Kendi, *Stamped from the Beginning: The Definitive History of Racist Ideas in America* (New York: Nation Books, 2016), 3.

6. Fox, "Brotherhood & Mrs. McGarry."

7. John LaFarge, SJ, "What is Interracial Justice," *The Collegiate Interracial Monthly*, November, 1950, AMP, Series 1, Box 1, Folder #6, MUA.

8. Interview with Rev. John Bloh, October 19, 2018, Sicklersville, NJ.

9. Letter from Anna McGarry to Alice McGinley, February 1969, Bloh papers.

10. Letter from Anna McGarry to Alice McGinley, February 1969, Bloh papers.

11. Edward Schmidt, "A Vocation for Neighborliness: Anna McGarry's Quest for Community in Philadelphia," *U.S. Catholic Historian* 22.2 (Spring 2004): 81–97, 82 citing Sigmund 1976 oral history.

12. Letter from Anna McGarry to Alice McGinley, February 1969, Bloh papers.

13. Letter from Anna McGarry to Alice McGinley, February 1969, Bloh papers.

14. Anna McGarry letter to Richard Dilworth, September 2, 1966, in AMP, Series 1, Box #2, Folder #12, Gesu Correspondence, MUA.

15. Jim Shea 1960 article, MUA.

16. Anna McGarry oral history conducted by Margaret Sigmund, January 1976, AMP, Series 2, Box #1, Folder #1, MUA.

17. Anna McGarry oral history.

18. Fox, "Brotherhood & Mrs. McGarry."

19. Fox, "Brotherhood & Mrs. McGarry.

20. George Yancy, "White Suturing, Black Bodies, and the Myth of a Post-Racial America," *ARTS, The Arts in Religion and Theological Studies* 26, no. 2 (March 2015): 5–14.

21. Dennis Clark, "Anna McGarry, 83, worker for interracial justice dies," *National Catholic Reporter*, January 20, 1978, Box 0106, Catholic Interracial Council of Philadelphia, Catholic Historical Research Center of the Archdiocese of Philadelphia, Philadelphia, PA.

22. Anna McGarry, "Radio talk on Station WJMJ," September 8, 1957, AMP, Series #1, Box, #1, Folder #9, Radio Broadcasts, MUA.

23. Anna McGarry, "Radio talk," September 8, 1957.

24. Undated letter from Anna McGarry to Ivey, AMP, Series 1 Box #2, Folder #12, Gesu Parish Correspondence, MUA.

25. Fr. Eugene McCreesh at dedication of Memorial of Anna McGarry, January 9, 1982, Anna McGarry Collection, Villiger Archives, SJPS.

26. Report on Gesu Home and Family Service Guild by Theresa A.M. McKinley, 1965, AMP, Series 1 Box #2, Folder #13, Gesu Parish Information 1964 and 1965, MUA.

27. "Our Neighborhood Association," AMP, Series 1, Box #2, Folder, #14, MUA.

28. Undated letter from Anna McGarry to Ivey, AMP, Series 1 Box #2, Folder #12, Gesu Parish Correspondence, MUA

29. Gesu Home and Family Service Guild report, 1963, AMP, Series 1 Box #2, Folder #12, Gesu Parish Correspondence, MUA

30. Undated letter from Anna McGarry to "Mother Mullen," AMP, Series 1 Box #2, Folder #12, MUA.

31. Anna McGarry letter to Board members of the National Catholic Council for Interracial Justice, September 20, 1963, AMP, Series 1, Box #1, Folder #16, MUA.

32. "Sample Agenda and Meeting Guide for Leaders in Racially Changing Neighborhoods," Anna McGarry Collection, Villiger Archives, SJPS.

33. Undated letter from Helen A to Anna McGarry, AMP, Series 1 Box #2, Folder#12, Gesu Parish Correspondence, MUA.

34. Tiffany Jana, "Calling-in versus Calling-out," *Medium*, February 18, 2021, https://aninjusticemag.com/calling-in-versus-calling-out-f032d8f5d94f.

35. Fox, "Brotherhood & Mrs. McGarry."

36. Letter from Robert Callaghan to Anna McGarry, October 8, 1959, AMP, Series 1 Box #2, Folder #1, Commission on Human Relations Correspondence 1953–1959, MUA.

37. Walter Fox, "Brotherhood & Mrs. McGarry."

38. Letter from Anna McGarry to Matthew Ahmann, May 9, 1962, AMP, Series Box 2, Folder 16, National Catholic Conference for Interracial Justice Correspondence, 1959–76.

39. Anna McGarry, "Ten Years in Retrospective," January 21, 1948, AMP, Series 1, Box #1, Folder #6, MUA.

40. Anna McGarry, "Ten Years in Retrospective."

41. Fox, "Brotherhood & Mrs. McGarry."

42. I use the word "riots" intentionally, following American historian Carol Anderson's description of "white rage" at any form of Black advancement, in this case Black people moving into suburban housing developments, without the federal assistance that whites received in doing so, in the 1950s. See Chapter 2 in *White Rage: The Unspoken Truth of our Racial Divide* (New York: Bloomsbury, 2016). See Jerry Jonas' 60-year retrospective in the *Bucks County Courier Times*, "60 Years Later, the Levittown Shame that Still Lingers," August 12, 2017: https://www.phillyburbs.com/story/lifestyle/columns/2017/08/12/60-years-later-levittown-shame/18206879007/.

43. "The Levittown Problem: Interracial Council Proposes Community Housing Forums," *Star Herald*, August 30, 1957, AMP, Series Box #1, Folder #6, MUA.

44. Sigmund oral history.

45. "Clark, Anna McGarry, 83, worker for interracial justice dies."

46. Sigmund oral history.

47. "Clark, Anna McGarry, 83, worker for interracial justice dies."

48. Anna McGarry letter to Board members of the National Catholic Council for Interracial Justice, September 20, 1963, AMP, Series 1, Box #1, Folder #16, MUA.

49. Anna McGarry letter to Board members of the National Catholic Council for Interracial Justice, September 20, 1963, AMP, Series 1, Box #1, Folder #16, MUA.

50. Undated "ROUGHT DRAFT OF SECTION 'B' proposed to AMERICAN BISHOPS at ECUMENICAL COUNCIL," AMP, Series Box 2, Folder #17, NCCIJ Information 1963–81

51. "ROUGH DRAFT OF SECTION 'B.'"

52. Anna McGarry undated later to Ivey, AMP, Series 1, Box #2, Folder #12, MUA.

53. For a critical history of the Catholic Interracial Council movement, see Lincoln Rice book. *Healing the Racial Divide: A Catholic Racial Justice Framework Inspired by Dr. Arthur G Falls* (Eugene, OR: Pickwick Publications, 2014).

54. Matthew Countryman, *Up South: Civil Rights and Black Power in Philadelphia* (Philadelphia: University of Pennsylvania Press, 2006), 32.

55. Gesu Home and Family Service Guild meeting minutes, October 23, 1957, AMP, Series 1 Box #2, Folder #12, Gesu Parish Correspondence, MUA.

56. Bryan Massingale, "The Magis and Justice," keynote address at the Ignatian Family Teach-In for Justice, Washington, D.C., November 7, 2017.

57. Robin DiAngelo, "White People Assume Niceness is the Answer to Racial Inequality. It's Not," *The Guardian*, January 16, 2019, https://www.theguardian.com/commentisfree/2019/jan/16/racial-inequality-niceness-white-people.

58. Camara Phyllis Jones, "Racism is a Public Health Crisis: Now that We See, What Do We Do?," 2020 Bray Health Leadership Lecture, Oregon State, https://health.oregonstate.edu/eid/camara-phyllis-jones.

59. adrienne maree brown, *Emergent Strategy: Shaping Change, Changing Worlds* (Chico, CA: AK Press, 2017), 146.

Laywomen as Church Patrons

Clare Boothe Luce, Marguerite Brunswig Staude, and Dominique de Menil

CATHERINE R. OSBORNE

Church buildings are always a negotiation. They begin as negotiations between pastor and congregation—what will people pay for?—and between pastor and builders—what is feasible on this site? What can we afford?—and, sometimes, between pastor and bishop. And after they are built, the next round of negotiation begins. What will be added or removed as pastors and congregants come and go? Some changes are not controversial, while others result in firestorms, even minor schisms, with the offended departing for a parish that better fits their aesthetic ideals.

While in this chapter I investigate a very special, very rare, type of lay female patronage of church art and architecture, I think it's productive to think of much of the aesthetic life of the church in the US as the outcome of lay patronage, and quite frequently of lay women's patronage, as the mothers of families squeezed their budgets to donate to their local parish building campaign or to major projects like the National Shrine of the Immaculate Conception.[1] Ultimately, much of the funding for most Catholic buildings was secured from the laity, and despite the high degree of control exercised by the pastor, we ought to constantly recall that not much could have been done without their parishioners' financial support. In the course of my research on American Catholic church buildings, I have heard a number of stories about elderly parishioners, the donor of an altar or statue, needing to be placated in the case of desired changes. The power field within a parish is far more complex after a closer look than it often is at first glance.

Nevertheless, although this chapter is largely about that same power field, the three projects I discuss here are qualitatively different from this broader variety of "lay women's patronage." Instead of the churches in question being assembled piecemeal from the patronage of many parishioners under the ultimate aesthetic direction of the clergy, all three of these mid-twentieth-century projects were funded almost entirely by extremely wealthy laywomen (with the financial and, in one case, managerial partnership of their husbands). Pharmaceutical heiress Marguerite Brunswig Staude conceived and pursued a "Chapel of the Holy Cross" for several decades, in various forms, before it was finally built in the Arizona desert in 1957. Clare Boothe Luce, with deep pockets derived from two rich husbands, funded and built St. Ann's, Palo Alto (dedicated 1955) as a memorial to her daughter. And Dominique de Menil and her husband Jean used their burgeoning oil fortune to transform the postwar campus of the University of St. Thomas in Houston, ultimately leading to the building of the Rothko Chapel (dedicated 1971). At the outset of these projects aesthetic control also rested with these women, who chose architects and artists and collaborated largely with them, rather than with clergy, to bring their visions to life. How, this chapter asks, did the immense wealth of these three women matter in their interactions with the institutional Catholic Church?

My three subjects employed different strategies, each highly gendered, for asserting their own considerable aesthetic expertise and for managing clerical relationships. Luce's letters are sterling examples of how an upper-class woman might deploy charm, even the suggestion of flirtation or seduction, in pursuit of her own ends. Staude was much less subtle, indeed quite aggressive, a fact not at all lost on her clerical partners but successful in its own way, up to a point. Dominique de Menil's self-presentation was much closer to Luce's, but with a twist due to her partnership with her husband, who took care of pugnacious assertion while Dominique soothed feelings. In the end, though, none of these strategies could produce successful final control over a Catholic church. Because these women were so deeply invested (emotionally and financially) in the projects, in all three cases the battle they engaged in to control the spaces once they were necessarily turned over to the clergy could end only one way: with the dissolution of the relationship.[2]

The Women

Marguerite Brunswig Staude and the Chapel of the Holy Cross

The Chapel of the Holy Cross (Anshen+Allen, 1957) is a Catholic "chapel of ease" located just outside Sedona, Arizona. A simple but dramatic concrete and glass structure, quite small on the inside although its exterior cross is ninety feet tall, it perches lightly in its spectacular setting amid the red rocks of the Coconino National Forest. The project was essentially the creation of the sculptor and pharmaceutical heiress Marguerite Brunswig Staude, who later recounted that she first had the idea in 1932, when, exiting St. Patrick's Cathedral in New York City, she compared it unfavorably both with Rockefeller Center and with the Empire State Building, in the latter of which she saw a "cross [that] seemed to impose itself through the very core of the structure." St. Patrick's having shamefully "exhausted itself in copying the Gothic instead of bravely pioneering," she became obsessed with the idea of a contemporary church.[3]

The project went through several iterations before becoming a reality in the late 1950s. Staude and her husband Tony scouted locations near their ranch in Arizona, finally settling on a site owned by the Forest Service.

She first had to secure a building permit, which, as a wealthy and well-connected resident of the state, she was able to do by enlisting Senator Barry Goldwater to introduce her to the Secretary of the Interior. After this, since she wanted the building to be a working Catholic chapel as a memorial to her parents, she needed ecclesiastical approval, and eventually struck a deal to donate the chapel to the diocese of Gallup, New Mexico, despite Bishop Espelage's interest in having the money go to Indian missions instead.[4] Staude hired her friends to provide the chapel's striking interior fittings, including Louisa Jenkins' tabernacle mosaic and Keith Monroe's 13-foot sculpture of the crucified Christ. After its opening to great acclaim, however, Staude's relationship with almost everyone else concerned—Monroe, a series of parish priests in Sedona, the diocese—deteriorated rapidly, as I discuss later.

Clare Boothe Luce and St. Ann's

The second project I am concerned with, the chapel of St. Ann in Palo Alto, California, is far more architecturally nondescript than the striking, award-winning Chapel of the Holy Cross. Its patron, Clare Boothe Luce, conceived of the project several years after the death of her teenage daughter in a car accident.[5] Ann Brokaw had been attending Stanford University, and Luce decided to build a chapel for Stanford's Newman Club as a memorial. In early 1950 she offered two possible plans to the Archbishop. The first was to gift $60,000 and allow the chaplain and the archdiocese

FIGURE 8: Marguerite Brunswig Staude (behind center car, in hat), priests, and other guests at the blessing of the future site of the Chapel of the Holy Cross on Coconino National Forest land outside Sedona, AZ, 1955. Photo: Courtesy St. John Vianney Parish, Sedona.

to decide on the architect, artists, and so on. The second was "to give me complete control of the choice of architect and decoration," in return for a gift of (she anticipated) around $250,000.[6]

This second plan was accepted, and in discussion with Archbishop Mitty of San Francisco, she informed him of her intention to have a *"modern . . .* adaptation of the architecture typical of the California area," and to "make this chapel as much of a gem in its small way as is Father Couturier's in France."[7] The reference is to the famous church at Assy, which had just been dedicated, and was generating significant controversy due to what was read as its aggressively modernist idiom. Marie-Alain Couturier, the Dominican who was the chapel's primary patron as well as one of the editors of the influential periodical *L'Art d'Église,* championed the use of the "best" art in Catholic churches, regardless of the faith commitment of the artists.[8] Though Luce hired the decidedly Catholic André Girard, a refugee from Nazism who had been the famous Catholic painter Georges Rouault's last pupil, to be the primary artist for

FIGURE 9: St. Ann Chapel, Palo Alto, CA, c. 1951. This photo, part of a set taken after the main building was complete but before André Girard's windows were painted, may record the first mass held in the building. Photo: St. Ann Chapel archives.

the chapel, her intention to make the chapel of St. Ann a rival, even in a small way, to Couturier's projects indicates her intention to place the chapel's aesthetics at the forefront. Indeed, Girard produced spectacular work in the chapel, including four great painted glass windows and fourteen seven-foot-high paintings of the Stations of the Cross.

The bones of the chapel were constructed very quickly and it held its first services in July 1951, although much work still remained to be done

It was formally dedicated in July 1955; however, Luce was still commissioning and paying for art and landscaping through the late 1950s, as well as negotiating with Girard over his proposed amendments to peeling paint on the chapel's windows. In 1962, she wrote the chaplain to commit annual funds for the next several years, although also to encourage the chapel to begin turning to Stanford alumni for gifts of chalices and the like. She felt that "now that the artistic integrity of St. Ann's has been established . . . no one would wish to make a gift not entirely in keeping with the spirit of the Chapel itself."[9] But she did not anticipate either the extensive changes that clergy and students wished to make in the aftermath of Vatican II, or the lack of control she herself would have once, as chaplain John Duryea reported in 1966, "all the expenses on the house and chapel" were "paid up."[10]

Dominique de Menil and the Rothko Chapel

The third project I discuss here is the internationally famous Rothko Chapel in Houston, Texas.[11] While in its completed form it is a nondenominational meditation chapel, the fourteen paintings by Mark Rothko and the original architectural design by Philip Johnson were commissioned by Jean and Dominique de Menil to serve as the chapel for the University of St. Thomas, a Basilian institution to which the de Menils were major donors throughout the 1950s and the first half of the 1960s. The de Menils were French Catholics (Dominique, from an old Huguenot family, converted when she married in 1931) who fled the Nazi occupation and established themselves in Houston. Between the wars they, like Luce, had become friends and disciples of Fr. Couturier, who interested them in collecting modern art—an interest they were increasingly able to indulge as their fortune, based on their shares in the Schlumberger Oil Company, grew apace through the postwar period.[12]

The de Menils were unusual figures in Houston on a number of axes. As French immigrants and devotees of social Catholicism, they felt an obligation and interest to use their fortune to advance the public interest in their chosen field of art and architecture, as well as elsewhere.[13] Accordingly, they not only commissioned and bought art for their own house, but developed a working relationship with the University of St. Thomas which included massive financial gifts specifically intended for the campus's architecture (Jean's special interest) and its art department (Dominique's). Maquettes of the campus from the late 1950s show that the chapel, though then rather vaguely conceived, was always intended to be the culmination of a "mall" plan. By December 1959, the de Menils had become specifically interested in Rothko; Dominique wrote to the Basilian scholar George Flahiff in Toronto that she had visited the artist and raised the concept of acquiring his rejected Four Seasons paintings, the color of which would "evoke the thought of sacrificial blood," for the St. Thomas chapel.[14] On April 17, 1964, Dominique's daybook records that she visited Mark

Rothko in his studio in New York City, and "asked him if he would consider making paintings for the Catholic chapel we were going to build at the University of St. Thomas. He said yes and seemed very pleased."[15] In February 1965, Rothko signed an agreement with the university to deliver "a sufficient number of paintings to illuminate the interior of the new chapel at the University of St. Thomas which is being designed by Philip Johnson."[16] In December it was agreed that this number would be ten murals, for which the de Menils would pay $250,000.

Between 1965 and 1968, however, that is, after the design was well advanced but before construction had begun, a complex break between the patrons and the university unfolded, and the fallout from this event included the withdrawal of both architectural plans and already completed paintings from the university into the de Menils' private collection. After an abortive attempt to place the chapel at another local educational institution, the couple eventually built it on their own, as an independent institution. Dominique dedicated it in 1971, and it now stands on the boundary between a museum created from the de Menil collection and the University of St. Thomas. After Jean's death in 1973, Dominique spent the next quarter-century developing the chapel's program in an ecumenical and interfaith direction, personally overseeing its transformation into a center where Christians, Jews, Muslims, Buddhists, Hindus, Zoroastrians, secular scientists, human rights advocates, and many others met and mingled.[17]

Controlling Catholic Space

These three projects collectively demonstrate a noticeable pattern. To begin with, each was the brainchild not of the clergy but of the patron. Luce was already intending to build a memorial to her daughter when she heard about the need for a Catholic chapel near the Stanford campus, and although the Stanford chaplain reached out to her early on, she attributed the idea ultimately to her friend Kathleen Norris.[18] She also made the archdiocese a financial offer they could not refuse in order to ensure her control over the building. The Basilians at the University of St. Thomas likewise needed a chapel, but it was the de Menils who fell in love with both Philip Johnson and Mark Rothko and conceived the particular form the chapel would take. Dominique said in 1978 that she had "always thought of building the chapel, giving it, and being done with that," but when push came to shove, they "realized that the Basilians didn't care" about keeping that particular chapel on campus.[19] Finally, the Chapel of the Holy Cross was not only unsolicited, but it also served no discernable need at all, and the local ordinary had to be wheedled into supporting it over what he considered the more urgent needs of his diocese. This pattern contrasts sharply with the typical genesis of American Catholic churches, which have nearly always been built in a context of great and immediate need, for example at the founding of a new parish or monastery or when a community outgrows its old church.

The early life of these projects was thus marked by a tension between the far greater emotional and financial investment of the donors (versus the institutional church) and the reality that a Catholic chapel, once consecrated, could not remain under the sole control of lay patrons. These two facts necessitated an intricate negotiation of power between donors and clergy, often leading to intense mutual irritation on both sides. In the case of the Rothko Chapel, relations broke down altogether over the question of lay control, not just of the chapel, but of the university. In the late 1960s, as matters were coming to a head, the de Menils collected newspaper clippings discussing the shift to lay control of the boards of both the University of Notre Dame and Fordham.[20] Finally the couple had a "searching conversation" with the University of St. Thomas's president, the physicist Fr. Patrick Braden, and "confirmed our ambition to build a nonsectarian college of which the Basilians would be a cornerstone: free to teach, yet not in the driver's seat." Braden replied that the Basilians wanted "to be a church-related college under their [i.e., the order's] management and control."[21] Though at this point the de Menils stated their intention to "remain interested in good architecture at St. Thomas and in the Rothko Chapel which transcends everything else," they also frequently expressed doubts that the university would be able to care for the paintings as they should be cared for following the withdrawal of massive ongoing financial support by the couple. The Basilians, meanwhile, were making a concerted effort to refocus the university away from the art program, which they felt had grown outsized due to the de Menil money. Patrick Braden was concerned that a Rothko Chapel on campus would draw more art lovers than mass-goers, in addition to being a security risk.

While less outwardly dramatic, perhaps because the buildings were built and occupied before a final break occurred, tensions could run very high between the other two patrons and the priests who supervised the chapels. Luce had the least contentious relationship, in many ways, but this was not because she and the Newman chaplain at the time of the chapel's construction, Fr. Tierney, agreed on aesthetics. In fact, they had distinctly different ideas, with Tierney wanting a more "traditional" look for the architecture and art. But Luce won this battle, and others, in part because she was canny enough to employ seduction rather than aggression in order to produce the result she intended in the first place. She coaxed Tierney into going along, writing him a few months after the plans were developed that, "I hope you are completely converted to modern architecture by now. Incidentally, I read a rather clever article by a great critic who suggested that a conversion to modern art is almost as startling as a conversion to Catholicism: i.e., one day ya hates it, and the next, nothing else will do."[22]

This was not the end of their disagreement, however. Tierney later commissioned a design for the walls and windows from the Los Angeles church decorating firm George Merrill and Associates, which (according to Merrill) "filled his [Tierney's] greatest expectations."[23] In this case, Luce exerted more raw power, having her secretary write a short note to Merrill that "unfortunately it is not the type of design that she has in mind for the Palo Alto chapel."[24] Tierney capitulated completely. He had to, in fact, since the Archbishop, perhaps a bit dazzled by Luce's money and influence, "often reminded [him] that everything must be submitted for [her] approval," which it was; she chose every one of the chapel's fittings, down to the vestments.[25] We might perhaps read some irritation into his statement, in the same letter, that "I am here only to help with the liturgical requirements," but whatever his personal feelings, he worked well enough from there on out with Luce's chosen artist André Girard, and Luce took care to smooth any ruffled feathers, commenting later that year that "your patience . . . has been saintly (You've had much to 'offer up' since St. Ann's started!)"[26] Luce's ability to control the chapel's aesthetics, however, waned in the later 1960s and 1970s, after she had turned over control of the building to the archdiocese and everything necessary had been paid for. Out of distaste for liturgical and aesthetic changes made in the period of post–Vatican II experimentation, she ultimately decided to withdraw her regular annual contribution from the chapel.

Overall, Staude's Chapel of the Holy Cross remains just as she intended it, as a Catholic chapel of ease, although mass is rarely celebrated there now that Sedona has a parish church of its own, and recently some substantial changes were made to the interior fittings. During her lifetime, though, she had a contentious relationship with the priests who supervised the chapel and with the artist Keith Monroe, whose 13-foot "Christus," also known as the "Atomic Christ" for its resemblance to the twisted, carbonized bodies of wartime bombing victims, dominated the chapel's interior during its early years. Despite Staude's having commissioned the sculpture, she began to disparage it in private almost immediately upon its installation. The artist Louisa Jenkins, a sometime friend of both Staude's and Luce's, who created the chapel's mosaic tabernacle doors, reported only six months after the chapel's opening that Staude disliked "the head of the Christ," and had hung it only after yielding to pressure from the other parties concerned. But she already wanted to either have the head changed or to take it down.[27] Over a decade later, this controversy resurfaced when Staude removed the head from the corpus during a visit to the chapel, promising to put a new corpus in its place, representing "the resurrected Christ," and move the "Christus" to a location somewhere in the red rocks near the chapel.[28]

Staude strongly implied to the press that the bishop and other ecclesiastical authorities agreed with her that "the crucifix, although it doesn't belong in a church, may on occasion be exhibited in museums." But in fact this episode demonstrates that there was an ongoing power struggle over control of the chapel, which crested in the early 1970s with the simultaneous dustup over the "Christus" and a several-years-long four-cornered argument between the Staudes, the diocese, the local Sedona community, and the Forest Service over what, exactly, could be done in and with the chapel and the land it rested on. In 1976, when the head had been missing for several years, Fr. Vincent Nevulis, the chapel's administrator, reported to Bishop McCarthy that Staude was arriving shortly to be present at a community meeting about the chapel's use, and he personally needed her presence "like a case of shingles!" He had recently told Staude that "if she didn't restore the cross, I would, without the head—with a sign explaining that she has the head buried on her estate in California."[29] The slow-motion breakdown of relations had included Staude's directing the chapel's caretakers (a lay couple) to "report directly to her on finances" and "authorizing expenditures" from California, thus circumventing Nevulis's theoretical control over the chapel.[30] Although the diocese did

manage to reassert firm control of the space, in part by requiring all finances to be reviewed *by* the diocese, the Christus was never restored to
the chapel, a victim of Staude's desire to be in sole control of visitors' aesthetic and spiritual experience.

This brings me to another reason why these three projects make for
an interesting entrée into the American Catholicism of the 1950s and
1960s. The latter end of this period was the exact time when laywomen
with far fewer resources were, often rather painfully, developing a sense
of themselves as actors in their own right rather than foot soldiers of the
church.[31] Not only do these three projects highlight the reality that power
in ecclesiastical spaces is a complex affair, with donors, local priests, diocesan administrators, and even neighbors and government bodies having their say, but they are also examples of a larger clash of values between
two communities of expertise: the clergy, who of course considered themselves expert in the administration and use of sacred space, and lay artists and art patrons, who felt that their aesthetic expertise as well as in
some cases their wealth granted them the right to determine the forms
and decoration of churches.[32]

The twentieth century, from the 1920s on, saw the development of a
class of American Catholics who, by dint of their profession or their highly
educated tastes, saw themselves as far more qualified than most clergy to
deal with the aesthetics of church life, a similar argument to that made
by, say, lay accountants who have recently argued that church finances are
far too important to be left in the hands of pastors whose degrees are in
divinity, not management. Documentary evidence from the mid-twentieth
century shows a spectrum of clerical opinion, running all the way from
chastened withdrawal from aesthetic pretension to the counter-assertion
of the clerical right to manage and control a church's visuals, even if "experts" (builders, sculptors, and so on) had to be brought in to do the actual
work. Laypeople, too, occupied a range of positions; some asserted that the
bishop had the perfect right to remove and add statues, crucifixes, and
the like at will, while simultaneously asserting that he could do this only
by virtue of his ecclesiastical office and not because he had any claim to
control Catholic taste. Others argued that the only "right" was the right
to good art in churches, and a bishop or priest without expertise in those
areas should stick to making sure the space was technically equipped for
liturgy.

The three projects I consider here occupy different points on this spectrum. All three women strongly asserted their artistic competence, calling not only on the fact that they were providing the money but on their reputations as collectors and patrons of the arts. While the arts were by no means a feminine domain to the same extent as "the home," they were an area in which many women both had, and were generally agreed to have, a high level of proficiency. Women might not have been the most decorated artists or the heads of the most prestigious museums, but many middle- and upper-class women received substantial practical and theoretical arts education, and often made careers as artists, teachers, and—as the century went on—museum and gallery employees and owners.[33] If they were wealthy enough, like de Menil, Luce, and Staude, they could also become patrons.

Of course, women's assertion of artistic expertise in conversation with men was as complex and delicate a matter as laypeople's' assertion of any control over a Catholic church space was, and my three subjects' approaches were similar in both arenas. Dominique de Menil generally took a more measured tone in meetings and letters than her husband. Many years after the split, Patrick Braden told the *New York Times* that "John shot from the hip. He was my particular nemesis. I could have worked with Dominique."[34] It is certainly true that Dominique understood her expected role and frequently, at least up to a point, played it. Her opening remarks at the dedication of the Rothko Chapel included the assertion that "I'm on the side of St. Paul who felt women should keep silence in church."[35]

But there is quite a bit of doubt about this assessment of de Menil, which feels performative and conventional, rather than realistic and descriptive. For one thing, her Pauline disclaimer preceded a two-single-spaced page address to the assembled dignitaries.

Another person in the same article as Braden's recollection described her as a "steel butterfly," and her personal correspondence in the Basilian archives, though rarer than Jean's solo letters, indicates that she consistently noted her own expertise and her gifts to the university. When several people complained about the showing of a series of Andy Warhol films on campus and Braden shared the letters with de Menil, she wrote back sharply that "during their life, Baudelaire and Flaubert were also accused of pornography. . . . Curiously enough, both your correspondents . . . write

FIGURE 10: Dominique de Menil at the dedication of the Rothko Chapel, Houston, 1971. Courtesy of Menil Archives, The Menil Collection, Houston. Photo: Hickey-Robertson, Houston.

'Warhole' instead of Warhol. . . . One cannot help wondering if they are qualified to talk about Andy Warhol."[36] At the height of the controversy between the de Menils and the University of St. Thomas Basilians, she wrote their superior in Toronto a short note, enclosing a copy of a speech she had given on behalf of the art department five years earlier. (The department in this period was entirely de Menil funded and managed. At one point, Dominique was even acting chair.) "You might be interested to see," she explained, "on pages three and four, that we had the same fundamental ideas as today."[37] She also enclosed an article from the *Saturday Review* which, Fr. Young had to acknowledge in his reply, was "a glowing tribute to your work at St. Thomas in the Art Department."[38]

Six weeks later a series of letters to various parties indicating the couple's decision to withdraw from the university were also signed first by Dominique, with Jean below; while we cannot read too much into this, it at least indicates that they intended to present a highly united front.[39] The following year she wrote Robert Indiana that while "we have lived under stress during the past two years," the separation from St. Thomas "has turned out to be good for our religious art project," i.e., the chapel.[40] Furthermore, Dominique's actions after Jean's death indicate essentially no interest in resuming the relationship with St. Thomas in the subordinate role Braden evidently had in mind. She had taken a lead role in the transfer of the art department and its assets to Rice University, and throughout the 1970s dedicated herself to the development of the chapel's ecumenical program and to the incipient museum, eventually known as the Menil Collection.

The Basilians at St. Thomas, indeed, never questioned the de Menils' claim to greater expertise in the arts; they did decide that they would rather maintain control of their university at the expense of providing it with an artistically great but contested worship space. Luce, meanwhile, took nearly complete control of the St. Ann space, determining the architectural form and all the decoration in collaboration with the architect and artists she hired, and quoting articles from art and architecture magazines in order to demonstrate to the clergy that she knew what she was talking about. When in the later 1960s a new clergyman asserted his own right to change the aesthetics to suit his theological vision, she chose to withdraw in protest. Staude, who had if anything a personality even more pugnacious than Jean de Menil's, began by promoting herself as the chapel's chief aesthetic muse despite the fact that all the design work was done by others (the architects and Keith Monroe) and she herself was most notable for providing the finances. She ended in semi-open warfare with the chapel's administrators; whatever the true causes of this breakdown of relations, she certainly expressed them to the press in the language of artistic expertise, giving a lengthy explanation of why the Christus was not aesthetically appropriate for the chapel even though Fr. Nevulis seems to have been determined to keep it in place.[41]

In all, these three projects provide relatively unusual documentation of long-term nonspiritual relationships between American laywomen and the institutional church in the mid-twentieth century, on the cusp of and immediately after Vatican II. This raises an important question: can the experiences of these very rich women tell us something about "laywomen" in general? Acknowledging the truly exceptional nature of these cases, I nevertheless would argue that they serve a useful and much broader function in that they tell us something explicitly about what is usually implicit and unspoken in more typical parish histories: the struggle between lay(women) and clergy for spatial control of the church. I mentioned the laity's role as fundraisers in the introduction to this chapter, but here I want to invoke the long-term experience of women in American Catholic churches, where they have historically spent significant time. Across at least two centuries American Catholic women have dropped in to pray in urban churches during the day when most men were working out of the neighborhood, they have cleaned and cared for objects and spaces including those they were often not permitted to touch or enter during liturgies, they have developed relationships with specific statues or paintings over a period of time. These experiences create an energy, a sense of ownership over one's own parish church, which has nevertheless been routinely violated by countless clerical decisions to add or remove sacred objects, to extend or withdraw approval to enter the sanctuary, or in cases becoming more routine in the twenty-first century, to close the entire church.[42]

Collectively, the three cases I discuss here provide clear documentation that, perhaps not surprisingly, the mid-twentieth-century US Catholic clergy was unused to engaging in negotiations with laywomen from positions of equal or even lesser power. But they also are a reminder that no matter how much money and education any laywoman had, she would be limited to two basic strategies in any scenario involving negotiation over a church: to persuade, or to withdraw. While these three stories reveal how each woman's relationship with the clergy was shaped by their own gendered strategies and by the clergy's positive or negative reaction to them as powerful, wealthy women, in the end the most single important factor in how events unfolded was not their gender, as such, but their lay status. There simply was no mechanism available for long-term lay control over a Catholic chapel, whether the donor was male or female. That the de Menil–St. Thomas relationship broke down not specifically over the chapel but around clerical or lay control of the university suggests the relevance of this point for considering other, broader spaces of lay-clerical tension today: around the control of church buildings, yes, but also around how allegations of clerical abuse are handled, around how lay employees of the church are treated, and around who maintains, and how, the Catholic identity of institutions such as universities and hospitals. The twin decisions of the Catholic Church both to refuse ordination to women, and to concentrate so much final power in clerical hands, ensures that all these will continue to be points of major tension in relationships between women and clergy.

Notes

1. For women's roles as funders see, in particular, Thomas A. Tweed, *America's Church: The National Shrine and Catholic Presence in the Nation's Capital* (New York: Oxford University Press, 2011).

2. Beyond the scope of this chapter, and this book in general, is another key type of women's architectural patronage: that of monastic communities. Hundreds of churches in the US were built under the active supervision and patronage of women religious, and of course these spaces also represented, and continue to represent, negotiation between the women and the male clergy who celebrate the sacraments in them. However, because women religious live and work in and around these churches once completed, the cases are qualitatively different from the three I discuss here.

3. Marguerite Brunswig Staude, "How the Chapel Came Into Being," pamphlet in the archives of the Chapel of the Holy Cross. This text was apparently written in the 1950s as the chapel was being built. However, it echoes statements Staude made in the 1930s, e.g., in a letter to Maurice Lavanoux, March 4, 1939, Collection of the Liturgical Arts Society (CLIT), 17/05, University of Notre Dame Archives.

4. There is very little surviving documentary evidence from any period before the 1970s, as far as I have been able to ascertain, and what the Staudes said on the subject to the press and in the chapel's publicity material is evidently not entirely reliable, making this the most challenging of the three projects to investigate. None of the three possible diocesan archives have yielded any material on the chapel's early life, and according to the couple's nephew, before his death Tony Staude destroyed whatever correspondence Marguerite kept. The chapel itself maintains a small scrapbook of newspaper clippings but no archive of original documents. A few letters in the Liturgical Arts Society's archives at the University of Notre Dame predate the 1960s, but other than these I rely here on newspaper articles and, carefully, on Kate

Ruland-Thorne's pamphlet "Upon This Rock: Marguerite Brunswig Staude and Her Sedona Chapel" (Sedona, AZ: Chapel of the Holy Cross, 1995), which hews closely to the story that Tony Staude wanted to tell. For the period of the 1970s there are several letters and other documents available in the archives of the Archdiocese of Phoenix; I consulted copies of these at St. John Vianney Parish in Sedona. For more on the Chapel of the Holy Cross see Catherine R. Osborne, *American Catholics and the Church of Tomorrow: Building Churches for the Future, 1925–1975* (Chicago: University of Chicago Press, 2018), 83–86.

5. On Luce and her conversion to Catholicism in the wake of this event see Rebecca L. Davis, *Public Confessions: The Religious Conversions That Changed American Politics* (Chapel Hill: University of North Carolina Press, 2021), 12–42.

6. This would be somewhere in the vicinity of $2,900,000 today. See Clare Boothe Luce to Kathleen Norris, April 12, 1950, Clare Boothe Luce Papers, Library of Congress (hereafter "CBL") 734/9. Indeed, the chapel's early financial records demonstrate that while the archdiocese played a role in holding and disbursing funds, these primarily came from donations from (separately) Clare and Henry Luce. See assorted correspondence and financial statements in CBL 12/7. These materials back up the general impression that Henry Luce supported his wife's venture—sometimes with large personal donations—but was uninvolved in producing the chapel, while Clare oversaw this in minute detail. Both Luces gave substantial cash gifts, and Clare transferred her own shares of Time stock on a number of occasions.

7. Clare Boothe Luce to Vincent Raney, May 8, 1950, CBL 734/6.

8. For Couturier and Assy, see Françoise Caussé, *La Revue "L'Art Sacré": Le Débat En France Sur L'art Et La Religion, 1945–1954* (Paris: Cerf, 2010), and Lai-Kent Chew Orenduff, *The Transformation of Catholic Religious Art in the Twentieth Century: Father Marie-Alain Courturier and the Church at Assy, France* (Lewiston, NY: Edwin Mellen Press, 2008).

9. Clare Boothe Luce to Fr. John Duryea, December 10, 1962, CBL 734/9.

10. Duryea to Clare Boothe Luce, January 29, 1966, CBL 734/9.

11. The literature on the chapel is extensive, but concentrates on the paintings and their production; viewers' experience of them; and the de Menils' spirituality, rather than the ins and outs of the chapel's Catholic politics. Additionally, much work has actually been produced by institutions associated with the de Menils. See among others Stephen Barnes, *The Rothko Chapel: An Act of Faith* (Houston, TX: Rothko Chapel, 1989); Laureen Schipsi, ed., *Art and Activism: Projects of John and Dominique de Menil* (Houston, TX: Menil Collection, 2010); Sheldon Nodelman, *The Rothko Chapel Paintings: Origins, Structure, Meaning* (Austin: University of Texas Press, 1997).

12. Schlumberger was Dominique's family company; Jean began working for them several years after the marriage.

13. They became involved in a variety of civil rights causes as well, up to and including donating to the local Black Panthers' breakfast program in the late 1960s.

14. These words are Flahiff's; G.B. Flahiff to Dominique de Menil, December 15, 1959, Menil Archives, Houston, Texas.

15. Menil Archives, Houston, Texas.

16. Mark Rothko to the Reverend John F. Murphy, CSB, February 13, 1965, Menil Archives, Houston, Texas.

17. For some of this later history see W. Andrew Achenbaum, "The Spiritual Landscapes of Dominique de Menil," *Journal of Religion, Spirituality & Aging* 21, no. 3, 145–58.

18. Luce to Norris, April 12, 1950: "bless you for having given me the idea." However, Luce also retained a copy of a letter from German professor Kurt Reinhardt (December 15, 1949), and another from then-chaplain Joseph Munier (June 17, 1948), who each suggested a Newman chapel. Luce rejected Munier's request at the time as she was still committed to a memorial for her daughter on campus; when she found the administration difficult to work with she returned to the chapel idea, perhaps spurred on by Norris.

19. "Notes from conversation with DdM," December 30, 1978, Menil Archives, Houston, Texas.

20. These are preserved in the Menil Archives in Houston, Texas, in a folder that was uncatalogued at the time of my visit.

21. John de Menil to William J. Young, C.S.B., October 22, 1968, Menil Archives, Houston, Texas.

22. Clare Boothe Luce to Fr. Tierney, September 5, 1950, CBL 734/9.

23. George Merrill to Clare Boothe Luce, January 25, 1952, CBL 734/2. Without getting too far into the details, I note here that the chapel's architect, Vincent Raney, had been suggested by the archdiocese, and was more of a traditionalist himself. It is not clear why Luce chose him as opposed to a more notable modernist, but she may have wanted a relatively inconsequential architect who would not pick too many fights over control with her artists. In this she miscalculated; Raney caused more headaches than Tierney, judging by the archival correspondence. However, Luce was swift to intervene when he seemed to be asserting too much control.

24. Secretary to George Merrill, February 29, 1952, CBL 734/2.

25. Fr. John Tierney to Clare Boothe Luce, March 14, 1952, CBL 734/2.

26. Clare Boothe Luce to Fr. Tierney, November 14, 1952, CBL 734/2.

27. Louisa Jenkins to Maurice Lavanoux, May 20, 1956, CLIT 33/02, University of Notre Dame Archives.

28. Gene Luptak, "Sedona's Crucifix of Despair Will Be Displayed Outdoors," *Arizona Republic*, July 6, 1973. The details of this event are murky, due

to the limited documentary evidence. A Sedona clergyman writing in the late 1990s could not get anyone who knew the details to discuss it with him, but reported that "local folklore" was that "Mrs. Staude . . . and her handyman came in from Los Angeles, went over to the chapel, and removed the Christus altogether." At this point, the statue was supposedly cut into pieces and disposed of in the desert, only the head surviving. The germ of the story, with Staude removing the head to California without telling anyone first, is apparently true, but the dismemberment story is almost certainly an embellishment. See David Gregory McMannes, "The 'Christus' and the Chapel of the Holy Cross," Palm Sunday 1997, http://www.episcopalnet.org/TRACTS/ThreeLives.html, accessed December 1, 2011.

29. Vincent Nevulis to +Eugene McCarthy, March 24, 1976, copy preserved in reference file at St. John Vianney parish, Sedona, AZ.

30. +Eugene McCarthy to John Simmons, April 29, 1976, copy preserved in reference file at St. John Vianney parish, Sedona, AZ.

31. Mary Henold, *The Laywoman Project: Remaking Catholic Womanhood in the Vatican II Period* (Chapel Hill: University of North Carolina Press, 2020).

32. On "expertise" in the mid-twentieth century generally, see Steven Brint, *In an Age of Experts: The Changing Role of Professionals in Politics and Public Life* (Princeton: Princeton University Press, 1994.) For a (waspish, but accurate) assessment of the effects of this cultural shift on American Catholicism in the same period, see Eugene D. McCarraher, "The Saint in the Gray Flannel Suit: The Professional-Managerial Class, 'The Layman,' and American-Catholic-Religious Culture, 1945–1965," *U.S. Catholic Historian* 15, no. 3 (Summer 1997): 99–118.

33. As Catholic examples of how this class of women helped to drive American aesthetics in the twentieth century see, for example, the material on Eloise Spaeth in Michael L. Krenn, *Fallout Shelters For the Human Spirit: American Art and the Cold War* (Chapel Hill: University of North Carolina Press, 2005), and on the arts in Katharine E. Harmon, *There Were Also Many Women There: Lay Women in the Liturgical Movement in the United States, 1926–59* (Collegeville, MN: Liturgical Press, 2013).

34. Grace Glueck, "The De Menil Family: The Medici of Modern Art," *The New York Times*, May 18, 1986, https://www.nytimes.com/1986/05/18/magazine/the-de-menil-family-the-medici-of-modern-art.html.

35. "Address made by Mrs. John de Menil at the opening of the Rothko Chapel, February 27, 1971," Menil Archives, Houston, Texas. This general assessment of Dominique has been repeated by a number of historians. For example, Achenbaum writes that "in a manner consistent with her upbringing and class, Mrs. de Menil deferred to her husband" until after his death, at which point she "came into her own" ("Spiritual Landscapes," 146).

36. Dominique de Menil to Father Braden, May 1968, General Archives of the Basilian Fathers, Toronto.

37. Dominique de Menil to Rev. William J. Young, CSB, September 5, 1968, General Archives of the Basilian Fathers, Toronto.

38. William J. Young, CSB, to Dominique de Menil, October 7, 1968, General Archives of the Basilian Fathers, Toronto.

39. E.g., Dominique and Jean de Menil to Patrick O. Braden, CSB, November 12, 1968, General Archives of the Basilian Fathers, Toronto.

40. Dominique de Menil to Robert Indiana, October 3, 1969, Menil Archives, Houston, Texas.

41. Luptak, "Sedona's Crucifix of Despair Will Be Displayed Outdoors."

42. For the explosive energy that can be released after such a perceived violation see John Seitz, *No Closure: Catholic Practice and Boston's Parish Shutdowns* (Cambridge, MA: Harvard University Press, 2011).

The Road to Friendship House

Ellen Tarry and Ann Harrigan Discern an Interracial Vocation in the US Catholic Landscape

NICHOLAS K. RADEMACHER

Ellen Tarry and Ann Harrigan were pioneering Catholic social activists in the US during the middle decades of the twentieth century. Tarry and Harrigan are both remembered for their respective contributions to the pursuit of racial justice in the US and in the Catholic Church. Their efforts coalesced briefly through their involvement with Friendship House, a Catholic interracial movement that Catherine de Hueck Doherty founded in Harlem, New York City, and which subsequently spread to several other locations across the US. Together, Tarry and Harrigan co-founded the Chicago branch of Friendship House. For different reasons, both Tarry and Harrigan were at first reluctant to undertake the initiative but through careful discernment of their life's purpose found themselves in Chicago to promote racial justice in church and society.[1]

The African American Tarry and the Irish American Harrigan made a distinct impression in the Bronzeville section of Chicago where they planted their headquarters. Few people were accustomed to seeing shared leadership across the color line because so few took that option even when it was available. This chapter explores how and why these two women took that option during a period in US history when legalized segregation persisted in some parts of the country and de facto segregation was entrenched in other parts. They overcame their respective resistance to the invitation to co-found Chicago Friendship House for different reasons and stayed for different periods of time.

Both women left a trace of their reasoning for taking the option to co-found and co-lead an interracial establishment at a time when such initiatives were vanishingly rare. Tarry revealed some of her discernment in *The Third Door: The Autobiography of an American Negro Woman*, which was published about fifteen years after the Chicago Friendship House was founded.[2] A skilled writer, Tarry provides a carefully curated recounting of the time before, during, and after her brief Chicago Friendship House period.[3] She dedicated a few pages to the time leading up to her decision to go to Chicago and an entire chapter about her time there. Harrigan, by contrast, never completed an autobiography and only attempted one after she was decades removed from the actual experience. Beyond a few short reflections on her time at Friendship House that appeared in print, she never published an extended autobiographical account of her life.[4] Nevertheless, scholars have access to her discernment process through the unedited pages of her private journal from 1940 which she deposited at the archives at the University of Notre Dame.[5] Exploring these Catholic laywomen's experiences and elements of their discernment sheds light on an underexplored area of US Catholic history related to the challenges and opportunities of interracial collaboration in the mid-twentieth century.[6] Likewise, their experience can serve as a resource for those discerning their course of action in a church and society that continues to struggle to overcome the same disease of racism today.

The first part of this chapter includes an exploration of Tarry's decision to go to Chicago as it appears in her autobiography, *The Third Door*. Tarry's autobiography provides the best insight into her motivation for co-founding Friendship House. In the book, Tarry's discernment unfolds within the context of her lived experience as a person of color in a racist context. She recounts her encounters with racism and white supremacy in church and society. At the same time, she communicates her commitments to preserve and celebrate Black history and culture and to pursue racial justice within the Catholic Church in the US and within the broader US context. She initially resisted the call to co-found the Chicago Friendship House in deference to her commitment to pursue racial justice as a journalist. Yet, in the midst of an intense eruption of anti-Black violence at the start of World War II, she accepted the invitation to co-found Friendship House in Chicago as another way to serve the Black community.

The second part of this chapter focuses on Ann Harrigan's unpublished 1940 journal, which includes reflections on the year leading up to her decision to make a full-time commitment to Friendship House. Harrigan's discernment unfolds against the same backdrop as Tarry's, of course, but her arrival to a full-time commitment to Friendship House is complicated for different reasons. She had to address and overcome a number of barriers that prevented her from choosing to go to Harlem and then on to Chicago, including but not limited to her geographical distance from the

Black community, her consequent intermittent contact with people within the Black community, and pervasive racism within herself and among many of her counterparts in the Irish American community. In light of these factors, and no doubt others, Harrigan's journal from 1940 reveals a process of intellectual, moral, and religious conversion that involved the ponderous process of ongoing personal transformation and the halting, imperfect translation of that personal transformation to social action. An examination of this single year in her life reveals a portrait of a woman who gradually integrated and transformed the Catholic practices that she had received from her mid-twentieth century Irish American Catholic community to commit herself full time to interracial work.

Ellen Tarry

Ellen Tarry was born in Birmingham, Alabama in 1906. She was raised in a Protestant family, but she was educated in a Catholic boarding school, where she was introduced to and subsequently entered the Catholic Church. After a brief teaching career, she pursued a career as a writer that led her to New York City in 1929. There, she became involved in the vibrant life of the Harlem Renaissance and found success as a journalist and as an author of children's books. Her children's books are notable, in part, because they are among the earliest such books published by a major publishing company that included Black characters as central characters in the stories.[7]

Tarry came into contact with Friendship House through Fr. Michael S. Mulvoy, CSSp, the pastor of her parish, St. Mark the Evangelist Catholic Church. Mulvoy introduced Tarry to Catherine de Hueck, who had founded the first Friendship House in the US in Harlem in 1938. Tarry was inspired by her engagement with the interracial community at Friendship House in Harlem. As Cecilia Moore explains, "Tarry was encouraged by their open exchange of ideas, fears, and dreams and found at Friendship House a community of Catholics like herself who wanted to use Catholic social teaching to dismantle racism and to bring more African Americans into the Catholic Church."[8] Subsequent to her contact with Friendship House, Tarry began to write about the Black Catholic experience in the US and in the Catholic Church both to preserve and lift up Black history and culture and also to challenge Catholics to do more to promote racial justice in church and society.[9]

Tarry's connection to Friendship House would take her to Chicago, where she would co-found a branch of the movement. Tarry's 1955 autobiography, *The Third Door: The Autobiography of an American Negro Woman*, is a valuable source of information about her decision to move from New York to Chicago. As Moore explains, "In *The Third Door*, Tarry focused on the personal, professional, political, and spiritual challenges she faced as a Catholic, and how she hoped to be part of a positive racial transformation of her church and society."[10] Helping to co-found Friendship House in Chicago was an expression of her desire to be part of that positive racial transformation.

Tarry's decision to move to Chicago appears to have been a natural outgrowth of her commitments at the time, but it was not an easy decision to make. She was conflicted about whether she should help to found such a project when she understood her vocation first and foremost as a writer. In *The Third Door*, Tarry reveals some of this inner conflict but does not disclose much detail about the discernment process. Further, Tarry left little personal information about her decision to co-found the Chicago Friendship House in her archival deposit in the Schomburg Center for Research in Black Culture at the New York Public Library.[11] Tarry's emphasis on privacy is part of a rhetorical strategy. According to Stephanie Brown's interpretation of *The Third Door*, "Tarry highlights her 'privacy' to frustrate the reader and reemphasize that she is in control of the narrative" and in doing so she resists attempts to objectivize her story "for sentimental identification or exoticization."[12] According to Brown, Tarry refused to concede that "her life needs to be an open book, let alone a best-selling one, to be politically or spiritually inspiring."[13] Both Moore and Brown recognize the book as both politically and spiritually relevant in spite of its tepid reception since its publication.

Privacy to the fore, Tarry does not disclose much in *The Third Door* relative to her discernment to co-found Friendship House Chicago with Ann Harrigan. Still, contours of the discernment process emerge in the pages leading up to chapter thirteen, "Memories of Chicago!" in which she chronicles her time there. Throughout the book, Tarry tells of her experience with racism in the Catholic Church in the US. For example, she relates an episode where she and a friend encountered segregated seating and white hostility while attending Mass at a Catholic parish during a research trip through the South. She also recounts her ambivalent early encounters with Friendship House. She explains that she was initially suspicious of de Hueck as a white woman, living in voluntary poverty in Harlem, purportedly in service of the Black community. Tarry explains how her perspective shifted from suspicion to trust the more she came to know de Hueck and the other people in the community. She was impressed by the theological dimensions of their conversations around "the Fatherhood of God, and the Brotherhood of Man," "the Negro and the Mystical Body," and "Christ in the Negro."[14] Still, she knew she had work to do in broadening Black participation in Friendship House and educating and forming the white young adults who attended Friendship House events. Tarry wrote, "But I would have to get more Negroes to help me and we would have to explain to these well-intentioned white boys and girls that, instead of working *for* the Negro, they would have to work *with* us."[15] She would level the same critique against Harrigan and de Hueck after the Chicago Friendship House was up and running.

"Signs of the Times" and "Angry Harlem," chapters eleven and twelve of *The Third Door*, represent the heart of Tarry's discernment process about whether to go to Chicago to co-found Friendship House. She recounts the indignities inflicted upon the Black community by the white community in the buildup to US involvement in World War II in 1940 and 1941. She wrote specifically about the "tension" that arose as the Black community was shut out from the emerging industrial effort to prepare the country for war.[16] She mentioned the proposed "March on Washington Movement" organized under the leadership of A. Philip Randolph to integrate the Black community in employment opportunities in mobilizing for the war. She notes with ambivalence that the mass protest was called off when Franklin Delano Roosevelt issued Executive Order 8802, which Tarry quoted at length in *The Third Door*, to the effect that, "there shall be no discrimination in the employment of workers in defense industries or Government because of race, creed, color, or national origin" and that employers and labor unions must make it so.[17] The executive order had minimal effect.

Tarry reported that "grumbling and unrest" abounded in Harlem during this time. "The Monday night meetings at Friendship House became more heated as reports of street brawls, riots, police brutality, and lynchings poured in from all parts of the country."[18] She documented a litany of violent acts, including the lynching of Felix Hall near Fort Benning, Georgia, and the murder of Henry Matthews by police in Birmingham,

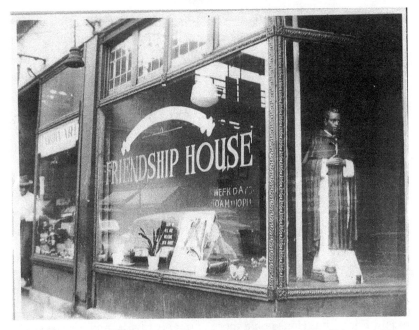

FIGURE 11: Storefront of Chicago Friendship House, 1946. Courtesy of Madonna House Archives.

Alabama.[19] In response, she and other Black members of Friendship House wrote up a "digest [of] the indignities our people had known from 1619 to 1942" that de Hueck would take with her to her meetings with bishops.[20] Tarry drew a direct line between this digest and the US Catholic bishops' 1943 statement concerning racism in the US.[21]

In the midst of this national and international nightmare, Catherine de Hueck informed Tarry that she had promised Bishop Sheil that both Tarry and Harrigan would go to Chicago to establish a Friendship House branch. Tarry declined the invitation. She was fulfilled with her work as a journalist. In fact, she had recently written a story about the wrongful prosecution and execution of Odell Waller in Virginia. Waller, a Black sharecropper, had been killed by electrocution for killing his white landlord in self-defense. After turning in her story on Waller, Tarry recounted, "I made up my mind to stick to my journalistic career and let some social worker co-direct Chicago's Friendship House." But de Hueck insisted. "She was convinced," Tarry recalled, "that I would be in a position to render even greater service to interracial justice in my position as co-director of Chicago's

Friendship House." Tarry was also approached by a priest from the bishop's office who commended her specific qualifications and familiarity with Friendship House operations. She recalled, "he told me my people needed me for this job," and that, "melted my resistance."[22] The signs of the times led Tarry to undertake this next step with the Friendship House movement, moving from Harlem, New York City to Bronzeville, Chicago.

Ann Harrigan

Ellen Tarry's path to and short-lived involvement in Chicago Friendship House may seem more than less direct in part because she presents it in a carefully prepared narrative. Harrigan's journey to Chicago might best be described as labyrinthine because her journal from the year 1940 is the closest source to her discernment process.[23] The journal puts the reader in medias res, January 1940, as Harrigan already had been involved in Friendship House intermittently over some time. She was feeling called to join Friendship House on a more permanent basis, and yet she could not deny a similar call to marriage and family life or making a commitment as a woman religious.

During this period, she vacillated between marriage, convent life, and a full-time commitment to Friendship House as a single person. She was, as she said of herself, "neither fish, nor flesh, nor good red herring." The phrase raises the question, of course: if she was none of these, what was she? She was self-consciously a work in progress, and she drew on the theological and spiritual resources of her day in order to determine next steps, rather than become locked into one or another particular pattern of action. During the discernment process she contravened, for a time, the social and cultural expectations of the communities she inhabited.

The phrase, "neither fish, nor flesh, nor good red herring," has a familiar ring but little is known about its origin or meaning. Read in the context of the entire journal year, Harrigan used the phrase to describe herself as not fitting in with the expectations of American culture, in general, or the established vocational expectations of her Catholic community, in particular. Understood in context, she used the phrase to simultaneously lament and celebrate that she was neither sister, nor housewife, nor radical lay Catholic, like Dorothy Day at the Catholic Worker or Catherine de Hueck at the Catholic interracial movement called Friendship House.

(Perhaps contrary to expectation, the radical Catholic option was already one among other viable courses of action for a laywoman in her vocational discernment by the late 1930s and early 1940s.)

Harrigan's vocational dilemma finds expression in her journal on the first day of the New Year. On January 1, 1940, Ann Harrigan recorded a prayer in her journal that frames the year to come. The prayer is an adaptation of the "Morning Offering," a prayer commonly recited daily by Catholics, especially in that time.

> O Jesus, thru the Immaculate Heart of Mary, I offer all the prayers, works, sufferings of this year, in union with the holy sacrifice of the Mass throughout the world, for all the intentions of thy Sacred Heart, especially for the Pope's intentions, and for Mama, Rita, Pete, Ed, and the rest of the family; for peace; for the success of Harlem work; and lastly that the whole world, including me, will learn to know ourselves and love you better.[24]

In this short prayer, Harrigan carries over some of her deepest longings from the year before and looks hopefully to the new year. Her Eucharistic spirituality, her commitment to her family, her work in Harlem, and her desire to know herself and love God better are all evident.

On the very next page, she introduces the underlying tension that seemed to obscure the clarity that she sought with respect to her vocation. She reflects on the New Year's Eve party that she attended the night before, "where all was noise, unhearable music, cramped quarters, dissatisfaction, envy." She acknowledged that the divide between flesh and spirit that she felt within herself was not unique. She described it as "this dickering with *la grande passion* interspersed with moments of high exaltation in working for Christ alone." She recounted the choice that was before her and concluded the New Year's Day journal entry with a quote that she attributed to St. Bernard: "What seek you that you will not find in Jesus Christ? . . . He is your spouse, friend, brother: Our Lord Jesus Christ is all you can and should desire."[25] While she accepted that principle axiomatically, she was less clear on how to live it out.

Harrigan was sorting out her vocation within the context of her particular place and time. She was born to Irish immigrant parents in 1910 in New York City. Her father worked as a carpenter while her mother raised the children and maintained the house. A Catholic priest sponsored scholarships that made it possible for Harrigan and two other promising alumnae from her high school to attend college. All three of the young women were encouraged to become women religious. She did not pursue a vocation as a woman religious, but the question surfaced for her repeatedly. She felt a greater call to marriage and to be a homemaker, a desire she traced back to her childhood, about age 15. After college, Harrigan passed the requisite exams for certification as a substitute teacher in the New York City public school system and served in that capacity from 1930 until 1937, when she passed the tests for permanent licensure. She held a full-time position at Grover Cleveland High School in Queens.

Up to this point, Harrigan's life followed the trajectory expected of a woman in her place in society. Harrigan's ambivalence around sex reflected the attitudes of the Irish Catholic community in the US at that time. As Jay Dolan explains in his history of Irish Americans, "Prescriptive literature enshrined the single woman's vocation to celibacy. This was an easier road to salvation than marriage." Consecrated virginity was upheld as the ideal, while marriage was the appropriate channel for those who were not called to celibate life.[26] It was not unusual for a second-generation Irish American woman to remain single or never marry.[27] She journaled often about her desire for physical intimacy and what she viewed as the frequent temptation to succumb to that desire.

Homemaking and teaching were socially acceptable occupations for Irish American Catholic women in the early twentieth-century.[28] In a mid-summer journal entry regarding the prospect of marriage and becoming a housewife, she disclosed, "I love domestic life—furnishing, cooking, planning—so what's keeping me back—Well, without love, it just isn't worth it—love makes all things easy. But otherwise, it is just a proposition and I'm against it."[29] Love was the measure as she sifted among the various forms of love available to her. Just a week earlier, while on retreat, she had written,

> More and more I see that it does not matter what we do—it is the spirit behind it—whether I work in Harlem, or live at home, teach in school or teach the missal—I am or should be—always ready to do all with zeal, intelligence, and above all love.

She recognized that God is the source and end of love. "I want to be poor, humble, hard-working. I want to love you and all in you . . . So, I say, come ahead and teach me, for I want you to enlarge my capacity for loving. Open wide my heart, the petty, paltry thing I call love—make me to see with thine eyes."[30]

In addition to considering a vocation as a woman religious or a housewife, Ann Harrigan also explored a third option, to join a radical Catholic community like Dorothy Day's Catholic Worker house or Catherine de Hueck's Friendship House. In 1933, Harrigan met Dorothy Day and became acquainted with and was inspired by the Catholic Worker community on Mott St. on the Lower East Side of Manhattan. Around the same time, she also became familiar with the work of Frank Sheed and Maisie Ward, whose lectures and publications fueled her intellectual curiosity and provided her with new ways to think about her inherited Catholic faith. Shortly thereafter, she met Catherine de Hueck and quickly became involved in Friendship House, an interracial apostolate that de Hueck had recently founded in Harlem. Taken together, Day, Sheed, Ward, and de Hueck helped Harrigan to assess and respond to prevailing communist philosophy and political theory that intrigued her by introducing her to alternative ways of being Catholic in the world.

A few weeks into 1940, she reflected on her various commitments. "I am neither fish, nor flesh, nor good red herring," she wrote, "I yearn to be something definite—a wife, a nun, a Harlem worker." She lamented that she was overstretched by her constant effort to be in so many places at one time and she did not feel as though she belonged in any of them. "But I'm an alien, an outsider, I do not fit, all my little plans shrivel up, are killed by frost. I have too many irons in the fire and they all suffer. O Lord, help me to love and understand you, to follow you blindly for there is no friend like you."[31] What was at stake for Harrigan, if anything, by not being "something definite"?

Harrigan held all three possibilities in balance. On February 3, 1940, she wrote, "What I must try to do perfectly is what I am attempting to do imperfectly now—live in the world but not of it—than which there is nothing harder, perhaps. The convent seems easy in comparison. But for those who have a vocation to it, it's hard, I suppose."[32] Her routine in 1940 was challenging. She recorded that, on Wednesdays, she was going from 6:15 in the morning until 11:30 at night, and consequently considered whether she should cut meditation and liturgy from her routine on Thursdays in order to get some extra rest. Still, Harrigan is honest enough to acknowledge that, while life in a convent might appear easy in comparison with her current routine, life as a sister would no doubt pose its own challenges were she fully immersed in that life.[33]

In part, she did not believe she was "pure" enough for the convent, given her history with men and the celibate ideal of the Irish American Catholic community in which she lived and breathed. She believed that her sibling, Helen, was a paragon of virtue as she took vows to religious life with the Religious Sisters of the Sacred Heart of Jesus in March 1940.[34] At her sister's vows ceremony, Harrigan reflected on the disruption her time in Harlem caused her family and the futility of her then current love interest. She stated plainly the dilemma she faced. "I am all over again—even now—*worried* about what I am going to do with my life—the time can be easily traced. Girl approaching 30 sees all friends marrying, going in convent, or living in H[arlem] or Mott St. Girl vacillates between [burning?] to marry Bill, or give it all up to go into the convent, or ditto and live in Harlem. It is an obsession with me."[35] Here, as elsewhere in her journal in 1940 and beyond, she felt drawn to religious life, to certain men, to marriage, and to a commitment like the one made by de Hueck and Day.

Between the two radical Catholic options in New York, Friendship House in Harlem or the Catholic Worker on Mott St., the former had greater appeal to Harrigan. Friendship House was located across the street from St. Mark's parish in Harlem. Here she, like Tarry, became acquainted with Fr. Michael Mulvoy, CSSp, who had invited de Hueck to establish Friendship House in Harlem. Under Mulvoy's leadership and on the strength of parishioners like Ellen Tarry, St. Mark's "came to be known as an activist parish" and "as a center for social justice" in Harlem.[36] In her visits to Harlem, Harrigan came into contact with an "African-American Catholic identity and culture in Harlem" that, as Moore explains, was being created by lay Black Catholics including "Billie Holiday, Claude McKay, Phillipa Duke Schuyler, Ellen Tarry and Mary Lou Williams."[37] Here, Harrigan must have come into contact with Tarry at least intermittently before they were invited to co-found a Friendship House branch in Chicago.

Harrigan consistently visited Harlem from her home in Brooklyn from the time she made acquaintance with the community. In the summer of 1939, Harrigan took on greater responsibility for the operation while de

Hueck was visiting Europe. In memory, the experience was exhilarating and added to the fulness of her life. She wrote in her 1940 diary,

> Who can measure God's goodness? My language is inadequate. But in everything—in Faith—above and beyond all others; in the careful, miniscule carrying of my soul—so delicately, so perfectly done. When I thought I was being ridden over rough shod; in my teaching, another example of stormy years to triumph is a sort of success; in music, in reading, in people—especially people—in food, in laughter, in clothes, in color, in variety—in the B[aronness Catherine de Hueck], in B[ill, a love interest], all the H[arlem] crowd—the pulse of life of blessed activity, that summer of 1939 in H[arlem].[38]

As with religious life and marriage, Harrigan carefully discerned between an idealized picture, a moment in time, and what a full-fledged commitment would be like. One year later, while on retreat, she reflected on that summer of 1939,

> What is success in the eyes of God? I am continually making adjustments in what it is—I just think I have it pat—and lo, a new horizon brings new perspectives—and I must recast the mold. But that is as it should be. I am in search of truth and as newer different aspects, or deeper strange meaning of Truth come to me—my preconceived notions conflicting with it fall away, e.g., my red hot zeal last summer was not tempered with a broad, long view. Prudence would have been difficult but salutary.

A year out from that experience, she acknowledges the pressure her absence from home placed on her family and meditated on the importance of serving both communities, in Harlem and in Brooklyn.

> You have given me a love for you, your poor, the eradication of injustice and inhumanity, the institution of charity, the rededication to your Mystical Body—but you have chained me to my home. I could break away, defy my mother, disregard my brothers and sisters, fly in the face of the world, and you know it. Instead, the harder thing is to straddle— to be a normal young woman who dresses and acts much the same as anyone else . . . but [who] must learn the harder road of detachment from all things while using them.

By way of conclusion, she challenged God, "If you wanted me in H[arlem], you could do it, you would do it." God had her in Harlem and with her family and in the public school, yet she perceived herself to be vacillating between home, work, and the Harlem community, all the while desiring to be more fully in one among these three.[39]

Whatever disruption her commitment to Friendship House had caused within her family to date, the situation was amplified on Trinity Sunday 1940 when she invited her friends from Harlem to visit the tidy apartment that she shared with her sibling, Rita. After Ann's friends visited, Rita discovered bedbugs in the house and immediately jumped to the conclusion that her sibling's guests from the night before had brought them. Ann was at a loss. She journaled, "Truly I don't know what to do—I put it in your hands, dear Jesus, for it wouldn't have happened if I hadn't tried to make interracialism social in fact, as well as in theory."[40] The bedbug situation became an ongoing problem in their apartment and Rita would not let Ann forget it. To resolve the emerging crisis, Ann unreasonably agreed to restrict Black visitors from entering the home and fired their Black housekeeper.

Racism combined with bourgeoise embarrassment over having a bug infestation no doubt played a factor in their interpretation and response to the situation. As Timothy Meagher explains, "American-born [Irish] women stood, like their immigrant mothers, for a future of ambition and respectability," which was represented by "'lace-curtain' middle class respectability."[41] According to historian Jennifer Nugent Duffy, social respectability and racial aptitude went together in the Irish Catholic community.[42] Indeed, racism was common among Irish American Catholics, and the Harrigan family, including Ann, was not immune from it. Meagher states plainly, "In the middle of the nineteenth century, Irish Americans earned a reputation as being among the most intensely racist people in America."[43] These attitudes persisted through the decades. Meagher continues, "The old values of group and neighborhood solidarity, virtues that enriched Irish American life in many respects, seemed to continue to also nurture Irish American (and other Catholics') resistance to cooperation with nonwhite people until well into the twentieth century."[44] Ann and Rita Harrigan seem to have been operating out of those very same biases in policing the boundaries of their Brooklyn home.

The bedbug situation was a recurring topic throughout Harrigan's diary in 1940. On July 11, Ann and Rita Harrigan were still dealing with an infestation that they could not seem to eradicate. The next day, Ann reflected on Matthew 5, the Gospel reading for daily Mass, wherein Jesus invites his disciples to live out of a universal love, one that extends beyond kinship ties. She wrote, "If this isn't clear on Jews, negroes, and all others commonly reviled, then I can't read anything." She concluded the entry for July with an Edwin Markham poem that she transcribed thus:

> They drew a circle that left me out
> Heretics, rebel, a thing to flout;
> But I and love had the will to win
> We drew a circle that took them in.[45]

Before the end of the year, Ann Harrigan drew the circle wide again around her home by inviting her friends from Harlem back for a visit. Rita became upset but Ann held her ground this time. "I got angry, of course," she wrote in her journal, and, at the same time, she implored God to transform Rita's racist attitude into love for neighbor. "I want her to see what I see. O Lord, can't you give it to her?"[46]

Beyond her apartment, Brooklyn, and Harlem, Harrigan was acutely aware of global events and the escalating conflict in Europe. She recorded the German bombing of England on May 25, 1940. She wrote,

> England was bombed last night. The face of Europe is a shambles, a human, terrorized, blasted, blasted wreck, seething with 3–5,000,000 refugee women and children. O God, this diabolic state. Will you not deliver us from it, as you have delivered us from our sins? I know and acknowledge that Europe, the world is what our rotten selfishness has made it . . . Hitler is certainly not dawdling.[47]

This news put her own problems into perspective. She described them here as "Just a ceaseless round of non sensical activities going to school plays, listening to talk about bed bugs, weariness, gossip, people, Dear Lord, I am yours—I want to be blindly obedient to you. But who are you?"[48] In the face of the destruction of World War II, she continued to pledge her allegiance to God but wondered about God's identity in the face of so much suffering.

The war further complicated her own discernment. She wrote later, "I am bewildered by the war, by what we should do, what I should do. It appalls me, the satanic evil of annihilation and total destruction." Yet, in the same entry, she continued to wonder about her own calling as she reports on her younger sister's friends marrying and having children. This observation gives way to a deeper insight into the foundation of her Christian vocation:

> I know that history is moved by far deeper causes than appear on the surface—that people too aren't what they seem, nor events—There is a hidden current of vitality—the supernatural life—which courses as it will through the Mystical Body—it is the stream that I must forever attach myself, and when I do forever, I shall no longer care what happens to me, except that I stay close to Christ.[49]

Here the question of fish, flesh, or good red herring totally faded away in light of an insight into the "hidden current of vitality" in which she participated as a member of the Mystical Body of Christ. She prayed that she would not be tempted by facile political allegiances, but remain committed to the work of Christ in the world. She wrote, "Dear Lord, [remain] inside me . . . so that I look neither to the right nor to the left. I put my life into your hands. Bless all I know, the whole world. Make peace again."[50] Harrigan internalized the global conflict and wondered how it would be made manifest in the US. She feared "that Hitler's ideas, not necessarily H[itler] would overrun and destroy church and society without resistance." She asked, implicitly having in mind her white community, "which of us in our comfort, apathy, self-complacency will move a finger to push back this tide of annihilation?" In the meantime, through her participation in conversations at Friendship House, she would have been acutely aware of the violence being afflicted on the Black community. She begged God to alleviate the suffering of the victims of war and wondered about the fundamental restructuring in society that would be required to transform society, both internal and external structures. She wrote, "and yet, am I wrong when I say that the world needs a radical change, a turning toward you? Is Rita [her sister] right that I revel in the idea, that I'm a crackpot etc."[51] Her participation in the "hidden current of vitality" within "the supernatural life which courses . . . through the mystical Body of Christ" continued to place her outside recognized social categories. Her sister named it, calling her a "crackpot." Still, Harrigan persisted.

Her desire to transform the world recurred throughout the year. As early as January 20, inspired by the Epistle of Peter, Harrigan identified an ambitious goal to Christianize the world. She wrote, "But when I read the Epistle of Peter who so perilously embarked on the Christianizing of the world—and who made the world over, because of his faith—I see we have need of more faith." She strove to interject Matthew 5 into her family system. She recognized that even Dorothy Day and Catherine de Hueck would need more faith to persevere in the face of the monotony of seeing the same problems and seeming never to surmount them. She knew that she herself needed more faith to continue the journey. She asked God to enable her "to love you as I should, to walk in your paths not mine, to be tested in your furnace and strengthened."[52]

In the final weeks of the year, she returned to the question of her identity and role, still unanswered, and began to name her mission. "I don't know who I am—I only know I burn and hunger for truth and justice and love and that in trying to get closer to these I am a sore thumb to myself and others. Sometimes I wonder if that is my mission—to make people sit up and think to jolt them out of complacent acceptance of the current status quo."[53] She did so through attentiveness to word and action. And on the last day of the year, Harrigan reflected back over the last 365 days and summarized her answer to the question with a single word, not a noun or an adjective to describe her role, but a verb to name what she did, "love." She wrote, "I see that at the beginning of this year I had 8 or 10 different aims—and this year I am going to have one—St. Augustine's own— 'instead of many methods, have one—love God, love, love and love.'"[54]

A prolific diarist, Harrigan also wrote publicly as a way to carry out her mission to "jolt [people] out of complacent acceptance of the current status quo." In August 1940, she authored a short article called, "The Dark Ghetto," for *The Councilor,* a publication of the Junior Councilor's of St. Mark's parish CYO in Harlem. Harrigan addressed her white brothers and sisters in the US and, more specifically, in the Catholic Church.

In this particular article, Harrigan pointed out plainly the reality of racial injustice in the US in order to call out her white readers with respect to systemic injustice in the country and also to call them to repentance and action for justice. The contents of her article and examination of conscience reflect her learnings from the Black community in Harlem that would be summarized in the document Tarry and others wrote for de Hueck and the bishops two years later. For example, Harrigan wrote, "Since 1929 we Americans have found it hard to get a job. Since 1619 negroes in America have found it almost impossible to get a job." She then outlined basic facts about discrimination in employment, housing, and education that disproportionately impacted the Black community in the US. She evoked the Constitution of the US and writings of Pope Pius XII to make the case for racial justice. Yet, even as she was trying to raise awareness about and responsiveness to racism among white US citizens, her language reflected her own need for growth as, for example, she distinguished between "we Americans" and the Black community so that the word, "Americans," stands for white people.

Beyond the recitation of facts, she includes an examination of conscience for her white Catholic readership. She included the following questions:

> Do I, as an employer, hire my employees because of their education, training, experience—or because of their color? As a Catholic, do I discriminate against the Negro in any way? As a Catholic, am I consciously or unconsciously adding to the pressure on the Negro, our brother in Christ, and therefore, am I, so to speak, putting pressure on Christ, adding to his cross and pain, injuring His Mystical Body, the Church, by thus giving scandal?

With these questions she sought to foster a moral reckoning among her white Catholic counterparts who may have read her article, her coreligionists, her neighbors in Brooklyn, her own sisters and brothers, and even herself. By this point, she was well situated to respond affirmatively to the invitation to help co-found the Chicago Friendship House.

Conclusion

In Fall 1942, Ellen Tarry and Ann Harrigan were in Chicago laying the foundations for a second branch of the Friendship House movement. The discernment process did not end for them when they joined Friendship House because the movement did not require permanent vows. Many of the same vocational questions remained for the women and men who wrestled with the decision whether to join the movement in the first place, such as, what tactics to pursue around direct action and advocacy; whether to remain on a permanent basis or come and go, especially should an emergency arise with one's family; whether to marry or join a religious community; and any number of other possibilities.

In "Memories of Chicago!," in *The Third Door*, Ellen Tarry recounted her preparation for, time in, and eventual departure from Chicago. While one might assume that Tarry and Harrigan would have been more acquainted with one another through their time at Friendship House in New York, it was not the case. Tarry only notes that Harrigan preceded her to Chicago and met her at the train station when she arrived. Her discussion of their collaboration in Chicago does not reflect any awareness of Harrigan's struggle with her own decision to take part in this initiative. Their strangeness to one another might be due in part to Tarry's regular travel for work and Harrigan's intermittent time with Friendship House in New York up to that point. Even when they were in Chicago together, Tarry makes clear in *The Third Door* that she did not disclose her misgivings directly to Harrigan and that, if Harrigan had misgivings, she did not disclose them to Tarry.[55]

Whatever the case, their collaboration in Chicago was complicated for many reasons, and Tarry's discernment led her to return to New York City once the Friendship House branch was up and running. In part, she felt that her presence was preventing Harrigan from growing in her knowledge and understanding of the Black community in Chicago. She wrote, "It would have been humanly impossible for anyone to try harder to understand a people and their habits than did Ann. I knew, however, that she would never have the understanding necessary to the smooth functioning of the center as long as I stood like a buffer between her and our Negro members."[56] Tarry did not find that de Hueck was receptive to her suggestions on how the center should be run. "The score was different with the 'B,'" Tarry wrote, "I was constantly making suggestions which I felt were sound, but they did not coincide with her views on how the center should be run."[57] While their friendship remained intact, Tarry felt she could not persist with a movement that did not take into account the community in which they were embedded. While she was concerned her departure from Chicago might jeopardize her friendship with de Hueck, she was just as concerned about how her participation in Friendship House impacted her relationship with the Black community there. She wrote, "neither could I afford to lose the respect of my people, and certain habits, customs, and policies had to be taken into consideration and the awareness thereof incorporated in the foundation on which we hoped to build a strong community center."[58] Her fundamental criticism of the project can be summarized in what she called a "fairy godmother approach," what she referred to as "working for" rather than "working with."[59] By the start of 1943, she was back in New York City to resume her work for racial justice in other ways.

On Harrigan's part, by choosing Friendship House, she made a more definite commitment to one of the various vocational options that she pondered throughout 1940. She was no longer, "neither fish, nor flesh, nor good red herring." She was "something definite." At the same time, of course, by becoming something definite, she forfeited the life that she was then presently living by straddling multiple roles. Harrigan remained with the movement until the end of the decade, when, motivated in part by internal dynamics at the house and her engagement to Nicholas Makletzoff, she embarked on another dimension of her Christian vocation.

Tarry's autobiography and Harrigan's journals provide insight into the discernment process of two Catholic laywomen whose paths crossed for a brief period of time when they chose to co-found an interracial center in Chicago at a time when such collaboration was rare. To be sure, their brief partnership points to the limits of interracial collaboration then and now. Although she eventually opted to move to Harlem, Harrigan struggled to overcome the de facto segregation of New York and the attending racism that infected her family and the broader white community in which she lived. Further, although Tarry commended Harrigan's efforts to understand the Black community, it is clear that Harrigan and Catherine de Hueck failed to listen carefully to or follow through with Tarry's advice about how to work with rather than work for the community they sought to serve. For her part, Tarry admirably drew boundaries around the limits of her capacity to educate her well-intentioned white counterparts in the movement, whether that be about the history and culture of the Black community or the best practices in collaborating with them in a project like Friendship House. Tarry's ongoing discernment led her to return to writing, which in turn led to several children's books and histories of the lives of saints.[60]

For both women, their Catholic identity and justice commitments converged in the context of the Friendship House movement. There, Tarry and Harrigan, among countless others, found a space where Black and white communities could meet to share and to learn about Black history and culture, to conduct social analysis to expose racial injustice, and to get to know one another through prayer, meals, and combined action for the common good. They also found a rare opportunity to learn, internalize, and practice theological insights that subverted racist attitudes and practices in church and society: our mutual membership in the Mystical Body of Christ, the affirmation that Christ is in everyone regardless of race, and the conviction that we are all daughters and sons of God. Their respective legacies deserve attention today as resources for discernment for those who recognize that the contemporary context calls for action as urgently as it did in Tarry's and Harrigan's time.

Notes

1. The word, "discernment" has a very specific meaning in a Catholic context, often evoked in reference to the Spiritual Exercises of St. Ignatius of Loyola. According to Bernard Lonergan, as theologian Patrick Byrne explains, "the spiritual exercises are concerned with the grace that makes people 'more and more fully and [ever] more consciously living members of Christ Jesus.'" While Tarry and Harrigan were not necessarily undertaking the spiritual exercises, this definition provides a concise understanding of what was unfolding within their lives as women of prayer who were committed to social action. See Patrick H. Byrne, "Discernment and Self-Appropriation: Ignatius of Loyola and Bernard Lonergan, S.J.," *Revista Portuguesa de Filosofia* 76:4 (2020): 1399–1424.

2. Ellen Tarry, *The Third Door: The Autobiography of an American Negro Woman* (New York: David McKay Company, 1955). The term "negro" appears throughout this paper only in direct quotations. The term was standard until the mid-1960s when the nomenclature shifted with the rise of the Black power movement.

3. See Stephanie Brown, "Bourgeois Blackness and Autobiographical Authenticity in Ellen Tarry's *The Third Door*," *African American Review* 41:3 (2007): 557–570.

4. Ann Harrigan, "Invading the South Side," *Commonweal* (May 19, 1944): 106–108 and "Living a Revolution at Friendship House," *Commonweal* (December 8, 1978): 777–779.

5. This paper emerges in part from a study of Harrigan's journal from 1940, held in the Harrigan collection at the University of Notre Dame. I am grateful for the support provided by a 2019 Cushwa Center Travel Grant to study this collection.

6. For recent account of Ann Harrigan's and Ellen Tarry's contributions to Catholic interracial work set against the backdrop of the broader Catholic

interracial movement, see Karen J. Johnson's *One in Christ: Chicago Catholics and the Quest for Interracial Justice* (New York: Oxford University Press, 2018) and Albert Schorsh's "'Uncommon Women and Others': Memoirs and Lessons from Radical Catholics at Friendship House," *U.S. Catholic Historian* (Fall 1990): 371–386. Schorsh and Harrigan were friends.

7. See Ellen Tarry, *Janie Belle* (New York: Garden City Publishing, 1940); *Hezekiah Horton* (New York: Viking Press, 1942); *My Dog Rinty* (New York: Viking Press, 1946); *The Runaway Elephant* (New York: Viking Press, 1950).

8. Cecilia Moore, "Keeping Harlem Catholic: African American Catholics and Harlem, 1920–1960," *American Catholic Studies* 114:3 (Fall 2003), 17.

9. Moore, "Keeping Harlem Catholic," 17–18.

10. Cecilia Moore, "Writing Black Catholic Lives: Black Catholic Biographies and Autobiographies," *U.S. Catholic Historian* 29, no. 3 (Summer 2011): 17–18.

11. Ellen Tarry papers, Sc MG 738, Schomburg Center for Research in Black Culture, Manuscripts, Archives and Rare Books Division, The New York Public Library.

12. Brown, "Bourgeois Blackness," 558.

13. Brown, "Bourgeois Blackness," 566.

14. Tarry, *Third Door*, 144.

15. Tarry, *Third Door*, 144.

16. Tarry, *Third Door*, 175.

17. Tarry, *Third Door*, 177.

18. Tarry, *Third Door*, 181.

19. Tarry, *Third Door*, 185–186.

20. Tarry, *Third Door*, 186.

21. Tarry, *Third Door*, 193–194.

22. Tarry, *Third Door*, 195.

23. I leave aside her late-in-life interpretations of this year because they are influenced by decades of hindsight. Her later interpretations of this period are valuable and important when examining the arc of her entire life, but they miss the crucial nuance available from a study of the quotidian events and reflection on those events that constituted that big picture. Parts of that big story have been told by scholars who have explored Harrigan's valuable contributions to Catholic interracial work at mid-century. For example, see Johnson, *One in Christ* and Schorsh, "Uncommon Women and Others," cited above.

24. Ann Harrigan, page one, Journal 1940. University of Notre Dame Archives, Notre Dame, IN. For 1940, Harrigan adapted a journal from 1930 so the days do not line up and frequently an entry would run across several pages. The reader of the journal must rely on Harrigan's annotations to determine what day it might be.

25. Harrigan, January 1, 1940.

26. Jay P. Dolan, *The Irish Americans: A History* (New York, Bloomsbury Press, 2008), 123.

27. Timothy Meagher, "Irish American Gender and Family," in *The Columbia Guide to Irish American History* (New York: Columbia University Press), 178. https://www.jstor.org/stable/10.7312/meag12070.11.

28. Meagher, "Irish American Gender and Family," 179.

29. Harrigan, Diary, July 16, 1940

30. Harrigan, Diary, July 7, 1940.

31. Harrigan, Diary, January 22, 1940.

32. Harrigan, Diary, February 3, 1940.

33. Harrigan, Diary, February 8, 1940.

34. Harrigan's entries for her sister's vows taking ceremony span February 29–March 1, 1940.

35. Harrigan, Diary, February 29, March 1, and Saturday, March 2, 1940.

36. Moore, "Keeping Harlem Catholic," 7.

37. Moore, "Keeping Harlem Catholic," 16.

38. Harrigan, Diary, January 11, 1940.

39. Harrigan, Diary, July 6, while she is on retreat.

40. Harrigan, Diary, May 19, 1940.

41. Meagher, "Issues and Themes in Irish American History," 180.

42. Jennifer Nugent Duffy, *Who's Your Paddy?: Racial Expectations and the Struggle for Irish American Identity* (New York: New York University Press), 72. The second chapter of Duffy's book is especially relevant here with respect to the development of Irish raced-based identity.

43. Meagher, "Irish Americans and Race," in the *Columbia Guide to Irish American History*, 214.

44. Meagher, "Irish Americans and Race," 231.

45. Harrigan, Diary, July 13, 1940.

46. Harrigan, Diary, November 1, 1940.

47. Harrigan, Diary, May 25, 1940.

48. Harrigan, Diary, May 25, 1940.

49. Harrigan, Diary, June 17, 1940.

50. Harrigan, Diary, June 20, 1940.

51. Harrigan, Diary, June 20, 1940.

52. Harrigan, Diary, January 20, 1940.

53. Harrigan, Diary, December 18, 1940.

54. Harrigan, Diary, December 31, 1940 (the top of the page is amended to read December 29 but the internal text identifies the day as New Year's Eve).

55. See Tarry, *Third Door*, 202, 209, 211.

56. Tarry, *Third Door*, 211.

57. Tarry, *Third Door*, 211.

58. Tarry, *Third Door*, 212.

59. For more on Tarry's critique of Friendship House, see Nicholas Rademacher, "Hierarchy and Democracy: The Friendship House Movement in the United States, 1938–1948," *U.S. Catholic Historian* 40, no. 2 (Spring 2022): 77.

60. See citations to Ellen Tarry's children's books above. Tarry's books on saints include the following titles: *Katharine Drexel, Friend of the Neglected* (New York: Farrar, Straus, & Cudahy, 1958); *Martin de Porres: Saint of the New World* (London: Burns and Oates, 1963); *The Other Toussaint: A Modern Biography of Pierre Toussaint, a Post-revolutionary Black* (Boston: St. Paul Editions, 1981).

From Grailville to the Universe

How the Grail Movement Widened the
Possibilities for American Catholic Laywomen

MARIAN RONAN

Because of the splendid film "Hidden Figures," many of us know of the Black women mathematicians who played pivotal roles in the US Space Race. And some also know that Marie Curie actually made greater contributions to modern physics than her husband. But who knows the stories of Catholic laywomen who had major impacts on the global Church?

In this essay, I lay out the history of one such significant but little-known group, the women of the Grail, especially in the United States.[1] In doing so I wish to bring to your attention the role of American Catholic laywomen, not only women religious, in global Catholic mission and ministry. I also hope to alert you to the ways in which the women of the Grail contributed to the education and formation of US Catholics beyond the boundaries of family and of the Catholic school system.

The Grail movement was launched in the US in March of 1940, when two women, Lydwine van Kersbergen and Joan Overboss, members of a Dutch Catholic laywomen's movement then known as the Society of the Women of Nazareth, arrived in New York City. The Nazis invaded the Netherlands two months later, severing communication between the two women and the group's leadership for the duration of the war.

A Dutch Jesuit, Jacques van Ginneken, had founded the Women of Nazareth in 1921. The purpose of the group was to employ the gifts of Catholic laywomen in the task of converting the world.

From the beginning, the group's identity had been a complicated one. Van Ginneken founded it with the expressed intention of using laywomen's extraordinary gifts in the battle to resolve the crisis in which Western society found itself. But he feared that the modern world with its many seductions would undercut the commitment required for the Women of Nazareth to transform the world, so he mandated that the lay group be led by a quasi-religious (that is to say, quasi-monastic) "fiery nucleus." The members of this core would be trained much as monks and nuns were, with a lengthy novitiate, severe ascetic practices, and the making of promises of "poverty, chastity and obedience," hopefully for life, but in any case, for as long as they belonged to the group. The group was also hierarchically structured, and the superior was called "Mother General." Yet van Ginneken also mandated that the Women of Nazareth be a lay group, not taking canonical vows, which would put them under the control of the Catholic hierarchy, or force them to have a male chaplain in residence.[2] As we shall see, this tension, not to say contradiction, would mark the hundred-year history of the group, eventually known as the Grail Movement.

The Women of Nazareth had initially worked with factory girls in the Netherlands and had planned to do lay missionary work in other countries. They also assisted van Ginneken with retreats for non-Catholics. But in 1928, J.D.J. Aengenent, the new bishop of the diocese in which the Women of Nazareth were located, in an attempt to push back against the growth of socialist youth groups locally, asked (well, ordered) the group to shift its focus to working exclusively with the Catholic girls of that diocese.

In obedience, the Women of Nazareth launched the Grail youth movement. Despite their initial ambivalence, the founding of the youth movement in 1928 turned out to be a "true watershed in the history of the Women of Nazareth."[3] Among other activities, the group held a series of massive dramatic presentations in the Amsterdam Olympic Stadium; during Easter of 1931, thirty-two thousand people witnessed three thousand girl actors from all over Holland perform a drama called "The Royal Road of the Cross;" two years later, ten thousand girls enacted a Pentecost play in that same stadium. By 1931, the group had "twenty-three urban centers, seventeen outposts in rural areas, six hundred and forty leaders, and eight thousand members."[4]

Because of the success of the Grail youth movement in the Netherlands, Catholic bishops began inviting the leaders of the Grail to launch the movement in other countries. In 1937, the social justice–oriented auxiliary bishop of Chicago, Bernard Sheil, visited the Grail while researching European youth movements, leading to a meeting between Lydwine van Kersbergen and George Cardinal Mundelein in Chicago in 1939 to discuss the lay apostolate. Mundelein welcomed the Grail to the US in 1940.

The following summer, with the help of Sheil, van Kersbergen and Overboss launched the first US Grail programs at Doddridge Farm, an archdiocesan-owned property in Childerly, Illinois, outside Chicago. Grail retreats and programs there attracted numbers of Catholic women and girls; the Grail's extraordinary embodiment of the liturgical renewal drew particular attention. Soon American Grail women were traveling from Doddridge Farm across the country to share the Grail message in parishes, dioceses, and Catholic women's colleges.

But things were never really satisfactory for the Grail in Chicago; while van Kersbergen and Overboss's primary aim was to train Catholic women for full-time work as lay apostles, Sheil, and Mundelein's successor, George Cardinal Stritch, required them to conduct summer camps for grade-school girls and share the property with Catholic Youth Organization programs for boys. Even as all this was unfolding, van Kersbergen became connected with the National Catholic Rural Life Conference, the Catholic embodiment of the "back to the land movement." Its leader, Monsignor Luigi Ligutti, urged her to move the Grail to a "real farm," and he connected her with Cincinnati archbishop, John T. McNicholas, who was considerably more receptive to the Grail mission than Sheil and Stritch had been. With McNicholas's help, the Grail in 1944 bought a 183-acre farm in Loveland, Ohio, northeast of Cincinnati, which McNicholas named "Grailville."

That first summer in Ohio the Grail conducted three training programs for Catholic lay women there and four others across the country. Then, on October 1, they opened the first "Year's School of Christian Formation," a rigorous, long-term residential program that prepared young women to go out and transform the world. The first year, there were three students; the second year, twenty-five. The Year's School and related programs not only helped the Grail to spread throughout the US—by 1962, an estimated fourteen thousand women had participated in Grail programs in the US— but also stimulated the growth of the Grail movement in other parts of the world. Thus began an educational endeavor beyond the boundaries of Catholic parishes and schools, one that would eventually "fertilize" communities around the world.

To grasp how a farm in southwest Ohio exerted such global influence, however, it's necessary to situate Grailville, and the Grail Movement, in the period when they began, the first half of the twentieth century, and even before then.

The Wider Context: The Catholic Church in the "Modern World"

A popular reading of the development of Roman Catholicism in the twentieth century is that the church "entered the modern world" at the Second Vatican Council (1961–1965). And it is certainly the case that the Catholic church had had a complicated and sometimes conflictual relationship with the "modern world," especially after the French Revolution, the revolutions of 1848, and the capture of Rome by the Italian State in 1870. The Vatican expressed its emphatic opposition to these developments in, among other things, the publication of the Syllabus of Errors in 1864, the condemnation of the Americanist heresy in 1899, and the Modernist heresy in 1907.[5]

At the same time, the Catholic church had been a major player in the modern world from the outset. The fourteenth-century papal bulls *Dum Diversas* and *Romanus Pontifex,* by declaring the conquest of Indigenous lands by Christian princes "just" and "lawful," contributed significantly to the "Doctrine of Discovery" that was used to justify colonization;[6] the Spanish Catholic monarchs, Ferdinand and Isabella, likewise sponsored Columbus's voyage to the "New World," an event some consider to mark the beginning of the early modern period.

It therefore follows that the Catholic church participated in modernity even as it opposed certain aspects of it. Indeed, in its efforts to defeat the evils of secularism and liberalism, the church called forth forces that contributed to its own modernization well before Vatican Council II.

One such development was the "lay apostolate," something that emerged, in part at least, from the recognition by the Vatican and the hierarchy that the laity are (almost) as much apostles as the clergy, and thus essential to the mission of the church. For example, as early as 1884, eighty-one years before the Vatican II document on the lay apostolate,[7] Pope Leo XIII acknowledged the important role of the laity in the church's fight against Freemasonry.[8] And in the decades that followed, especially after World War I, the hierarchy began acknowledging and promoting the laity's apostolic role, using the term "Catholic Action" to describe it.[9] In the first encyclical after his election, for example, in 1922, Pope Pius XI strongly promoted the laity's role in Christianizing all aspects of the increasingly secularized modern world.[10]

Certain tensions existed, however, between the Vatican's recognition of the essential role of the laity in the battle against "modernity" and its desire to retain control over that same laity. Pope Pius XI expressed the tension in 1931 in his, in many respects, galvanizing social encyclical "Quadragesimo Anno," when he described "Catholic Action" as "the participation of the laity in the action of the hierarchy."[11] Many lay associations that eventually came into existence, for example, here in the United States, the Holy Name Society, the National Council of Catholic Women, and the National Council of Catholic Men, did in fact remain under the control of the bishops, though this was less the case with some other lay groups.[12]

At the heart of the lay apostolate was the theology of the Mystical Body of Christ, based in the Pauline teaching that all are "one body" with a "single Spirit."[13] But in the promulgation of this theology, too, the Vatican struggled to retain control over the laity, as when Pope Pius XII, in his 1943 encyclical on the Mystical Body, used distinctly hierarchical and juridical terms to describe the relationship between head and members in that "one Body."[14] All this notwithstanding, because of the teaching's stress on the unifying role of the Spirit and on the mystical rather than purely organizational nature of Christ's Body, the church, the theology of the "Mystical Body of Christ" introduced a strikingly more unified vision of humanity and a groundbreaking understanding of the church itself as a vital force for social and cultural change. These had a particularly energizing impact on Catholics in the US.[15] The various papal calls for "Catholic Action," the dynamizing new theology of the Mystical Body, and the growth of an increasingly educated middle class led to the emergence of a considerable number of lay Catholic movements and communities between the 1890s and the 1950s.

One noteworthy dimension of the lay apostolate is the Catholic Intellectual Revival. The revival was a cluster of intellectual, cultural, and spiritual movements formed to counter the anti-religious rationalism of the Enlightenment and the wider evils of the modern world. Perhaps the single most significant figure in the Catholic Revival was a member of the clergy, John Henry Cardinal Newman, but it was also powered by the literary work of laymen such as G.K. Chesterton and Christopher Dawson in Britain and Charles Péguy, Léon Bloy, and Jacques Maritain in France. By the 1920s, the Catholic Revival was underway in the US as well, with the foundation of the lay Catholic journal, *Commonweal*, in 1924, the reconstruction of the Sodality of Our Lady in the late 1920s, and the 1933 opening of the New York branch of the British lay publishing house Sheed and Ward, to make the classics of the European Catholic Revival available to US Catholics.[16]

Another factor contributing significantly to the "modernization" of the Roman Catholic Church before the Second Vatican Council was the Liturgical Movement. This movement to revive and transform the liturgy and the communal prayer life of the church emerged from the renewal of European Benedictine monasticism in the 1830s. By the 1920s, the liturgical renewal had made its way to the US, through initiatives at St. John's Benedictine Abbey in Minnesota.[17] Some consider their publication of the first issue of the liturgical journal *Orate Fratres* in November 1926 to be the beginning of the US liturgical movement.[18] But Pope Pius X (1903–1914) had already energized certain aspects of the liturgical renewal, urging more frequent reception of communion, reducing the age of children's First Communion, and declaring participation in the liturgy to be the source of the true Christian spirit.

Though some aspects of these earlier phases of the liturgical renewal may seem romantic and medieval, the effects of its emphasis on the communal nature of prayer and worship were quite the opposite. Already by the late 1930s, letters to the editor of *Commonweal* were demanding that the Dialogue Mass, launched by the Benedictines in Germany in 1924, be celebrated every Sunday in all parishes.[19]

A third major development within Roman Catholicism well before Vatican II was the turn to social action. Stimulated by various anti-Catholic actions beginning in Germany in the 1840s, Catholic concern with social justice came further into focus with the publication in 1891 of Pope Leo XIII's "Rerum Novarum," the first Catholic social encyclical. By the early decades of the twentieth century, clergy and laity alike were calling for Catholic social and political engagement in response to industrialization, urbanization, and poverty. After World War I, the Social Action Department of the National Catholic Welfare Council (NCWC)—now called the US Conference of Catholic Bishops—pushed for various social reforms. In the early 1920s, the NCWC Social Action Department established the Rural Life Bureau, focused on poverty in rural areas; this bureau, in turn, morphed into the National Catholic Rural Life Conference (NCRLC).[20] During the Depression, Luigi Ligutti, a pastor active in the NCRLC, spoke out continually about the plight of the rural worker and secured federal funds to build homes for unemployed miners; by 1941, he had become head of the organization. Also during the Depression, the NCWC held seventy US conferences that addressed industrial problems. Lay groups also played a significant role in the Catholic turn to social action. These included the Catholic Worker, founded in 1933, Friendship House, an interracial apostolate founded in 1938 comprising a network of urban centers across the US, and the Grail Movement.[21]

As noteworthy as each of these pre-Vatican II developments are in themselves, the Intellectual Revival, the Liturgical Movement, and Catholic social action, it would be difficult to overstate the extent to which they were interconnected. Dorothy Day, the charismatic leader of the Catholic Worker, is known primarily for her commitment to social justice, yet for her, the liturgy was the core of that work. Less than a year after the publication of the first issue of *The Catholic Worker* newspaper, Benedictine Dom Virgil Michel, a driving force behind the Liturgical Movement in the US, noted in *Orate Fratres* that the *Catholic Worker*'s editors had "caught the spirit of the Church's liturgy and admirably link up their restatement of the Church's social doctrines with the inner life of the Church." Michel had good reason to praise this Catholic Worker synthesis, since for him, too, the liturgy, the Mystical Body of Christ and the reconstruction of the social order were fundamentally connected.[22]

Along these same lines, at the 1941 meeting of the Liturgical Movement, the Rev. Martin Hellreigel, a national leader in the liturgical renewal, complained because the gathering was being held at the same time as the annual meeting of the NCRLC and he wanted to attend both.[23] Similarly, a leader of the Catholic Intellectual Revival, Sheed and Ward co-publisher Maisie Ward, wrote regularly for *Orate Fratres* and considered the Dialogue Mass an essential building-block of the lay apostolate.[24]

In the decades before Vatican II, these components of the lay apostolate, the Intellectual Revival, the Liturgical Movement, and Catholic social action converged remarkably in the International Grail Movement. The Grail's earliest incarnation, the Women of Nazareth, had been explicitly founded as a part of the lay apostolate, and their ministry focused from the outset on serving the poor and disenfranchised, working with Dutch factory girls and planning to start a university for women in the Dutch East Indies (now Indonesia) based in Javanese rather than European culture and languages. Such an egalitarian approach by European missionaries was rare at the time.[25]

The founder, Jacques van Ginneken, an internationally known psycho-linguist and ethnologist and the only Jesuit ever elected to the Dutch Royal Academy of Sciences, might himself be characterized as a force in the European Catholic Intellectual Revival. Van Ginneken's vision of a mythical, profound, and vigorous Catholicism was in line with those of radical Catholic thinkers such as Léon Bloy, Jacques Maritain, Cardinal Newman, G.K. Chesterton, and the Dutch Catholic author, Gerard Brom.[26] In addition, Lydwine van Kersbergen, one of the first members of the Women of Nazareth and founder of the Grail in Great Britain and Australia as well as the US, had studied the Oxford Movement in Britain after completing her PhD at the University of Nijmegen in 1936.[27]

During the 1920s and 1930s the Women of Nazareth and the Grail Youth Movement were not explicitly involved in the European Liturgical Movement. Yet as Katharine Harmon argues, the Grail's massive dramatic performances in the Amsterdam Stadium beginning in 1929, with many thousands of girls dressed in bright colors enacting the Christian message and dancing to Gregorian chant, launched the Grail as "one of the most courageous and public realizations of Catholic Action in the years between the world wars."[28]

Almost immediately upon its arrival in the US in 1940, the Grail became integrally involved in the liturgical-intellectual-social action of the American church. To illustrate the speed with which this occurred, consider that one of the US founders, Lydwine van Kersbergen, attended the convention of the NCRLC in 1941, only a little more than a year after the Grail's arrival in North America, and the other founder, Joan Overboss, spoke at the National Liturgical Week meeting at St. Meinrad's Abbey in Indiana in 1942.[29] Indeed, the Grail's first direct contact with the American church was a 1936 letter from van Kersbergen to Dorothy Day.

After the Grail was established in the US, in the summer of 1943, before the Grail's historic move to Grailville, Day participated in a three-week Grail course devoted to the principles and practices of rural living. Day mentioned enjoying the instructions in liturgical music by Dom Ermin Vitry, on the Mystical Body of Christ by the liturgist and founder of the US Jocist movement, the Rev. Reynold Hillenbrand, on religious-rural questions by Monsignor Luigi Ligutti, and on women by Lydwine van Kersbergen. She also welcomed the Grail's integrated approach to all of these questions, "meditating *and* breaking bread, praying *and* extracting honey, singing *and* making butter."[30]

With the 1946 publication of the Grail's booklet, *Program of Action: A Suggested Outline for the Lay Apostolate of Young Women*, the importance of the Catholic Intellectual Revival to the Grail became even more apparent. The first obligation in the battle against the evils of secularism, the program asserted, was learning the literature of the Catholic Revival, including the works of Sorokin, Berdaeyev, and Maritain. This was to be followed by engagement in the lay apostolate itself, modeled on the examples of the Desert Fathers, Benedictine Monasticism, and other movements for the transformation of church and society. The booklet also included a particularly sobering description of the modern condition by Professor Frank O'Malley of Notre Dame, a leader in the US Catholic Revival who spoke frequently at Grailville before Vatican II.[31]

In her interview for *Women of Vision*, US Grail co-founder Lydwine van Kersbergen likewise mentions readings at Grailville of Paul Claudel plays, such as *The Tidings Brought to Mary*, T.S. Eliot's *Murder in the Cathedral*, and the works of European writers such as Charles Péguy, Josef Pieper, Romano Guardini, John Henry Newman, G.K Chesterton, and Eric Gill, as well as religious dance led by Dom Ermin Vitry.[32] A number of US women also drawn to Grailville and the Grail had themselves been shaped by Catholic action, liturgical renewal, and Catholic Revival experiences. Dorothy Day sent a number of women to the Grail from the Catholic Worker, in some cases because she believed they were more suited to the Grail's culture than to that of the Catholic Worker. Marie Sutter-Sinden came to Grailville from the St. Louis parish of Msgr. Martin Hellreigel, one of the leaders in the US liturgical renewal, and Mary McGarry Kane, a future president of the US Grail, had been active in Catholic interracial work in Philadelphia before moving to Grailville with her husband.[33] And as the Grail movement spread from Grailville to city centers across the country beginning in the late 1940s, the operation of Grail art and book shops also manifested the Grail's investment in the Catholic intellectual and artistic revival.

In the years that followed, the US Grail continued and extended this multifaceted commitment, based in the theology of the Mystical Body of Christ, through its communal formation programs at Grailville and its

FIGURE 12: Marian Ronan has participated in the Grail movement since 1965 and has written extensively on the history of the Grail. Photo by Elizabeth M. Robinson. Courtesy of the author.

work in nine city centers across the country. In addition, the Grail stressed the essential function of women in this apostolate, something that distinguished it from all the other US Catholic lay groups of the time. For while women like Dorothy Day and Catherine de Hueck Doherty of Friendship House played pivotal roles in Catholic social justice activism, and a significant number of women made invaluable, if too often unacknowledged, contributions to the liturgical renewal, the Grail Movement has highlighted the essential place of women in the transformation of church and society from its founding in 1921 to its current work in nineteen countries around the world.[34]

At Grailville, in particular, these developments, including the lay apostolate, the Catholic Intellectual Revival, Catholic social action, the liturgical renewal, and of course, the Grail's identity as a women's movement, exerted enormous impact on women not only from the US but from around the world who lived, worked, studied, and prayed there beginning in 1944. This global impact is seldom mentioned in historical studies.

Before I move to the story of this international impact, however, let me mention that I myself began participating in the Grail movement in 1965, my senior year in high school, precisely because of what I perceived to be these extraordinary intersectional commitments. I was primarily attracted by the extraordinary liturgical life of the Grail: its liturgies and, in particular, the singing of Gregorian chant and the Grail's own sacred music, all of which seemed the fullest expression of the Second Vatican Council that I had ever encountered. Through my subsequent involvement in the Philadelphia Grail, I became more and more aware of and active in racial justice issues, and eventually in the development of feminist theology, in which the US Grail played a pivotal role. But now, back to Grailville . . .

Grailville's Impact on the Founders

Of the sixteen founders of the International Grail Movement whose profiles comprise *Women of Vision*, twelve visited Grailville at least once, and seven speak at length in their interviews about Grailville's impact on them.

The first of the founders profiled is Lydwine van Kersbergen. It may seem counterintuitive to discuss Grailville's impact on van Kersbergen since, as the person who made the decision to buy Grailville, her influence on Grailville would seem more significant than Grailville's on her. But in her interview, van Kersbergen speaks very clearly about that very impact on her; she had grown throughout her time in the Grail, but in America, she had grown the most. And not just "in America," but specifically at Grailville. She goes on to say, "The most beautiful years of my life have been the years at Grailville—living in community, fasting and feasting together . . . (and being) touched and impressed by . . . the young women who were with me."[35]

———

This vision of building a worldwide laywomen's movement, brought to realization in the Year's School of Christian Formation under van Kersbergen's leadership, significantly stimulated the growth of the Grail Movement internationally. In her travels in Africa and elsewhere between 1940 and

1965, van Kersbergen encouraged women to come for training at Grail-ville, with the hope that these women would then take the idea of the movement back to their home countries. She also believed the international presence at Grailville brought a rich, reciprocal dimension to the learning experiences of American women. Finally, van Kersbergen admitted, she had always been searching for an integrated life, inclusive of "training, the liturgy, the land"—and at Grailville, she had found it.[36]

Like Lydwine van Kersbergen, another Grail founder profiled in *Women of Vision*, Mary Louise Tully, can in one sense be said to have had as much influence on Grailville as Grailville had on her. Tully was the first American member of the Grail; she met and joined the movement in Europe, while she was traveling, before the outbreak of World War II. Tully's parents were financially well off, and after returning to the US, Tully gave van Kersbergen $22,000 for the down payment on the property, an amount she had obtained from her parents as her inheritance.[37]

Tully herself got most of her Grail formation at the Tiltenberg, the international Grail headquarters in the Netherlands, and at Doddridge Farm, the first Grail center in the US. She had never spent a great deal of time at Grailville. But while she was living at Grailville for a short period in the mid-1940s, the bishop of Hong Kong visited and invited the US Grail to send women to help build up the lay apostolate in China. Tully subsequently became the first Catholic lay missionary in China. While there she lived in a hostel for Chinese girls and with Chinese families. She also arranged for several young Chinese women to go to Grailville for training and spoke about the impact that being at Grailville had on those young women: "It awakened them to possibilities they hadn't even thought of before."[38]

Another founder profiled in *Women of Vision*, Frances van der Schott, was one of the first members of the Women of Nazareth to visit Grailville after it started in 1944. Van der Schott had been part of a team of Dutch women who had founded the Grail in Australia in the late 1930s. After the Nazi invasion of the Netherlands, communication between the Grail in Australia and the group's Dutch leadership was severed, as it was for the US Grail. But the Australian leaders decided in 1944 to send van der Schott to Grailville, "to make contact with what was going on with the Grail in other places." Van der Scott comments on the rigorous training she received at Grailville, and especially at Superflumina, the house in nearby Foster, Ohio, where future leaders were sent for intensive spiritual formation. She comments on the "marvelous discussions and speakers she encountered at Grailville." She also talks about the significant differences that emerged in the Grail in different countries during the war. In particular, she mentions how the Grail in the US had become more identified with the lay reality, whereas in Britain, the Grail had moved increasingly toward the more traditional practices of the original Women of Nazareth and had finally separated from the international movement to become a canonically recognized "secular institute," something like a Catholic religious order.

When, at the end of 1945, van der Schott returned to Australia, she helped to shape the community at the Grail's formation center there to live "more as they did at Grailville . . . more open and less separate from others, no more stress on the Ladies of the Grail. We did meditations the way they did at Grailville and began to till the earth."[39] Van der Schott's time at a farm in southwest Ohio had a major impact on the Grail in a country halfway around the world.[40]

Another visit to Grailville, this one in 1951–1952, actually shaped the very postwar identity of the International Grail Movement. This occurred when Rachel Donders, the Dutch head of the Women of Nazareth and the Grail Youth Movement, arrived finally at Grailville after visiting Grail groups around the world, to assess what the Grail had become during the war. As Donders recalls in her interview, Grail women up to that time had gone to the various countries to prepare young women to convert the world, but not to start a movement. Even at Grailville, young women had received apostolic and spiritual formation to change the modern world, but there was no wider Grail movement.

During her visit to Grailville in 1951–1952, Donders met with van Kersbergen and other women in US leadership and together they decided that the reconfiguration of the Grail as an international laywomen's movement would provide a new identity for the groups who until then were connected in such different ways around the world. It would no longer be a youth movement, but a laywomen's movement made of nucleus members who had made promises of poverty, celibacy and obedience, as well as married members and single members. The head of the movement would now be called the international president, not Mother General, and she would work with two international vice-presidents. When Donders returned to the Netherlands, the Women of Nazareth there were open to the idea, and even the bishop responded positively. The International Grail Movement, as it has been known since World War II, was born, and Grailville was its birthplace.[41]

In the summer of 1957, two Portuguese women, Maria de Lourdes Pintasilgo and Teresa Santa Clara Gomes, visited Grailville after attending a meeting in El Salvador of Pax Romana, the international Catholic students' association. Pintasilgo had just been elected the first woman president of the group. As she recalled, "Grailville was fantastic. We arrived at the beginning of a summer program and the first evening there was a presentation of Tolstoy's "What Men Live By." At the end of a few days, Teresa, who was twenty-one at the time, said, 'This is for me.' Just like that!"[42]

That was in August, and by October, Pintasilgo and Gomes had called together a group of young women from the Catholic Action group in Lisbon to start the Grail there. A few years later, Pintasilgo became a member of the International Grail Vice Presidency team, serving for two terms. Pintasilgo and Gomes both went on to become members of the Portuguese legislature, with Pintasilgo, becoming in 1979 the only woman prime minister in the history of the country.[43] The Grail in Portugal continues to this day, and one of its younger members recently served on the International Leadership Team.[44]

Another Grail founder, Elizabeth Namaganda of Uganda, spent three years at Grailville in the late 1950s. Namaganda found her time at Grailville exciting, describing it as a place where she got "real formation." She was especially impacted by the liturgy at Grailville, but also by what she learned about different cultures, and about religious education. When she returned to Uganda, she introduced liturgical practices there that she had learned at Grailville and that would become common in the church after Vatican II, for example, the Dialogue Mass.[45]

When Rebecca Nebrida, the founder of the Grail in the Philippines, was in the US studying theology and liturgy at the University of Notre Dame in 1957, she met Audrey Sorrento, a US Grail leader, and the future director of Grailville, who was also studying liturgy there. Sorrento took Nebrida to Grailville, and Nebrida enrolled in the Year's School.

Nebrida was deeply impressed with the new thinking and exposure to the latest theology at Grailville. She recalled visits by some of the best pre-Vatican II theologians: Jean Daniélou, Gerald Vann, Bede Griffith, and others. And, like many other women, myself included, Nebrida was deeply influenced by the music at Grailville, and especially the singing of Gregorian chant. In 1973, Nebrida, along with Jeannette Loanzan and Nebrida's sister Teresa, started the Grail in the Philippines. She especially wanted to share with people what she had learned at Grailville and at Notre Dame, that God is a God who loves us, not a punishing God.[46]

Another significant figure, Eileen Schaeffler, the first American to head the US Grail and then become president of the International Grail, spoke in her interview of the impact of her learning, at Grailville, for the first time, a lifestyle very much in touch with organic principles of life. She also stressed Grailville's unique impact on the International Grail, in particular because of its size and the number of Grail programs that were offered there, as well as the sense of community among the women, the bonding of their energy, and most fundamental of all, the infusion of the practical with the spiritual. So powerful was Grailville's impact on Schaeffler, in fact, that after six months in the Year's School, she went home and ended her engagement to be married and dedicated the rest of her life to the mission of the Grail.[47]

Several others of the International Grail founders profiled in *Women of Vision* visited Grailville, but much more briefly than the founders' visits already discussed. Imelda Gaurwa, the Tanzanian Grail leader who was the first African to serve on the International Presidency Team, attended the Grail International General Assembly at Grailville in 1971.[48] And Bep Camanada, the Dutch woman who was one of the founders of the Grail in Brazil, visited Grailville and several Grail city centers in the US on her way to start the Grail in São Paulo. She said it was there that she "came in contact with lay women in church and society." She described the experience as "marvelous."[49] And Magdalene Oberhoffer, another president of the International Grail, speaks not of her own visit to Grailville, but of how Ugandan women's notions of themselves were completely overturned when they saw two US Grail members trained at Grailville driving the tractor they brought with them to Uganda. The Ugandan women had never seen a woman drive a tractor. They were so impressed, they marched behind it in a kind of celebratory procession![50]

In addition to its effects on a number of the founders profiled in *Women of Vision*, Grailville fertilized the International Grail in other ways. From its very beginnings, women came from around the world to study at Grailville, taking their training back with them to their home countries. And in 1950, the Grail started the first lay mission training center in the US at Grailville; by 1963, over a hundred American women were serving on Grail teams in Asia, Latin America, and Africa. Then, in 1974, Grailville served as a base for the "Cultural Exchange Meetings on Africa," in which thirteen African women participated. For five months, these women traveled around the US, leading twenty-six workshops in different locations and meeting with their counterparts in US and UN educational, medical and social service agencies, returning periodically to Grailville to rest and regroup.[51] Similarly, since the 1990s, a number of African Grail women have attended a series of permaculture workshops at Grailville, and in 1995–1996, two US Grail members, went to Uganda to conduct permaculture workshops there.

Conclusion

A certain ambiguity has marked the Grail Movement from its inception. Founded as a lay movement, but with a "fiery core" who made promises (not vows) of poverty, chastity and obedience and underwent rigorous spiritual training, the Grail has elicited curiosity, and sometimes skepticism, from the church as well as the wider public. One Dutch member initially sought out the Women of Nazareth because of rumors about the group sharing housing with a Dutch Catholic men's group also founded by van Ginneken.[52]

Nor did the Grail's move to the US resolve that ambiguity: a year and a half after van Kersbergen and Overboss's arrival, an article in *Time* magazine described the women as "Nuns in Mufti" and a "new religious order."[53] And lest that article seem too old to signify very much, in January of 2016, the liberal *National Catholic Reporter* newspaper, published an interview with "Sister Imelda Gaurwa, the First Tanzanian Grail Sister," in which the Grail is described as "an international order."[54] Gaurwa is one of the Grail founders profiled in *Women of Vision*, and she mentions specifically joining the Grail because it was *not* a religious order.[55] What Gaurwa seems to have said may perhaps be attributed to her advancing age and health problems but reflects the ongoing ambiguity nonetheless.

In some respects, the US Grail continued that ambiguity. In part because of the severed communications between the two founders of the US Grail and their superiors in Europe during the World War II, and perhaps also because of American egalitarian tendencies, the US Grail emphasized the lay rather than the quasi-religious dimension of the group's identity from the outset. Yet in 1951, the international president of the Grail, Rachel Donders, to strengthen the group after the departure of the English Grail, mandated the dedication of the first twelve members of the "fiery core" of the Women of Nazareth in the US, thus introducing the historic tension between the "inner circle and the outer circle," the "nuns in mufti" and the laity, into the US Grail. This tension would then spread from Grailville to the rest of the world.[56]

It might seem that repeated questions about whether the Grail is a lay organization or a congregation of Catholic sisters would at least mean that the Grail's denominational identity is unambiguous, but neither is that the case. In the "Afterword" to his 1989 study, *The Grail Movement and American Catholicism 1940–1975*, Alden Brown argues that by 1975, the Grail in the US had effectively moved beyond the bounds of "Catholic affiliation," based on the fact that in 1979, it had begun welcoming Protestant members, and in 1975, expanded to include members of other religions as well.[57] While the move in the US from a Catholic to an ecumenical or even "spiritual" identity has spread to some other countries, the Swedish Grail, for example, is primarily Lutheran, in others the Grail membership is still entirely Roman Catholic.[58]

Some ambiguity also attends Grailville itself. For some, the US Grail was primarily identified with its training of young women on the farm. Yet by 1963, more than two hundred women were living in nine Grail "city centers" across the US and in Toronto, with thousands more gathering regularly for meetings in those centers. Some of the teams at those centers were deeply involved in interracial work and in the civil rights movements. I myself first became active in the Grail at its center on Chester Avenue in West Philadelphia, where the Grail had been working in community organizing and racial justice since 1954. I also trace my environmental work back to my five years on the Grailville staff, for example, to discussions we had with the eco-theologian Thomas Berry.

In fact, there had always been a tension between Grailville's rural identity and a certain urban orientation. Van Kersbergen herself was at first hesitant about Monsignor Ligutti's urging to locate the Grail on a farm.[59] Subsequently, in Britain, at the first meeting of international Grail leaders (including van Kersbergen) after the war, the founder, Jacques van Gin-neken, opposed the organization of the US Grail around a farm, though van Kersbergen was not deterred.[60] On the other hand, the co-founder of the US Grail, Joan Overboss, was primarily committed to the Grail's urban apostolate and worked from time to time as a laborer in Detroit factories.

It would be difficult to argue today that the International Grail, with its approximately nine-hundred members worldwide, is having as massive an impact as the Grail youth movement with its "six hundred and forty leaders and eight thousand members" in the Netherlands had in the 1930s.[61] It would be similarly difficult to argue that the current US Grail, with its approximately two-hundred-twenty-five members and fifteen women exploring membership, operates on the same scale as the movement did in the 1960s. At this point, even Grailville, the national center and inspiration of the US Grail since 1944, is facing serious challenges, with rising deficit forcing sales of property.

Yet neither can it be denied that the lives of many of the nine-hundred or so current members of the International Grail and their communities have been deeply affected by the women from around the world who trained at Grailville over the years and then went home to start the Grail. They have opened and staffed schools and hospitals, taught the Christian faith, farming, and women's empowerment, served in Parliament and even, in one case, became the Prime Minister of Portugal. Nor can it be denied that here in the US, the women of the Grail expanded the understanding of what Catholic laywomen could do and where they were able to do it. May their history inspire American Catholic laywomen toward similarly heroic work today and in the years to some.

Notes

1. This article is drawn from Marian Ronan and Mary O'Brien, *Women of Vision: Sixteen Founders of the International Grail Movement* (Berkeley, CA: Apocryphile Press, 2017).

2. Janet Kalven, *Women Breaking Boundaries: A Grail Journey* (Binghamton, NY: State University of New York Press, 1999), 35–36, 175–176.

3. Rachel Donders, *History of the International Grail 1921–1979* (Loveland, Ohio: Grailville, 1983), 6.

4. Alden Brown, *The Grail Movement and American Catholicism 1940–1975* (Notre Dame, IN: The University of Notre Dame Press, 1989), 9.

5. "The Syllabus of Errors Condemned by Pius IX," *Papal Encyclicals Online*, accessed November 13, 2021; R. Scott Appleby, *"Church and Age Unite" The Modernist Impulse in American Catholicism* (Notre Dame, Indiana: The University of Notre Dame Press, 1992), 7–8 and throughout.

6. "Preliminary study of the impact on indigenous peoples of the international legal construct known as the Doctrine of Discovery," United Nations Economic and Social Forum, Ninth Session of the Permanent Forum on Indigenous Issues, 19–30, April 2010, accessed November 13, 2021, https://www.un.org/esa/socdev/unpfii/documents/E.C.19.2010.13%20EN.pdf.

7. Pope Paul VI, "Apostolicam Actuositatem," November 18, 1965. The Vatican Archives, accessed November 13, 2021, http://www.vatican.va/archive/hist_councils/ii_vatican_council/documents/vat-ii_decree_19651118_apostolicam-actuositatem_en.html.

8. Pope Leo XIII, "Humanum Genus," April 20, 1884. The Vatican Archives, accessed November 13, 2021, http://w2.vatican.va/content/leo-xiii/en/encyclicals/documents/hf_l-xiii_enc_18840420_humanum-genus.html.

9. Brown, *The Grail Movement*, 10.

10. Pope Pius XI, "Ubi arcano Dei consilio," December 23, 1922. The Vatican Archives, accessed November 13, 2021, https://www.vatican.va/content/pius-xi/en/encyclicals/documents/hf_p-xi_enc_19221223_ubi-arcano-dei-consilio.html.

11. James M. O'Toole, *The Faithful: A History of Catholics in America* (Cambridge, MA: Harvard University Press, 2008), 146.

12. Jay Dolan, *The American Catholic Experience: A History from Colonial Times to the Present* (Garden City, NY: Doubleday and Company, 1985), 395–396; Debra Campbell, "The Struggle to Serve: From the Lay Apostolate to the Ministry Explosion," in Jay Dolan, R. Scott Appleby, Patricia Byrne, and Debra Campbell, eds., *Transforming Parish Ministry: The Changing Roles of Catholic Clergy, Laity, and Women Religious* (New York: Crossroad Publishing, 1990), 212–213.

13. Eph. 4:4.

14. John W. O'Malley, *What Happened at Vatican II* (Cambridge, MA: Harvard University Press, 2008), 85.

15. Arnold Sparr, *To Promote, Defend and Redeem: The Catholic Literary Revival and the Cultural Transformation of American Catholicism 1920–1960* (New York City: Greenwood Press, 1990), 105.

16. Campbell, "The Struggle to Serve," 226–227.

17. Steven M. Avella and Jeffrey Zalar, "Sanctity in the Era of Catholic Action: The Case of St. Pius X," *U.S. Catholic Historian* 15:4 (Fall 1997): 57–80

18. Timothy P. O'Malley, "Re-Reading *Orate Fratres*: The American Liturgical Movement Is Born (1926–27)," University of Notre Dame Blog Network, September 20, 2012. No longer accessible.

19. Campbell, "The Struggle to Serve," 226.

20. Dolan, *American Catholic Experience*, 380–381.

21. Campbell, "The Struggle to Serve," 240–241.

22. Harmon, *There Were Also Many Women There*, (Collegeville, MN: Liturgical Press, 2012), 51, note 62.

23. Harmon, *There Were Also Many Women There*, 223.

24. Harmon, *There Were Also Many Women There*, 136–137

25. Brown, *The Grail Movement*, 21.

26. Marjet Derks, "Female Soldiers and the Battle for God: Gender Ambiguities and a Dutch Catholic Conversion Movement," in Patrick Pasture, Jan Art, and Thomas Buerman, eds., *Gender and Christianity in Modern Europe: Beyond the Feminization Thesis* (Leuven, Belgium: Leuven University Press, 2012), 180.

27. Kalven, *Women Breaking Boundaries*, 39; Brown, *The Grail Movement*, 25.

28. Harmon, *There Were Also Many Women There*, 35.

29. Brown, *The Grail Movement*, 28–29; Harmon, *There Were Also Many Women There*, 51, note 134.

30. Brown, *The Grail Movement*, 23, 41–42.

31. Brown, *The Grail Movement*, 52–53; Sparr, *To Promote, Defend and Redeem*, 123–142.

32. Ronan, *Women of Vision*, 16, note 16.

33. Mary E. Gindhart, telephone conversation, August 26, 2006.

34. See Harmon, *There Were Also Many Women There*, for a thorough exploration of women's roles in the Liturgical Movement; for the Grail's focus on women, see Kalven, *Women Breaking Boundaries*, 217–231 and throughout.

35. Ronan, *Women of Vision*, 16.

36. Ronan, *Women of Vision*, 9–21.

37. Kalven, *Women Breaking Boundaries*, 70.

38. Ronan, *Women of Vision*, 72–86. .

39. In England and Australia, the Women of Nazareth had been called "the Ladies of the Grail" rather than the "Women of Nazareth"; the term was shortened to "the Grail" in the US. *Women Breaking Boundaries*, 311, note 2.

40. Ronan, *Women of Vision*, 37–51.

41. Ronan, *Women of Vision*, 22–36.

42. Ronan, *Women of Vision*, 199.

43. Though as the head of a transitional government, Pintasilgo's tenure was brief. "Obituary: Maria de Lourdes Pintasilgo," *The Independent*, July 13, 2004, accessed November 13, 2021, http://www.independent.co.uk/news/obituaries/maria-de-lourdes-pintasilgo-550094.html.

44. Ronan, *Women of Vision*, 155–169, 199–212.

45. Ronan, *Women of Vision*, 214–228.

46. Ronan, *Women of Vision*, 184–198.

47. Ronan, *Women of Vision*, 102–118.

48. Ronan, *Women of Vision*, 259.

49. Ronan, *Women of Vision*, 94.

50. Ronan, *Women of Vision*, 141.

51. Kalven, *Women Breaking Boundaries*, 150, 269.

52. Ronan, *Women of Vision*, 57–58.

53. "Nuns in Mufti," *Time*, July 21, 1941, accessed November 13, 2021, http://content.time.com/time/magazine/article/0,9171,765827,00.html.

54. Melanie Lidman, "Q & A with Sr. Imelda Gaurwa, the First Tanzanian Grail Sister," *The National Catholic Reporter, Global Sisters Report*, January 21, 2016, accessed November 13, 2021, http://globalsistersreport.org/blog/q/q-sr -imelda-gaurwa-first-tanzanian-grail-sister-36661.

55. Ronan, *Women of Vision*, 235–236.

56. The last US Grail member joined the Nucleus in 1975, but half of the approximately one hundred members of the Grail in Tanzania were Nucleus members in 2016. Mary E. Gindhart, telephone conversation, August 26, 2006.

57. Brown, *The Grail Movement*, 174–175.

58. "Where We Are: Countries: Sweden," The International Grail, accessed November 12, 2021, https://www.thegrail.org/index.php?option=com _content&view=article&id=82&Itemid=108 We Are: Countries: Tanzania," accessed November 13, 2021, http://www.thegrail.org/index.php?option=com _content&view=article&id=83&Itemid=109.

59. Brown, *The Grail Movement*, 28–29.

60. Brown, *The Grail Movement*, 55.

61. Brown, *The Grail Movement*, 9

Laywomen Enacting the Mystical Body

SANDRA YOCUM

A striking feature of US Catholic literature written from the 1930s through the 1960s is Catholics' confidence that they had a culture and that culture possessed the power to transform every aspect of contemporary secular society. For all the discussions of American Catholic insularity, a number of women, lay and religious, participated in a complex network of social, economic, political, and religious movements in which bishops, priests, religious, and lay people committed themselves to transforming twentieth-century US Catholicism so that lay Catholics could, in turn, engage and thereby transform contemporary secular culture. A principal standard-bearer of this complex network from the 1930s through the 1960s was the Roman Catholic Church, under the guise of the Mystical Body of Christ. This Body dedicated itself to the work of Catholic Action.

The ecclesial metaphor has its origins in Paul's reflections on the Church as the Body of Christ. Among certain twentieth-century Catholics, the metaphor generated complicated narratives that gave shape and meaning to nearly every aspect of their daily lives. These narratives share much in common with the "spatial stories" that Michel de Certeau describes in *The Practice of Everyday Life*.[1] "Two sorts of determinations," on the one hand, "place," and, on the other, "space," gives shape to these stories. Certeau, in his inimitable style, offers a bemusing definition of "place"—"*being-there* of something dead." Place appears fixed, unchanging, settled, like St. Peter's Basilica, a memorial marking the apostle's grave. The second, "space," is determined through "*operations*" that "specify 'spaces' by the actions of historical *subjects*" in relation to a specific place. More simply, "space" is a "*practiced place*." St. Peter's Basilica becomes a space of revivified apostolic authority when the pope teaches, most potently when he speaks *ex cathedra*, from the chair of Peter. This narrative of papal authority remains a familiar, even if contested, spatial story among Catholics.

Few spatial stories are fixed or stable. As Certeau explains, they "carry out a labor that constantly transforms places into spaces and spaces into places. They also organize the play of changing relationships between places and spaces." He continues, "The forms of this play are numberless, fanning out in a spectrum reaching from the putting in place of an immobile and stone-like order . . . to the accelerated succession of actions that multiply spaces. . . ."[2] Once papal pronouncements appear as written texts, they too function as places, fixed, stable, and unchanging, in one sense, but also quite portable in another. Through "the actions of historical *subjects*," these "places" become "spaces," which are not entirely stable or fixed. Certeau's use of "play" captures something of the creative energy among Catholics, including laywomen, whose actions multiply spaces, i.e., "practiced places" of Mystical Body performing Catholic Action.

Placing the Mystical Body's Catholic Action

Which lay activity constituted Catholic Action remained under constant debate. In his *U.S. Catholic Historian* article on Catherine de Hueck and Catholic Action, Nicholas Rademacher notes that even Fulton Sheen admitted difficulties in identifying what was and was not Catholic Action despite repeated papal efforts to clarify. In his 1931 *Non abbiamo bisogno* (We do not need . . .), Pius XI states emphatically: Catholic Action "does not wish to be nor can be anything other than 'the participation and the collaboration of the laity with the Apostolic Hierarchy.'"[3] Yet, earlier papal pronouncements about Catholic Action contributed to its expansive purview. In his 1905 encyclical, *Il Fermo Proposito* (The firm purpose . . .), for example, Pius X explained to Italian prelates Catholic Action's ultimate purpose: "to restore all things in Christ."[4] Restoring all things in Christ includes not only saving souls but also attending to "Christian civilization in each and every one of the elements composing it."[5] Taking their lead from Pius X's restoration project, Catholics could identify almost any activity as Catholic Action. Sheen proffered "that, in spite of its ambiguities, the term Catholic Action has definite meaning when it is understood 'in terms of the Church, or the Mystical Body of Christ,' which includes 'a kind of juridical incorporation' of the laity into the Church."[6] Sheen's observations resonate in striking ways with Certeau's describing the "operations" of spatial stories, which include "marking boundaries." Such stories provide an "everyday role of a mobile and magisterial tribunal in cases concerning their delimitation." According to Certeau, these boundary-making "operations" become even clearer when "made explicit and duplicated by juridical discourse."[7] The laity's "Catholic Action" gained a "place," or as Sheen describes it, a "juridical incorporation" in the Church through the spatial stories of the Mystical Body of Christ.

Appeals to the church as Mystical Body of Christ, however, produced its own ambiguities. In prefatory remarks to the 1943 encyclical, *Mystici Corporis Christi*, Pius XII observes, "Much indeed has been written" about this "sublime doctrine."[8] The pope intends not only to recommend the image as doctrinally proper, but also "to exclude definitively the many current errors with regard to this matter."[9] These errors zigzag between "'popular naturalism'" and a "false 'mysticism.'"[10] To overemphasize, on the one hand, "the body" reduces the church to a mere "natural" or human institution void of its supernatural dimension; to overemphasize, on the other hand, the "mystical" obscures the church's visible reality under the pontiff's vicarship. After clarifying the necessary synergy between mystical and body, he exhorts all "members of the Mystical Body of Jesus Christ" to recognize

> the obligation of working hard and constantly for the building up and increase of this Body. We wish this to be borne in mind especially by members of Catholic Action who assist the Bishops and the priests in their apostolic labours—and to their praise be it said, they do realize it—and also by those members of pious associations which work for the same end.[11]

Pius XII's inclusion of "pious associations" hardly discourages capacious views of the Catholic Action of the Mystical Body of Christ.

The Mystical Body's story, as the corporate "historical subject" of Catholic Action, involves an exceedingly complex place. As a physical place, the Roman Catholic Church exists as an international visible society, hierarchically ordered, located in geographically defined parishes, with auxiliary institutions including convents, schools, orphanages, and hospitals as well as "pious associations," all located within geographically defined bishop-led dioceses all united under the headship of the Pope located at the Vatican. These places received further definition through multiple fixed discourses, from Scripture to papal pronouncements to canon law to the Roman missal to the catechism, together constituted "a mobile and magisterial tribunal." The Mystical Body of Christ enacts Catholic Action, a spatial story in which these places become spaces of lay activity. In some cases, these spaces of lay activity in turn become fixed, stable places. John Courtney Murray's 1946 exposition, "Towards a Theology for the Layman," illustrates the interplay between space and place.

> There is the theological movement towards a wider intelligence of the doctrine of the Mystical Body of Christ, the liturgical movement towards a more active participation in the liturgy of the Mystical Body of Christ, and the social movement towards a more universal participation in the hierarchical apostolate of the Mystical Body of Christ.[12]

Embedded in this quote is the unfolding of the story: theology's account of "the doctrine of the Mystical Body." The Mystical Body in turn enacts this theological story. On the one hand, it transforms places like local churches into spaces, "practiced places," signified as "liturgical movement." The "movement" consists in "active participation in the liturgy **of** [not **in**] the Mystical Body." In Murray's telling, the "Mystical Body" possesses a kind of corporate agency that enacts liturgy. On the other hand, as Murray's description suggests, some spaces become places. A "social movement" wends its way toward "universal participation in the hierarchical apostolate of the Mystical Body of Christ." It moves toward "place," the "stability" and "fixed location" of the church's settled teaching signified in its "hierarchical apostolate."

Murray invokes the "hierarchical apostolate" with no mention of "Catholic Action." The first installment of what is a two-part essay provides a possible reason. Murray intentionally opts for small "'a' Catholic action" since it "designates simply the laity as called to support and prolong the apostolate of the hierarchy; it omits the question of their mode of organization. And we shall take Catholic action in this sense as covering the active function of the laity in the Church."[13] Murray's option describes laity as "historical subjects" operating in a myriad of "multiple spaces." He also refers to "the development of the doctrine of Catholic action," which he links to "a double pressure—one from without upon the Church, and, answering it, another from within, a vital upsurge of the Church's own conquering life."[14] His expansive story of Catholic action suggests the possibility of interplay between places and spaces that could very well involve "each and every one of the elements" in modern civilization that Pius X hoped the laity might conquer for the church.

Thus far, the storytellers, including the Jesuit American intellectual, John Courtney Murray, have been the ordained. The principal "historical *subjects*" of these spatial stories, the laity and more particularly laywomen, performed their own versions. Certeau, citing other scholars, notes how these spatial stories delimit, i.e., mark boundaries. In marking boundaries, their "primary function is to *authorize* the establishment, displacement, or transcendence of limits. . . ."[15] What follows are a small sample of American Catholic laywomen who told such stories "to *authorize* the establishment, displacement, or transcendence of limits" in their own enacting of the Mystical Body of Christ.

Women Authorizing the Mystical Body of Christ

Eva J. Ross provides the first example. Who exactly is Eva J. Ross? Born in Northern Ireland in 1903, she received a degree from Bedford College, London, in 1930, and that same year, immigrated to the US. She taught in a number of small Catholic women's colleges, Nazareth College in Kalamazoo, Michigan, and then Maryville and Fontbonne Colleges, while pursuing her master's degree in sociology from St. Louis University. After completing her master's thesis in 1934, she moved to New Haven, where she taught at Albert Magnus (1935–1936) and then the College of St. Elizabeth in New Jersey (1936–1939) while completing a doctorate in sociology at Yale University. She graduated in 1937. Her dissertation topic, "the cooperative movement," remained her lifelong academic specialty and is the subject of her major substantive book, *Belgian Rural Cooperation: A Study in Social Adjustment* (1940).[16] In 1940, she joined the faculty at Trinity College in Washington, D.C., where she served as chair of the sociology department until her death in 1969. Her accomplishments include co-founding the *American Catholic Sociological Review* and her election as president of the American Catholic Sociological Association in 1943, eight years prior the American Sociological Association electing a woman.[17] In 1961–1962, she received a Fulbright to pursue her study of rural cooperatives, this time in Colombia. She published numerous textbooks that introduced sociology to a host of Catholic high school and college students.

Dr. Eva Ross authorized an official and distinctive Catholic lay agency in a 1940 *Catholic Educational Review* article, "Training for Catholic Action." The article identified specific "historical *subjects*" who perform the Mystical Body's spatial story, Catholic Action. "The word *laity* means laypeople, so that priests and religious cannot take part in the actual work of Catholic Action, although of course they can be auxiliaries to it." In explaining the obvious, Ms. Ross hints at the less obvious significance of an official ecclesial-sanctioned role for the laity. "The word *apostolate*" informs this role, and "the restoration of all the activities in this world to Christ is of the essence of Catholic Action."[18] More specifically, the laity participate in the hierarchy's three-fold apostolate: "to teach the doctrine of Christ and to sanctify the souls of the faithful, and thus to help the hierarchy to fulfill its third function—the government of the Church."[19] The papal intent in defining Catholic Action as participation in the hierarchy's apostolate was not to transform the ecclesial order but the secular. Dr. Ross suggests otherwise.

> We needed not only a renewal of the age-old Pauline doctrine of the union of Christians in the Mystical Body of Christ, not only a renewed appreciation of the liturgy and what it means; we needed an official position within the Church to give us courage to live again in the zeal and the spirit of the early Christians.[20]

The sociologist Ross shares the theologian Murray's singling out the doctrine and its liturgical enactment as key in the Mystical Body's spatial story. Earlier in the article, she directly links Catholic Action to the Eucharistic liturgy. "Catholic Action is a union with the sacrifice of the Mass—an extension of the work of Calvary, not by passive worship, but through sacrifices and through deeds—a life of example to others, which is also a life of work for others."[21] She appeals to the episcopal authority of Bishop Meyers who spoke about the Mass in these terms at the Sodality of Our Lady summer school. Ross's third point contrasts with Murray's external facing "social movements." The laywoman focuses on the effects of gaining "an official position within the Church." In Eva Ross's telling, Catholic Action authorizes the laity's transcending the present to revive "the zeal and the spirit of the early Christians." In Pius X's promotion of Catholic Action to restore Christian social order, he probably had in mind reviving the spirit of medieval papacy's Christendom rather than early

Christian laity's zeal. Ross's sociological accounts of economic cooperatives resonate with at least one account of early Christians; they shared
all things in common.

US Catholics introduced to sociology through one of Ross's high school
and college textbooks learned about the social order through her ecclesial lens. Her 1966 high school text, *Living in Society*,[22] published only three
years prior to her death, provides evidence of her enduring commitment
to bringing an explicitly Catholic perspective to sociology. The seventeen-
chapter text provides a wide-ranging overview of sociology, organized
around individual and society, social institutions, and national and international social problems. In explaining "the influence of environment" on
the individual, for example, she states, "As we know, all men the world
over are equal in the sense that all are composed of body and soul and are
made in the image and likeness of God." She notes all also suffer "the effects of original sin" and benefit from Christ's redeeming work.[23] The text
makes occasional references to papal teaching but no explicit mention of
the Mystical Body. Ten of the seventeen chapters recommend for supplemental reading either Virgil Michel, OSB., et al., *The Christian in the World*
(1939) or Virgil Michel, OSB., *Christian Social Reconstruction* (1937). Some
chapters recommend both.

In the chapter, "Religious Organizations," under the subheading "Basic
Social Institutions," Catholic Action appears in the section highlighting
how the US Catholic Church "is particularly flourishing." She describes a
"highly organized institution," mentioning the parish, diocesan, papal system as well as "numerous organizations for religious and social purposes."[24]
After describing "religious congregations" and "secular institutes," Ross
states, "*Catholic Action is the official organization for the Catholic laity to help
in the apostolate of the hierarchy.*" It requires episcopal recognition and "must
have some apostolic work, and must aim at the spiritual improvement of its
members."[25] As in her 1940 article, the sociologist Eva J. Ross establishes
the clear limits of lay activities that qualify as official "Catholic Action" and,
in doing so, lays claim to an official space in the Church's social organization
as Mystical Body of Christ. As will soon be clear, many other Catholic
laywomen identified other fixed places from which emerged the "spaces"
of the Mystical Body enacting Catholic Action/action.

The second laywoman, Dorothy Day, in contrast to the infrequently
referenced Dr. Eva Ross, serves as a primary historical exemplar of US

Catholic laywomen's initiative and activism. As with many other aspects of Day's Catholicism, she cites an unusual source for her understanding of the doctrine of the Mystical Body of Christ. In the middle section, "Natural Happiness," of her 1952 autobiography, *The Long Loneliness*, she gives an account of her coming to understand the "doctrine of the Mystical Body." In the chapter, "Love Overflows" she recollects with horror and sorrow the August 1927 executions of Nicola Sacco and Bartolomeo Vanzetti. Day includes a page-length excerpt from Vanzetti's last letter in which he identifies himself and Sacco as workers: "a good shoemaker and a poor fish peddler." The final quoted line: "That last moment belongs to us—that agony is our triumph" anticipates and celebrates their executions in ways that echo gospel accounts of Jesus's crucifixion. Day attributes a very particular lesson to that event. "All the nation mourned. All the nation, I mean, that is made up of the poor, the worker, the trade unionists—those who felt most keenly the sense of solidarity—that very sense of solidarity which made me gradually understand the doctrine of the Mystical Body of Christ whereby we are the members one of another."[26] Day recollects a feeling, not a text, experienced twenty-five years earlier. Her expansive understanding of who holds membership in the Mystical Body arises "gradually" not from reading papal teaching but from memorializing two innocent men executed, quite literally the "*being-there* of something dead." Her gradual understanding eventually included a pacifist response to America's entrance into the World War II. "What the Mystical Body of Christ produces in Dorothy's thought is the radical effacing of the difference between us and them."[27] Facing sharp criticism from other Catholic Workers, Day never yielded her pacifist stance, later manifest in her refusal to cooperate in civil air raid drills. Joining others, she sought refuge in a New York City public park rather than an air raid shelter. For her, to attack another person is to attack the body of Christ just as to serve another person is to care for the body of Christ. The Catholic Worker Houses of Hospitality became that "practiced place" where one offered direct service to Christ embodied in every person who crossed the threshold.

Among the many laywomen who crossed the threshold was Helen Caldwell Day (no relation to Dorothy Day). Caldwell Day, like Dorothy, converted to Catholicism as an adult. In *Color, Ebony*,[28] this African American woman gives an account of the many twists and turns in her conversion. Helen had come from her mother's home in Memphis to New York

City to study nursing. Initial attraction to Catholicism arose from baptizing at-risk newborns. Eventually she received Baptism. Shortly after entering the church, she married George Day, and then became pregnant. The couple soon separated and eventually divorced. Helen returned to her mother's home in Memphis with her two-week old son. After two months, she returned alone to New York City to complete her nursing studies. Following a hospital chaplain's advice, she volunteered at St. Joseph's House of Hospitality.

Seeing past the chaos and filth that repelled her, Helen came to admire those who joined the ranks of Catholic Workers. They were "very ordinary people who had found a great truth. . . . Their discovery had revolutionized their own lives, as well as the lives of a lot of other people, and aimed at revolutionizing the whole of society . . ." Their pursuit of sanctity through voluntary poverty fueled this revolution. Their efforts had "not made them angels." Yet, Helen desired what they had. "In all their poverty they were richer than I—and I knew I wanted to be poor—as they were poor."[29] Dorothy Day, in Helen's telling, embodied this revolution of sanctity. Helen recalls "a warmness about her, a tenderness—woman, mother." She marvels at Dorothy's ability to recognize "in this insolent beggar, smelling of whiskey, the Person of Christ. She sees in this brown girl [Helen] His [Christ's] sister—nay, more, a member of His Mystical Body."[30] Caldwell Day expresses the semiotic power of "the Mystical Body of Christ" that elevates her to more than the happenstance of family. She gains membership in a space, a "practiced place," of revolution. Her words resonate with the opening lines of *Restoring All Things to Christ: A Guide to Catholic Action.*

> It was Peguy who said: 'When an idea takes to itself a body, the result is revolution.' Catholic Action is all of this, and even more. Christ, the Verbum Dei, took to Himself a Body and became man; His Mystical Body, which is the Church, lives on and is in every age and at every period of history a revolution, both personal and corporate.[31]

In her personalist revolution, Dorothy Day never sought the official moniker of Catholic Action. In eschewing episcopal approbation, she also avoided the constraints of hierarchical oversight. She did have the advantage of being a white woman with a cosmopolitan past in a cosmopolitan city where such movements could thrive regardless of official episcopal approval.

Helen Caldwell Day, by contrast, did seek clerical approval for her work in Memphis. *Not without Tears* offers her account of that work.[32] Nineteen months in New York sanitariums recovering from tuberculosis while her son, Butch, recovered from polio in a Memphis hospital led her to "adopting new values and new ways of thinking about things." Helen quickly learns the major obstacles she will face in living out those values in segregated Memphis. In her first encounter with a local priest, Father Paul, pastor of St. Joseph's parish, "very kindly" informed her, "Negroes did not attend services there, not even the Mass, *St. Joseph's* parish! (St. Joseph, Patron of the Universal Church, pray for us!)." He gave her communion and "promised to visit her at her home." After recounting the painful episode, Helen speaks directly to her readers: "That is a terrible, ugly thing, isn't it? You who love the Church and see in her Christ's Mystical Body will tremble."[33] The same pastor had reassured Memphis's white citizens that his establishing a Catholic school for Black children would not upset the status quo. "He was being 'prudent,'" Caldwell Day observes and then continues, "The only thing he forgot was that kind of prudence has no place in the Mystical Body of Christ, in the life of the Church."[34] Helen Caldwell Day exercised her place in the Mystical Body to call out another member who happened to be ordained.

Caldwell Day found a handful of Memphis Catholics who shared her interests, in particular, a young white man, Jim. Using the *Catholic Worker* subscription list, they organized an "interracial Catholic Action or discussion group"[35] As she explained, "A member might be white or colored, Catholic or non-Catholic, so long as he was interested in the life of the Church as the Mystical Body of Christ and the welfare of the members therein."[36] Fifteen people gathered to discuss *Mystici Corporis*. Finding a priest-chaplain, required for official Catholic Action groups, proved difficult. One priest claimed time constraints, recommended another priest, and then called him to warn about the group and its radical interracial plans. Finally, a Josephite, Father Coyne, accepted the invitation.

In her telling, the Mystical Body of Christ became a space, a practiced place, not of racial harmony but of struggle. Her memoir of the four years in Memphis, *Not without Tears* relates the many challenges with searing honesty. She recounted the difficulties in addressing racism in the Catholic Action study group. ". . . the racial problem is more than a problem of color. It is a problem of housing, of wages, of work, of families, of many different things. . . . We wanted to be interracial as the Church is inter-racial, because the truth is too big for any one people. And because Christ is in all and loves all."[37] She describes with great poignancy the difficulty in believing "the doctrine of the Mystical Body sometimes, when we have grown up in the loneliness of hatred and suspicion, distrust and prejudice. . . . like a monster lurking ready to pounce, is the demon of prejudice, waiting for one to step over the faint line that is still there and forget one's place, so that this unity, good as it is, is not enough." Unity in the Mystical Body had nothing to do with color blindness, as she makes clear: "we wanted not to forget color, but to have it not matter."[38] Caldwell Day made painfully clear in story after story how much it did matter.

The courage of her actions in 1950 segregated Memphis and racially charged America cannot be overstated. Her activism included memo-rizing the Supreme Court ruling that prohibited enforcing segregated seating on interstate public transportation, reciting it if challenged on middle-of-the-bus seat choices on cross-country bus trips. On one trip, she and a companion moved in the face of immediate violence. On another, other Black women seated in the back spoke loudly to each other about her causing trouble.

In Memphis, she sought and received Bishop Adrien's permission to es-tablish Blessed Martin House of Hospitality. It opened January 1952 in a rented storefront and in 1954 moved to a house that Dorothy Day helped to finance. Its location in a purportedly dangerous area made it affordable. Blessed Martin House's primary work of mercy was offering poor work-ing mothers a place of safety and care for their children. Besides the usual house of hospitality problems of finances, mission focus, and difficult guests, she faced constant criticism and second-guessing from whites and Blacks. Helen's commitment to Catholic Worker practices of voluntary poverty, works of mercy, and social action exacerbated suspicions. She stood against segregation even in her worship, going to a nearby white par-ish for Mass where she sang in the choir. Bishop Adrien soon demanded that she halt public actions promoting racial justice and fair labor prac-tices and concentrate on caring for the poor. The House closed in June 1956.

Caldwell Day's membership in the Mystical Body by virtue of her bap-tism granted her the authority to tell its story. The Mystical Body delimited a divinely sanctioned space that demanded displacing the color line that demarcated every aspect of her life, from riding the bus to attending Mass.

Toward the end of *Not without Tears*, Helen spoke fondly of students from a local Christian Brothers school who "entered not only into the work of the house, but also into its spirit." They composed and mimeographed a newsletter, "Impact," a name describing the effect of the doctrine of the Mystical Body of Christ on their "sense of responsibility" for the house and for "the problems of the Negro people in their midst." Caldwell Day praised their "open and genuine humility and charity that . . . shamed prejudice out of others, who might otherwise have been awed by or resentful of the white skins God gave them."[39] For four years, Blessed Martin House provided a space to test the limits and possibilities of the Mystical Body of Christ. The principal animator of that space was Helen Caldwell Day. Soon after Brother Martin closed, Helen moved to California with her new husband, Jessie Riley, in 1957. Together they raised five children and remained active in their local parish. Helen drew upon her life experiences to create dynamic programing about Black culture and life for the local public libraries. She died on December 15, 2013.[40]

Caldwell Day is one of many Catholic women who sought to form young adult Catholics in living the Mystical Body of Christ. Sister Marie Philip Haley, from the College of Saint Catherine, Saint Paul, Minnesota, a women's college, provides an interesting contrast in the intentional formation of college-age women into the Mystical Body of Christ. In the *Journal of Religious Instruction* (June 1941) under the title, "An Attitude Scale in Religion for Catholic Colleges," Haley described a questionnaire on religious attitudes, previously tested, and revised to clarify ambiguous questions. An unnamed theologian, presumably male, reviewed the revised survey "for his criticisms and suggestions, and under his guidance a scoring key was constructed." Incoming first-year students answered a series of randomly ordered statements, indicating their agreement, disagreement, or neutrality. Students knew the test intended "to show how college students feel about various religious, social, and personal problems."[41] The responses when scored fell under one of ten theological categories. Completion of the survey, as Haley described it, promoted a student's self-understanding, if honestly answered. Since each statement had a correct response, self-understanding here meant not simply awareness and acceptance of one's own views but acknowledging and changing incorrect ones. To determine whether appropriate change had occurred, these same students responded to the same statements four years later, immediately prior to graduation.

Sister Marie Philip Haley listed the categories and provided sample statements under each category. The formula used was x attitude versus y attitude, e.g., "preponderance of emotion *versus* intellect and will in worship." Under this category, one statement, using the first-person singular, described feeling more prayerful when an organ played softly in the background. The correct answer was "disagree."[42] In reviewing all the categories, it appears that Saint Catherine's promoted attitudes that would make for successful and urbane Catholics who understood themselves as located within the Mystical Body and committed to Catholic Action. So, under the category, "The Church regarded primarily as an organization *versus* the Church as a living organism, the Mystical Body of Christ with solidarity of all members and diversity of function," all correct responses should advance the latter ecclesial image. Another category championed Catholic Action, the major corollary of the Mystical Body. Another category discouraged "Prudery" and encouraged an "appreciation of the 'whole man [sic].'"[43] This category focuses on forming a more sophisticated laywoman ready to engage contemporary US society on Catholic terms. The final category recapitulates this aspiration. "Religion as a matter of Sundays and prayer-time *versus* religion penetrating every act of man." To score well in this category, the respondent should agree that "washing dishes and dusting" ought to be performed with care since all actions done for others "have their share in building up the Body of Christ in men."[44] Given that only women took this particular survey, it is impossible to ignore the transformation of the Mystical Body into a spatial story confirming gender roles.

Catholic networks of meaning embed simple household activities with multivalent significance. The survey itself suggests that Catholic women's colleges introduced these mostly white and more privileged women students to potentially competing understandings of faithful Catholic women, whose religious commitments demand active use of their wills and intellects against prudery as well as passive acceptance of certain prescribed functions in the Mystical Body of Christ. In her speech, "The Education of Sister Lucy," a source of inspiration for Sister Formation, Sister Madeleva Wolff situated all postwar college-age Catholic women squarely in the Mystical Body performing Catholic Action but in a very different world than when Pius X called for restoring the social order.

Let us remember that Lucy and her generation have been fed on the Blessed Sacrament all their lives. They have grown up on the doctrine of the Mystical Body of Christ. They are militant in Catholic action. They think and move with the instancies of aviation and television. They think in terms of super-atomic power. They are in spirit and truth children of God. We must form and educate them in terms of these potencies. We must not frustrate the magnificence of their qualities by our lower-geared Victorian traditions and training.[45]

Less than ten years later, the Jesuit sociologist Joseph Fichter, offers a less flattering picture of the college-educated Catholic woman. She has learned "the best techniques of analysis and criticism" as well as "the liturgy and the Mystical Body of Christ." Her understanding arises from "principles, plans and blueprints in an idealistic way, and she may pretend to be shocked that the pastor is not 'up' on these matters."[46] In other words, these college-educated Catholic women may be a source of friction in their parishes rather than acquiescing to their pastors' demands.

Mary Daly offers an example of such a Catholic college alumna who for a period of her life inhabited a spatial story of the Mystical Body of Christ and eventually became a source of friction well beyond her parish. Mary Daly received her first PhD in 1954 from Saint Mary's Graduate School of Sacred Theology, a school which Sister Madeleva established to develop women's potencies in theology. Her final paper, "Theology and Holiness," provided a Thomist-inspired defense of the vocation of the lay theologian.[47] The introduction quotes Leon Bloy—"there is only one misery . . . not to be saints." Her neo-scholastic argument unfolds in three parts. The first examines theology's effect on a theologian's holiness. The second, or middle part, treats "the effect of the theologian acting as such upon the growth in holiness of the other members of the Mystical Body, real or potential, whom he [sic] inevitably influences" (2). The third part traces holiness's effects "on the increase of science of the theologian" (2). Daly's argument, rooted in Thomist teleology of charity, regards theological study as a means to "perfecting the condition of love, insofar as it more perfectly presents the lovable object to the will" (7). Studying Sacred Doctrine also "perfects the theologian as a man [sic] of vision, although probably not of visions," given that he is circumscribed by "laws, which are determined by Divine Wisdom and made known through revelation and the experience of the saints" (14). Theologians ultimately assist "the Roman Pontiff and the Bishops of the Church, who are the only teachers divinely constituted in the Church of Christ" (15). Her discussion grounded in Thomistic explanations has little to distinguish it from other defenses of the lay apostolate as participation in the hierarchy's apostolate.

Yet Daly has a deeper concern—the link between the spiritual (holiness) and the intellectual (theology) in the individual theologian. Inspired by the example of the Angelic Doctor whom she believed had nearly perfected the union between theology and holiness, Mary Daly exhorts her readers to consider the enormous influence of individual theologians quite apart from the hierarchy.

> The activities of men whose minds are ordered to God then, whether they be theologians or those taught by them, will be more and more like the activity of the perfect Peacemaker, who is subsistent Wisdom. This can hardly fail to influence the real members of the Mystical Body, and even potential members still remote from the Church (18).

Whatever one thinks about the subsequent work of Mary Daly, the radical post-Christian feminist philosopher, one can hardly deny a certain ironic truth in her first attempt at a dissertation. She has not failed to influence real members of the Mystical Body and even potential members in her pursuit of Wisdom.

Women Authorized to Establish, Displace, and Transcend the Mystical Body

Given the ubiquity of appeals to Mystical Body and Catholic Action, its seemingly rapid disappearance after the Second Vatican Council is striking. The reasons are as complex as the multiple spaces the Mystical Body and its Catholic Action/action inhabited. What follows are some brief explorations featuring the writings of Catholic laywomen in the conciliar and post-conciliar period. Sally Cunneen's 1968 *Religion: Catholic; Sex: Female*, provides a few clues.[48] The first clue is how little the image appears in her accounts of the survey responses that make up the book's content. The second, and more telling, is how it appears. In the chapter, "The Women Who Wrote This Book," a "California mother," Catholic convert, after a ten-year sojourn as "a disciple of Vedanta," explains her Catholic sensibility. "I am always a part of the Church, but the way I feel this is not as a member of an institution, but as part of the Mystical Body of Christ . . ." She compares it to being "one in the human family," or always feeling like a woman whether performing "some specifically female function such as childbirth or menstruation or intercourse . . . [or] something 'neutral' like driving a car or weeding or typing a news-story."[49] In "The Proof is in the Parish," a sixty-year old married woman from Skokie, Illinois, captures a crucial distinction: "I am often impatient with the structural Church, but this in no way disturbs my commitment as a member of the Mystical Body—or, as we now say, the people of God. The Mass is basic for me; the Eucharist is real; the known union with Christ is experienced."[50] Like the "California mother," the Illinois woman introduces the distinction between the institutional structure and Mystical Body. She also understands the metaphor as interchangeable with "People of God." Finally, a third contribution from "a young research assistant in a private library in Washington" appears in "Inside/Outside the Church/World." She identifies women for whom "the Church is neither building, nor hierarchy, nor even people of God." It is "primarily symbolic—pointing always to the Other, the Sacred . . ." In considering theologies, she warns "against a tendency to identify description—with reality" and calls for "more ecumenism, the end of institutionalism, the beginning of personalism. We are all ministers to each other; consequently more thought about the Mystical Body would prepare people for these changes. God's manifestation is unlimited. The Church has no monopoly."[51] Like the other examples, this presumably youngest participant has dissolved the "place," i.e., the fixed and stable institution. One of the two determinations in the spatial story of the Mystical Body of Christ and its Catholic Action has disappeared.

Sydney Callahan's *The Illusion of Eve* (1965) offers another possible reason, especially for laywomen, to abandon the Mystical Body's story.[52] Callahan repeatedly returns to the Pauline insistence on male headship (1 Cor. 11:3): a serious challenge for Christian feminists. Callahan raises the question in recounting a common Catholic narrative about marriage. It is "a union paralleling the union of Christ and the Church; man is the head of woman as Christ is the head of the Church. Paul teaches that Christ is the head of His body the Church, and this teaching, the doctrine of the 'Mystical Body' is important in Christianity." She asserts that this complex doctrine is easily misunderstood and then raises a crucial question. "How closely does the analogy—man is the head of woman as Christ is the Head of His Church—correspond to the doctrine of the Mystical Body?" She then quotes the Ephesians text: "'a husband is head of the wife, just as Christ is head of the Church, being himself savior of the body' (Eph. 5:23)." She continues, "The crucial question turns on the meaning of 'just as.' A literal analogy cannot work since Christ is divine, husbands are not—and Christ, not the husband, saves the wife. How then does the analogy apply?"[53] Later she distills the question to the following: "Is Christ to God as woman to man?" Callahan acknowledge the passage's usefulness in defending a "strong anti-feminine tradition" among Christians.[54]

In a subsequent chapter she appeals to the Body of Christ metaphor in defense of husbands and wives possessing distinct "vocations to serve Christ in active roles of authority in the world." Even in her positive appeal to "the Pauline metaphor of the mystical body," she immediately adds in parentheses, "(and it is a metaphor which should be used sparingly)"[55] Callahan later champions another Christian space, the "practiced place," which "emphasizes Resurrection and Paradise as the Christian ideal for the here and now" rather than a future goal. If Resurrection and Paradise have come into the world through Christ, "then—women, work and sex take on different values." She appeals to another Pauline text, frequently cited by other Christian feminists, to challenge normative gendered roles. "In Christ there is neither slave nor free, Jew nor Greek, male nor female—nor is there a special work that each must do. These old divisions are no longer operative or limiting. There is variety and diversity in Christian life and work, but it is a variety and diversity that arises from the diversity of individual vocation, talents and gifts rather than necessity."[56] Callahan's concern anticipates heated debates about the application of the Ephesian analogy in the spatial stories entitled "Theology of the Body." Pope Francis, in his apostolic exhortation, *Amoris Laetitia*, characterizes the analogy as "imperfect," and yet "inspires us to beg the Lord to bestow on every married couple an outpouring of his divine love."[57] Later, he cautions against "lay[ing] upon two limited persons the tremendous burden of having to reproduce perfectly the union existing between Christ and his Church, for marriage as a sign entails 'a dynamic process . . . one which advances gradually with the progressive integration of the gifts of God.'"

Quoting John Paul II, Francis's account of this analogy as "imperfect" opens up a space in which Callahan's "variety and diversity" might find a "practiced place."[58]

It seems untoward to end a paper on Catholic laywomen with a post-conciliar papal debate. Rather, I want to return to Mary Frances Daly in the spirit of Certeau's numberless forms of play between place and space in spatial stories. In her "recollections," *Outercourse*, Daly recalls what she learned while studying at Saint Mary's College. ". . . the Speaker was a hedge on the campus that caught my attention one shimmering, dewy morning. The hedge added to the message given to me years before. It not only Announced its be-ing to me. The hedge Said: 'Continued existence.'" She then goes on to explain this encounter.

> The meaning of the Original message Unfolds even as I am writing this, and my Memory of my Moment of Hearing the hedge Dis-closes itself as *Metamemory*. That is, it is Deep, Ecstatic Memory of participation in Be-ing that eludes the categories and grids of patriarchal consciousness. Spiraling into the Past, carrying Vision forward; Memory that recalls Archaic Time, Re-calling it into our be-ing; Memory beyond civilization (*Wickedary*).[59]

I do wonder whether the hedge might have caught a few lectures concerning being and essence in the thought of Thomas Aquinas at St. Mary's Graduate School of Sacred Theology. I also wonder if a mystical body reappears in a new form. In her "*Feminist Postchristian Conclusion to the Feminist Postchristian Introduction*" of *The Church and the Second Sex*, Daly

> suggest[s] that what women require is *ludic cerebration*, the free play of intuition in our own space, giving rise to thinking that is vigorous, informed, multidimensional, independent, creative, tough. Ludic cerebration is thinking out of experience. . . . I mean the experience of be-ing. *Be-ing* is the verb that says the dimensions of depth in all verbs, such an intuiting, reasoning, loving, imaging, making, acting, as well as the couraging, hoping, and playing that are always there when one is really living.

The choice is between the "male-identified professional, or else one tries to make the quantitative leap toward self-acceptable deviation as ludic cerebrator, questioner of everything, madwoman, and witch."[60]

From certain vantage points, the Mystical Body narrative moves with centripetal force toward the fixed point of centralized papal authority, described with ironic clarity in Mary Daly's first foray into doctoral studies. From another vantage point, the mid-twentieth century American Catholic narrative seemed to explode with the centrifugal force of the Mystical Body's Catholic action in the world. Assertive laywomen went out and about with this "mobile and magisterial tribunal" to create spaces for themselves to enact the Mystical Body's Catholic Action/action. Their stories served "to *authorize* the establishment, displacement, or transcendence of limits" in that permeability of natural/supernatural boundaries expressed in the paradoxical notion of a "mystical body." These militant Catholics sought to situate themselves in the natural sphere in an attempt to order it to the supernatural, to bring into reality the Mystical Body of Christ and in doing so transcended certain limits long established for lay Catholic women.

Notes

1. Michel de Certeau, *The Practice of Everyday Life*, translated by Steven Rendall (Berkeley: University of California Press, 1984; paperback ed. 1988), 117.

2. Certeau, *The Practice*, 118.

3. Accessed February 23, 2021, https://www.vatican.va/content/pius-xi/en/encyclicals/documents/hf_p-xi_enc_29061931_non-abbiamo-bisogno.pdf, par. 5.

4. Accessed February 23, 2021http://www.vatican.va/content/pius-x/en/encyclicals/documents/hf_p-x_enc_11061905_il-fermo-proposito.html, par. 11.

5. *Il Fermo Proposito*, par. 6.

6. Nicholas Rademacher, "'Allow me to disappear . . . in the fetid slums': Catherine de Hueck, Catholic Action, and the Growing End of Catholic Radicalism," *U.S. Catholic Historian* 32, no. 3 (Summer 2014): 79–80.

7. Certeau, *The Practice*, 122

8. *Mystici Corporis Christi*, accessed February 14, 2021, https://www.vatican.va/content/pius-xii/en/encyclicals/documents/hf_p-xii_enc_29061943_mystici-corporis-christi.html, par. 8.

9. *Mystici Corporis Christi*, par. 11

10. *Mystici Corporis Christi*, par. 9.

11. *Mystici Corporis Christi*, par. 98

12. John Courtney Murray, SJ, "Towards a Theology for the Layman: The Pedagogical Problem," *Theological Studies* 5 (1944): 373.

13. Murray, "The Pedagogical Problem," 64.

14. John Courtney Murray, SJ, "Towards a Theology for the Layman: The Problem of Its Finality," *Theological Studies* 5 (1944), 65.

15. Murray, "The Problem of Its Finality," 123.

16. Michael R. Hill, "Bio-Bibliography: Eva J. Ross—Catholic Sociologist," *Sociological Origins* 1, no. 2 (1999): 107. All the biographical information is taken from Hill, "Bio-bibliography: Eva J. Ross," 106–110. Accessed on February 3, 2021 from University of Nebraska—Lincoln Digital Commons@ University of Nebraska—Lincoln.

17. Ruth A. Wallace, "Bringing Women In: The ACSS/ASR Story," *Sociological Analysis* 50 (Winter 1989), 409.

18. Eva J. Ross, "Training for Catholic Action," *Catholic Educational Review* (1940), 20.

19. Ross, "Training for Catholic Action," 21.

20. Ross, "Training for Catholic Action," 24.

21. Ross, "Training for Catholic Action," 21.

22. Ross, *Living in Society* (Milwaukee: The Bruce Publishing Company, 1966).

23. Ross, *Living in Society*, 35

24. Ross, *Living in Society*, 90–91.

25. Italics in the text. Ross, *Living in Society*, 92.

26. Dorothy Day, *The Long Loneliness* (New York: HarperOne, 1952), 147.

27. William T. Cavanaugh, "Dorothy Day and the Mystical Body of Christ in the Second World War" from the Selected Works of William T. Cavanaugh, DePaul University, 462.

28. Helen Caldwell Day, *Color, Ebony* (New York: Sheed & Ward, 1952).

29. Caldwell Day, *Color, Ebony*, 123.

30. Caldwell Day, *Color, Ebony*, 126.

31. John Fitzsimons and Paul McGuire *Restoring All Things to Christ: A Guide to Catholic Action* (New York, Sheed and Ward, 1938), vii.

32. Helen Caldwell Day, *Not without Tears* (New York: Sheed and Ward, 1952), 3.

33. Caldwell Day, *Not without Tears*, 175.

34. Caldwell Day, *Not without Tears*, 176.

35. Caldwell Day, *Not without Tears*, 177.

36. Caldwell Day, *Not without Tears*, 11.

37. Caldwell Day, *Not without Tears*, 11–12.

38. Caldwell Day, *Not without Tears*, 13.

39. Caldwell Day, *Not without Tears*, 238.

40. Amanda W. Daloisio, "Remembering Helen Caldwell Riley Day," *Black Catholic Messenger*, November 29, 2020, https://www.blackcatholicmessenger.com/remembering-helen-caldwell/.

41. Marie Philip Haley, "An Attitude Scale in Religion for Catholic Colleges," *Journal of Religious Instruction* (June 1941): 921.

42. Haley, "An Attitude Scale," 921.

43. Haley, "An Attitude Scale," 923–924.

44. Haley, "An Attitude Scale," 925.

45. "The Education of Sister Lucy Young Religion Teachers," NCEA April 21, 1949 *Symposium of Theories and Practices for the Ed. and Training of the Young Religious Teacher*, 10.

46. Joseph H. Fichter, SJ, "Educated Catholic Women," *America* 97 (April 20, 1957): 65–66.

47. Saint Mary's College Archives, Box 204. Page numbers appear in the text.

48. Sally Cunneen, *Religion: Catholic; Sex: Female* (New York: Holt, Rinehart and Winston, 1968).

49. Cunneen, *Religion: Catholic*, 7.

50. Cunneen, *Religion: Catholic*, 45.

51. Cunneen, *Religion: Catholic*, 157.

52. Sydney Callahan, *The Illusion of Eve* (New York: Sheed and Ward, Inc., 1965).

53. Callahan, *The Illusion of Eve*, 45.

54. Callahan, *The Illusion of Eve*, 46.

55. Callahan, *The Illusion of Eve*, 97.

56. Callahan, *The Illusion of Eve*, 170.

57. *Amoris Laetitia*, https://www.vatican.va/content/dam/francesco/pdf /apost_exhortations/documents/papa-francesco_esortazione-ap_20160319 _amoris-laetitia_en.pdf, par. 73.

58. *Amoris Laetitia*, par. 122.

59. Mary Daly, *Outercourse: The Be-dazzling Voyage Containing Recollections from My Logbook of a Radical Feminist Philosopher (Be-ing an Account of My Time/ Space Travels and Ideas—Then, Again, Now, and How)* (New York: Harpers San Francisco, 1992), 51, 52

60. Mary Daly, *The Church and the Second Sex with the Feminist Postchristian Introduction and New Archaic Afterword by the Author* (Boston: Beacon Press, 1985), 49, 50.

Acknowledgments

We would like to thank the editorial staff at Fordham University Press, especially Fredric Nachbaur, John Garza, Courtney Lee Adams, Jr., Kem Crimmins, and Erica Messina for their assistance in preparing the manuscript for publication. We are grateful to the external reviewers whose valuable feedback improved the volume. Additionally, we thank University of Dayton graduate students Hunter Doiron, Lillian Hynfield, and Emily Lawrence who assisted us in our editorial work at various stages of production. We are especially grateful for Hunter's assistance in conducting additional research during the revision process and assisting with the preparation of the index. Finally, we are thankful to the contributors of this volume who persevered through the pandemic to bring this book to fruition.

Contributors

VAUGHN A. BOOKER is the George E. Doty, Jr. and Lee Spelman Doty Presidential Associate Professor of Africana Studies at the University of Pennsylvania. His first book is *Lift Every Voice and Swing: Black Musicians and Religious Culture in the Jazz Century* (NYU, 2020).

BRIAN J. CLITES is an assistant professor in the Department of Religious Studies at Case Western Reserve University, where he also serves as associate director of the Baker-Nord Center for the Humanities.

DAMIAN COSTELLO is Director of Postgraduate Studies at NAIITS: An Indigenous Learning Community. He is the author of *Black Elk: Colonialism and Lakota Catholicism* (Orbis Books, 2005).

NEOMI DE ANDA is the executive director of the International Marian Research Institute and associate professor in the Department of Religious Studies at the University of Dayton.

KATHERINE DUGAN is associate professor of religious studies at Springfield College (MA). She is the author of *Millennial Missionaries: How a Group of Young Catholics is Making Catholicism Cool* (Oxford, 2019) and is currently working on an ethnographic study of Catholics who practice Natural Family Planning.

KATHARINE E. HARMON is associate professor of theology at Holy Cross College in Notre Dame, IN and author of *There Were Also Many Women There: Lay Women in the United States Liturgical Movement, 1926–1959* (Liturgical Press, 2012).

ANNIE HUEY is a doctoral candidate at the University of Dayton. She is currently writing her dissertation, which is part biography and part thematic analysis of Katherine Burton's life and works.

MAUREEN H. O'CONNELL is professor of Christian ethics at La Salle University. Her most recent book is *Undoing the Knots: Five Generations of American Catholic Anti-Blackness* (Beacon Press, 2021).

CATHERINE R. OSBORNE holds a PhD in theology from Fordham University and a BA in art history from Swarthmore College. She is the author of *American*

Catholics and the Church of Tomorrow (University of Chicago Press, 2018) and the co-editor of *American Catholic History: A Documentary Reader* (NYU Press, 2017).

NICHOLAS K. RADEMACHER is professor in the Religious Studies Department at the University of Dayton. He is co-editor of the journal *American Catholic Studies* and author of *Paul Hanly Furfey: Priest, Scientist, Social Reformer* (Fordham, 2017).

MARIAN RONAN is research professor of Catholic studies at New York Theological Seminary in New York City. She is author or co-author of seven books, most recently, with Mary O'Brien, *Women of Vision: Sixteen Founders of the International Grail Movement* (Apocryphile Press, 2017).

SANDRA YOCUM is University Professor of Faith and Culture at the University of Dayton. Her publications have addressed a wide range of topics in nineteenth, twentieth, and twenty-first century US Catholicism, including papal authority, clergy sexual abuse, intellectual life, theological education, historiography, and spirituality.

Index

CATHOLIC PRACTICE IN THE AMERICAS

James T. Fisher and Margaret M. McGuinness (eds.), *The Catholic Studies Reader*

Jeremy Bonner, Christopher D. Denny, and Mary Beth Fraser Connolly (eds.), *Empowering the People of God: Catholic Action before and after Vatican II*

Christine Firer Hinze and J. Patrick Hornbeck II (eds.), *More than a Monologue: Sexual Diversity and the Catholic Church. Volume I: Voices of Our Times*

J. Patrick Hornbeck II and Michael A. Norko (eds.), *More than a Monologue: Sexual Diversity and the Catholic Church. Volume II: Inquiry, Thought, and Expression*

Jack Lee Downey, *The Bread of the Strong: Lacouturisme and the Folly of the Cross, 1910–1985*

Michael McGregor, *Pure Act: The Uncommon Life of Robert Lax*

Mary Dunn, *The Cruelest of All Mothers: Marie de l'Incarnation, Motherhood, and Christian Tradition*

Dorothy Day and the Catholic Worker: The Miracle of Our Continuance. Photographs by Vivian Cherry, Text by Dorothy Day, Edited, with an Introduction and Additional Text by Kate Hennessy

Nicholas K. Rademacher, *Paul Hanly Furfey: Priest, Scientist, Social Reformer*

Margaret M. McGuinness and James T. Fisher (eds.), *Roman Catholicism in the United States: A Thematic History*

Gary J. Adler Jr., Tricia C. Bruce, and Brian Starks (eds.), *American Parishes: Remaking Local Catholicism*

Stephanie N. Brehm, *America's Most Famous Catholic (According to Himself): Stephen Colbert and American Religion in the Twenty-First Century*

Matthew T. Eggemeier and Peter Joseph Fritz, *Send Lazarus: Catholicism and the Crises of Liberalism*

John C. Seitz and Christine Firer Hinze (eds.), *Working Alternatives: American and Catholic Experiments in Work and Economy*

Gerald J. Beyer, *Just Universities: Catholic Social Teaching Confronts Corporatized Higher Education*

Brandon Bayne, *Missions Begin with Blood: Suffering and Salvation in the Borderlands of New Spain*

Susan Bigelow Reynolds, *People Get Ready: Ritual, Solidarity, and Lived Ecclesiology in Catholic Roxbury*

Katherine Dugan and Karen E. Park (eds.), *American Patroness: Marian Shrines and the Making of U.S. Catholicism*

Sandra Yocum and Nicholas K. Rademacher (eds.), *Recovering Their Stories: US Catholic Women in the Twentieth Century*

Printed in the USA
CPSIA information can be obtained
at www.ICGtesting.com
LVHW051229210524
780834LV00004B/611